This collection of essays explores key dimensions of Faulkner's widespread cultural import. Drawing on a wide range of cultural theory, ten major Faulkner scholars examine closely the enduring whole of Faulkner's oeuvre in clearly written and intellectually provocative essays. Bringing into focus the broader cultural contexts that give his work its resonance, the collection will be particularly useful for the student seeking a critical introduction to Faulkner, while serving also the dedicated scholar interested in discerning recent trends in Faulkner criticism.

Together, these essays map Faulkner's present-day meaning by exploring his relations to modernism and postmodernism, to twentieth-century mass culture, to European and Latin American fiction, to issues of gender difference, and, above all, to the conflicted scene of U.S. race relations. Neither assuming in advance his literary "greatness" nor insisting that his canonical status be revoked, the essays ask instead, What is at stake, today, in *reading* Faulkner? What company does he keep? In what ways does his work intersect with current debates on race and gender? How does his practice respond to today's questions about the individual subject's insertion within broader cultural activities? Why, in short, should we read him now?

THE CAMBRIDGE COMPANION TO
WILLIAM FAULKNER

CAMBRIDGE COMPANIONS TO LITERATURE

The Cambridge Companion to

WILLIAM FAULKNER

Edited by Philip M. Weinstein
Swarthmore College

CAMBRIDGE
UNIVERSITY PRESS

PUBLISHED BY THE PRESS SYNDICATE OF THE UNIVERSITY OF CAMBRIDGE
The Pitt Building, Trumpington Street, Cambridge CB2 1RP, United Kingdom

CAMBRIDGE UNIVERSITY PRESS
The Edinburgh Building, Cambridge CB2 2RU, United Kingdom
40 West 20th Street, New York, NY 10011-4211, USA
10 Stamford Road, Oakleigh, Melbourne 3166, Australia

First published 1995
Reprinted 1995, 1996, 1997

Printed in the United States of America

Typeset in Trump Mediaeval

A catalogue record for this book is available from the British Library

Library of Congress Cataloguing-in-Publication Data is available

ISBN 0-521-42063-6 hardback
ISBN 0-521-42167-5 paperback

CONTENTS

v

Part II. The World in the Texts

PREFACE

Not just "another book on Faulkner": when I accepted Cambridge University Press's invitation to edit this *Companion to William Faulkner*, I insisted on that distinction. Free to gather together many of the best Faulknerians writing in the 1990s, I sought to convert the potential defects of an anthology into its virtues. The absence of a single guiding argument could become the presence of several provocative introductions. In place of a sustained, unified intelligence (engaged peripherally with other points of view), this book could foreground encounter itself – difference. It could emphasize what most literary studies pay lip service to but actually work to conceal: that the entity we call "Faulkner" exists, publicly, only in the plural, differentially construed according to the operative critical approach. *The Cambridge Companion to William Faulkner* is dedicated to introducing, to a broadly literate audience, several of the most compelling "Faulkners" of our time.

These various Faulkners are by no means the arbitrary constructions of willful critics. Rather, my nine fellow contributors come to Faulkner through critical procedures with their own cultural history, and I have urged these contributors to attend self-consciously to the orientations enabling their thought. All of them have – while revising their own work – read one or more of the neighboring essays, and at certain points specific convergences of ideas and claims take place. Taken together, this range of orientations gestures toward the broader discursive field within which current commentary on Faulkner is being generated. The *Companion* makes no pretense of mapping that field exhaustively, but it does acknowledge that the field is necessarily prior to the writer being discussed within it. Ideally, the *Companion* sheds light simultaneously on the present-day significance of Faulkner's work and on many of the particular questions cultural critics of the 1990s have counted as significant.

In the Introduction I discuss in detail the kind of argument – its assumptions and implications – each contributor is making. But the point to emphasize here is that the volume as a whole is committed to producing an *accessible* Faulkner. This is no simple task, since making him accessible cannot mean making him "easy" (that would be a betrayal of his work's deliberate transgressions), nor can it mean reducing the terms of critical approach to a single vocabulary of assumptions and goals (that would be a betrayal of the tonic range of questions his work engages in the critical practice of the 1990s). Rather, "accessible" must mean the presentation of a Faulkner whom first-time readers can recognize, a Faulkner not trammeled up in a thick weave of previous commentaries and scholarly footnotes. And it must mean a Faulkner not uniquely pursuing his esoteric dreams but, instead, a Faulkner immersed in his broader culture's compelling debates. Readers already interested in such debates will recognize them here, and they will find in the *Companion*'s various Faulkners both a "citizen" (however reluctant) of his time and place and a respondent (however reluctant) to our time and place.

Getting ten Faulknerians to collaborate on one volume has not lacked its frustrations, but this joint enterprise has been mainly an occasion of intellectual enrichment. Poring over one another's work, each of us ensconced hundreds (or thousands) of miles distant from each other, we persevered in our own parodic version of *Absalom*'s Jefferson/Cambridge project of multiple authorship. I am grateful to each contributor for this provocative and unpredictable interchange. Likewise,

I am grateful to Julie Greenblatt and T. Susan Chang (both at Cambridge University Press) for seeking out this volume and for then adroitly seeing it through. Finally, without the extraordinary achievement of William Faulkner there would have been no common focus for our energies, no body of texts through which we severally rehearse what it means to be subjects in culture, no "companion" to make possible this *Companion.*

CONTRIBUTORS

ANDRÉ BLEIKASTEN is Professor of American Literature at the Université de Strasbourg. His major work on Faulkner began with book-length studies in the 1970s of *As I Lay Dying* and *The Sound and the Fury*, followed by many essays in scholarly journals and collections, culminating in *The Ink of Melancholy: Faulkner's Novels from* The Sound and the Fury *to* Light in August (Indiana, 1990). His essay in this volume appeared in an earlier form in *Faulkner, His Contemporaries, and His Posterity*, ed. Waldeman Zacharasiewicz (Tübingen: Francke, 1993).

CHERYL LESTER is Associate Professor at the University of Kansas, where she teaches cultural studies, modern literature, and African-American literature and culture. She has written several essays on Faulkner and is currently completing a manuscript entitled *Faulkner and the Great Migration*, to be published by Cambridge University Press.

JOHN MATTHEWS is Professor of English at Boston University. His contributions to Faulkner studies include the editorship of the *Faulkner Journal* and his major study *The Play of Faulkner's Language* (Cornell, 1982). He has published widely in the scholarly journals on Faulkner and others, has written The Sound and the Fury: *Faulkner and the Lost Cause* (Twayne, 1991), and is now completing a study of framing devices in American literature.

RICHARD C. MORELAND, Associate Professor of English at Louisiana State University, is the author of *Faulkner and Modernism:*

Rereading and Rewriting (Wisconsin, 1990). He has also written scholarly essays on Faulkner, Morrison, and the teaching of cross-cultural encounters in the new canon. He is currently at work on a project entitled "Domination and Democracy in Twain, Eliot, Ellison, and Morrison."

PATRICK O'DONNELL is Editor of *Modern Fiction Studies* and Professor of English at Purdue University. His work centers on modernism and postmodernism, and he has edited a number of anthologies focused on twentieth-century culture. His book-length studies include *Passionate Doubts: Designs of Interpretation in Contemporary American Fiction* (Iowa, 1986) and *Echo Chambers: Figuring Voice in Modern Narrative* (Iowa, 1992).

CAROLYN PORTER is Professor of English at the University of California, Berkeley. She has taught and published on a wide range of American writers and issues. Her work on Faulkner began with *Seeing and Being: The Plight of the Participant Observer in Emerson, James, Adams, and Faulkner* (Wesleyan, 1981), and it has continued in the form of scholarly essays for conferences and in journals.

RAMÓN SALDÍVAR is Professor of English and Comparative Literature at Stanford University. He is the author of *Figural Language in the Novel: The Flowers of Speech from Cervantes to Joyce* and *Chicano Narrative: The Dialectics of Difference*. His teaching and research focus on literary criticism, nineteenth- and twentieth-century comparative literary studies, Chicano narrative, and cultural studies.

WARWICK WADLINGTON is Joan Negley Kelleher Centennial Professor of English at the University of Texas. His publications include *The Confidence Game in American Literature* (Princeton, 1975), *Reading Faulknerian Tragedy* (Cornell, 1988), and *As I Lay Dying: Stories out of Stories* (Twayne, 1992), as well as many scholarly essays on American fiction and culture.

PHILIP M. WEINSTEIN is Alexander Griswold Cummins Professor of English at Swarthmore College. He teaches and publishes on American, British, and comparative fiction. His books include *Henry James and the Requirements of the Imagination* (Harvard, 1971), *The Semantics of Desire: Changing Models of Identity from Dick-*

ens to Joyce (Princeton, 1984), and *Faulkner's Subject: A Cosmos No One Owns* (Cambridge, 1992).

JUDITH BRYANT WITTENBERG is Professor of English and Acting Dean of the College at Simmons College. She teaches widely in American literature and culture. Her central work on Faulkner began with *Faulkner: The Transfiguration of Biography* (Nebraska, 1979), has continued in the form of many essays in scholarly journals, and is currently embodied in her serving as President of the Faulkner Society.

CHRONOLOGY OF WILLIAM
FAULKNER'S LIFE AND WORKS

1897 William Cuthbert Falkner, first of four sons of Murry C. Falkner and Maud Butler Falkner, is born on September 25 in New Albany, Mississippi. Murry Falkner is an administrator for the railroad built by his legendary grandfather, William C. Falkner — a man known as the "Old Colonel" and widely remembered for his achievements as soldier, landowner, lawyer, businessman, politician, and writer. (The family name was spelled "Falkner" until WF added the "u" in 1919.)

1902 The Falkner family moves to Oxford, Mississippi.

1914 After an indifferent secondary education (ceasing after the tenth grade), WF accepts a mentor relationship with Phil Stone (four years older), reading widely in classics and contemporary literature. Stone will serve for many years as a sometimes unwanted adviser, helping WF get his early works published.

1916–17 WF begins to write verse and to submit graphic and literary work for the University of Mississippi yearbook.

1918 WF and Estelle Oldham, childhood sweethearts, do not manage to elope. She marries Cornell Franklin. WF attempts to enlist in the U.S. Air Corps to fight in World War I, is rejected because of insufficient height, goes to Toronto and (masquerading as an Englishman) joins the Royal Air Force training program. He returns to Oxford after the war, feigning war wounds and military exploits (his flight training was actually completed only in December, a month after the armistice).

1919–20   WF enrolls as a special student at the University of Mississippi, studies French, writes a play entitled *Marionettes*, completes his first volume of verse – *The Marble Faun* – which (with Phil Stone's help) will eventually be accepted for publication.

1921–23   WF works in a New York bookstore managed by Elizabeth Prall, Sherwood Anderson's future wife. He returns to Oxford to serve as university postmaster, a job he notoriously mishandles; in 1923 he is fired from it.

1924   *The Marble Faun* is published in December.

1925   WF travels to New Orleans and is introduced (through Elizabeth Prall) to Sherwood Anderson and his literary circle, a group associated with the avant-garde literary magazine *The Double Dealer*. WF spends six months with this group, developing a serious interest in writing fiction, not poetry, and completing his first novel, *Soldiers' Pay*, a "lost generation" story centering on the betrayals of a war-wounded aviator. Anderson's publisher, Horace Liveright, accepts it for publication. WF spends the second half of 1925 traveling in Europe, living in Paris, reading contemporary literature, and writing reviews; he returns to Oxford by Christmas.

1926   *Soldiers' Pay* is published in February.

1927   WF's second novel, *Mosquitoes*, set in New Orleans and attentive to the avant-garde arts scene, is published in April by Liveright.

1928   Liveright refuses WF's third (and most ambitious to date) novel, *Flags in the Dust*. This novel inaugurates WF's fictional history of his own region and is accepted eventually by Harcourt, Brace, on condition that it be shortened. Throughout the 1920s, WF continues to see Estelle Oldham Franklin and her two sons during her visits to Oxford. He begins writing *The Sound and the Fury* in the spring and finishes it by early fall.

1929   Shortened and renamed, *Flags in the Dust* is published as *Sartoris* in January. WF begins writing *Sanctuary*.

The Sound and the Fury, his first indisputable modernist masterpiece, is rejected by Harcourt, Brace but accepted by Cape and Smith. Estelle Oldham Franklin's divorce is finalized in April; WF marries her in June. *The Sound and the Fury* is published in October. During this fall, WF works nights at a power plant, completing a first draft of *As I Lay Dying* (his next modernist masterpiece) in under seven weeks.

1930   *As I Lay Dying* is published in October by Cape and Smith, giving WF's fictional county its name of Yoknapatawpha. WF buys Rowan Oak, an elegant Oxford estate. In need of funds (a need that will continue for the next twenty years), WF begins aggressively to market his short stories along with his novels, the former often paying better.

1931   *Sanctuary,* begun before publication of the two previously completed masterpieces and first conceived as a potboiler, is heavily revised before being published in February. Its sexual violence attracts the attention of Hollywood, and WF soon begins an off-and-on twenty year history as a scriptwriter for MGM and Warner Bros. (The film versions of Hemingway's *To Have and Have Not* and Chandler's *Big Sleep* both contain much Faulknerian dialogue.) *These Thirteen,* a collection of WF's stories, is published in September.

1932   *Light in August,* WF's first major treatment of racial turmoil, is published in February by Smith and Haas.

1933   WF's second volume of poems, *A Green Bough,* is published in April. Jill Faulkner is born in June. *The Story of Temple Drake,* a film version of *Sanctuary,* is released.

1934–35   *Doctor Martino and Other Stories,* a collection of detective stories, is published in April. WF works on *Absalom, Absalom!,* his most ambitious novel about the South so far, as well as his most deliberately modernist work, both in Hollywood and in Oxford. He interrupts *Absalom* to complete *Pylon,* a brief, feverish novel about daredevil stunt pilots, in a few months, then re-

turns to *Absalom* after the death of his youngest brother, Dean, in an air crash. (WF, himself an amateur aviator, had encouraged Dean to learn to fly.) *Pylon* is
published in March 1935.

1936   *Absalom, Absalom!*, is published in October by Random House, thereafter WF's permanent publisher.

1938   *The Unvanquished*, a collection of Civil War stories, is
published in February. WF writes *The Wild Palms*, a
hybrid novel composed of two intertwined stories. He
buys a farm outside of Oxford.

1939   *The Wild Palms* is published in January. WF is elected
to the National Institute of Arts and Letters. Despite
previous attention from French critics such as Malraux
and Sartre, WF only now begins to receive searching
commentary from American critics.

1940   *The Hamlet*, the first novel of the Snopes trilogy, is
published in April.

1942   *Go Down, Moses and Other Stories*, WF's broadest and
most sustained scrutiny of black–white relations, is
published in May.

1946   Malcolm Cowley's edition of *The Portable Faulkner* is
published in May by the Viking Press. Except for *Sanctuary*, WF's novels are out of print; Cowley's ably introduced volume makes WF's work inexpensively available to a large reading public.

1948   *Intruder in the Dust*, a sequel to the Lucas Beauchamp
materials of *Go Down, Moses*, is published in September. The novel's overt interest in Southern racial turmoil secures large sales and signals WF's willingness to
speak out on social issues. WF is elected to the American Academy of Arts and Letters.

1949   *Knight's Gambit*, a collection of detective stories, is
published in November.

1950   *Collected Stories* is published in August. WF wins the
Nobel Prize for Literature, travels with his daughter Jill
to Stockholm, and delivers his famous Nobel Prize acceptance speech.

1951   *Collected Stories* is awarded the National Book Award.

Requiem for a Nun, a reprise of the Temple Drake materials in *Sanctuary*, written in a form both novelistic and theatrical, is published in September. France awards him the Legion of Honor. From this point on, WF's work receives critical (indeed "canonical") attention and brings him financial security. Increasingly, he writes and speaks out on political (especially racial) issues, his position costing him support from many fellow Southerners because of his attack on racism, while disappointing liberals because of his gradualist approach to desegregation. WF travels extensively during the 1950s as a sort of cultural ambassador for the State Department.

1954   *A Fable*, WF's most premeditated novel, a story of World War I in terms of the Christ fable, is published in August. It wins the Pulitzer prize.

1955   *Big Woods*, a collection of stories, is published.

1957   *The Town*, the second novel of the Snopes trilogy, is published in May. WF teaches as writer-in-residence at the University of Virginia. He will alternate residence between Charlottesville and Oxford until his death.

1959   *The Mansion*, the final volume of the Snopes trilogy, is published in November.

1962   *The Reivers*, Faulkner's last and deliberately light-hearted novel, is published in June. A month later, on July 6, WF dies unexpectedly (probably of a heart attack) in a clinic at Byhalia, Mississippi, where he had been recurrently hospitalized for alcoholism and more recently for treatment following the last of many horseback-riding accidents. His funeral takes place the next day in Oxford.

1963   *The Reivers* wins the Pulitzer prize.

ABBREVIATIONS FOR TEXTS CITED

AA   *Absalom, Absalom!: The Corrected Text.* 1936. New York: Vintage International, 1990.

CS   *Collected Stories of William Faulkner.* New York: Random House, 1950.

ESPL   *Essays, Speeches and Public Letters*, ed. James B. Meriwether. New York: Random House, 1966.

FAB   *A Fable.* New York: Random House, 1954.

FMS   *Faulkner's MGM Screenplays*, ed. Bruce F. Kawin. Knoxville: University of Tennessee Press, 1982.

FU   *Faulkner in the University*, ed. Frederick L. Gwynn and Joseph L. Blotner. New York: Random House, 1959.

GDM   *Go Down, Moses.* 1942. New York: Vintage International, 1990.

LA   *Light in August: The Corrected Text.* 1932. New York: Vintage International, 1990.

LG   *Lion in the Garden: Interviews with William Faulkner, 1926–1962*, ed. James B. Meriwether and Michael Millgate. New York: Random House, 1968.

SF   *The Sound and the Fury: The Corrected Text.* 1929. New York: Vintage International, 1990.

SL   *Selected Letters of William Faulkner*, ed. Joseph L. Blotner. New York: Random House, 1977.

TH   *Thinking of Home: William Faulkner's Letters to His Mother and Father, 1918–1925*, ed. James G. Watson. New York: Norton, 1992.

US   *Uncollected Stories of William Faulkner,* ed. Joseph L. Blotner. New York: Random House, 1979.

WP   *The Wild Palms.* 1939. New York: Vintage, 1966.

WILLIAM FAULKNER

PHILIP M. WEINSTEIN

Introduction

What do we do and why when we think Faulkner? This is the
personal (but never just personal) question I asked all of the
contributors to ponder as they thought about their essays for
this *Companion*. In responding to it, they have aligned their
work, roughly, within one of two groups: "the texts in the
world" or "the world in the texts." The five essays that make
up Part I explicitly press beyond the art of Faulkner's texts in
order to comment on the larger "world" those texts inhabit,
envisaged here as contextual social activities and processes
within which Faulkner's practice may reveal its broader cultural dimensions. These essays sketch out a range of contexts
– modernism, postmodernism, the "culture industry," a canon of twentieth-century European novelists, the noncanonical
practice of Latin American fiction of the same period – that
permit us to consider Faulkner's comparative identity. To put
the matter differently, these first essays identify several of the
current "theaters" in which Faulkner's texts are most interestingly performed.

The three essays that constitute Part II operate otherwise,
probing more deeply into the textual behavior of three of
Faulkner's canonical masterpieces – *The Sound and the Fury,
Light in August,* and *Absalom, Absalom!* These essays attend
in detail to a discrete text's formal moves, but they go beyond
New Critical procedures in their insistent focus on "the world
in the texts," especially the larger social problematics of race,

1

gender, and subject formation. A fourth Faulknerian text – *Go Down, Moses* – receives sustained attention as well, in the essays of Patrick O'Donnell and Warwick Wadlington. Finally, this introduction and Wadlington's conclusion, conceived more as "metacommentaries" on the practice of Faulknerian commentary, move outside the alignment of either group. Taken together, all ten essays aspire to be a composite (though necessarily incomplete) "profession" of Faulkner studies today, by circulating around the following concerns:

1. What is at stake in reading Faulkner? How does the apparently private act of reading function in the broader dynamic of cultural reproduction and revision?

2. What (from the perspective of the 1990s) does it mean to call Faulkner a modernist? What (largely European) alignment of forms and concerns is thus asserted? How is this alignment reaccented when we contrast Faulknerian practice with other fictional practices of the same period?

3. What would constitute a postmodernist interpretive lens, and how would such a lens map Faulkner's work in ways that differ crucially from the New Critical celebration of Faulkner that was founded on modernist premises and remained canonical in U.S. criticism from the 1950s well into the 1980s?

4. How would a postmodernist axis of priorities remap the relation of Faulkner's high-culture achievement to the burgeoning forms of popular culture – movies, magazine stories, best-selling novels – within which it made its way and negotiated its accommodations?

5. How does Faulkner's work explore the construction of human subjectivity (that personal space of thinking, feeling, and doing that – with whatever qualifications – we insist on as the domain of our private identity and that fiction has long taken as its special province)? How do Faulkner's texts produce the "traffic" between this interior resource and the larger culture's incessant demands on the individual?

6. In what ways does Faulkner's fiction – the passionate work of a white American male of the early twentieth century

– participate in, and shed light on, his own culture's differential structures of race and gender? Going beyond the facile critical alternatives of blindness to, or rebuke of, these differential structures, how might we read the fissures within his work determined by the pressures of race and gender so as to deepen our understanding of his culture's normative procedures and of his complex insertion within them?

7. Within what larger, nonliterary cultural narratives is Faulkner's practice tacitly embedded? How might his work look when understood within racial/historical perspectives not his own?

Richard Moreland's opening essay identifies at the outset some of the issues that circulate more indirectly through all the subsequent ones. Moreland candidly inquires into the relations among the three central activities he himself performs when he is thinking Faulkner: reading, writing, and teaching. He then seeks, speculatively rather than insistently, to reconceive these activities as dimensions of texts themselves: the "readerly" text of realism (a text that passes on to us the world substantially constituted as we already seem to know it), the "writerly" text of modernism (a text that seems radically to refuse the commonly perceived world of the status quo), and the "participatory" text of postmodernism (a text that recognizes our complicity in the cultural arrangements – however ironic our stance – that we both identify within and import into the texts to which we attend). Moreland tellingly analyzes the ways in which Faulkner's work generally – and *Light in August* specifically – activates with fluid unpredictability all three novelistic stances. "The world of [Faulkner's] work," he writes, "does not feel natural, comfortable, or recognizable in the cultural way that realist work feels to many readers. It does not effectively contain its society's self-criticisms and discontents, or reduce those conflicts to terms an individual character, narrator, or reader can resolve." In other words, although both the "real" and its critique are compellingly produced in Faulkner's practice – we read of a cultural landscape both easily recognizable and disturbingly charged with social ills – his texts at the same time undermine any simple commitment to reform. They thus leave in their reader a sense of malaise – "a critical dissatisfaction with what the culture in general or any of us as individuals alone already knows how to say." This pervasive resistance on the part of Faulkner's texts to effective diagnosis and cure Moreland happily terms a "critique of critique."

Patrick O'Donnell also probes the sense of unresolvable impasse that characterizes Faulkner's modernist major phase: his experimental texts between *The Sound and the Fury* (1929) and *Absalom, Absalom!* (1936). O'Donnell draws on two conflicting dimensions of European modernism in general: the writer's urge to escape the contaminating practices of the world he has inherited, by way of a monumental and formally stunning (antirealistic) replacement of that world (Joyce's Dublin, Proust's Combray, among others); this urge followed by his concomitant ironic awareness that the refused historical world always returns, however repressed, to haunt its brilliant replacement. O'Donnell sees this tension writ large in *Absalom, Absalom!*, Faulkner's tragic modernist masterpiece. He then explores *Go Down, Moses* (1942) as an implicitly postmodern, transitional text in Faulkner's career, in which this double bind of modernism (the transcendent urge, its subsequent betrayal) yields to a more contingent and resilient vision of ongoing histories, black and white, female and male, that quietly elude the either/or dynamic of Faulkner's tragic modernism. As O'Donnell puts it, "To return to Quentin's metaphor of the interconnected pools, these 'postmodern' moments frequently appear in the form of a ripple effect – a movement along the surface of the text far removed from the nascent occurrence that initiated the series, yet one that profoundly puts into question the fatality of events and their aftermath often seen as characteristic of Faulkner's fiction."

Finally, in this opening triad of contextual essays, John Matthews subtly analyzes the impact of larger market pressures on Faulkner's artistic practice. Drawing on Adorno and Horkheimer to theorize the emergence of the "culture industry" (the unparalleled development in the United States of mass-produced and mass-consumed art forms during the mid-twentieth century), Matthews examines closely some of the vicissitudes of Faulkner's Hollywood writings during the 1930s. His argument resembles Moreland's and O'Donnell's in its refusal of a simple binary opposition that would pit the Olympian detachment of the high-modernist masterpiece, on the one hand, against the ideologically contaminated practices of mass culture, on the other. (This stereotypical opposition organizes our most widely shared narrative of the "great writer" – such as Fitzgerald or Faulkner – ensnared by "Hollywood commercialism.") Attending to the transformative history of "Turnabout," one of Faulkner's rare stories actually to be made into a film, Matthews shows that Faulkner's much revised script neither slavishly submitted to commercial pressures nor sublimely transcended them. Rather, it managed, by reflecting wittily on its own manner of rehearsing social co-ordinates, to distinguish its uncoerced behavior from the "culture industry" norms it necessarily encoded. Matthews pursues this argument as part of a larger project of reconceiving the ways in which the aesthetic practice of high modernism encounters mass-market cultural forms spawned by twentieth-century modernization. We have wanted too often to polarize this encounter. We are just learning – thanks to essays like this one – to chart a more complex dynamic of submission and resistance.

The next two essays seek to assess Faulkner's work, first, within a twentieth-century European novelistic perspective and, second, as culturally illuminated by the related practice of a Chicano writer (Américo Paredes) exactly contemporary with Faulkner. In the first of these two pieces, André Bleikasten shrewdly interrogates the current critical convic-

tion that the significance of a writer's work is determined in
the last instance by his cultural insertion. Noting that Faulkner's novels have for more than a half century reached and
moved a huge European readership whose knowledge of the
American South is restricted to what they learn from his
pages, Bleikasten speculates that Faulkner's work possesses
an aesthetic power that survives translation and crosses cultural borders with impunity. He then gathers together the rare
European novelists – a dozen in all – whose work has
achieved, in his view, an equivalent mastery and reach. Modernists all, these writers nevertheless lack the unifying commitment to realism that permits us to join nineteenth-
century writers as divergent as Balzac, Dickens, Tolstoy, and
James. With fine discrimination Bleikasten shows how Faulknerian practice maintains a creative tension between a poet-
ic/experimental impulse and a mimetic/representational impulse. Faulkner thus produces novels that draw powerfully on
fiction's primitive resource – storytelling itself – while all
along calling into question the authority of the stories they do
not cease to unfold. Bleikasten concludes with a modernist
pairing as compelling as it is unexpected: Kafka and Faulkner,
both "children" of Dostoevsky, compassionate masters of the
uncanny, of mesmerizing tales that are simultaneously transparent and opaque.

Ramón Saldívar's comparative frame is equally modernist,
but his project could hardly differ more from Bleikasten's.
Rather than attend to the dimensions of Faulkner's artistic
mastery, Saldívar is intent on the unmanageable inflection of
class, race, and ethnicity on subject formation within Faulkner's protagonists. The representation of the subject-in-
culture is Saldívar's focus, and he turns to Sutpen in *Absalom,
Absalom!* as Faulkner's paradigm case. Saldívar brings to the
Haiti portion of Sutpen's career a cluster of concerns that
reveal as never before the specifically cultural components of
subject formation. Using colonial and postcolonial theory, he
charts the fatal differences – for Sutpen – between (1) a coloni-

al culture (Haiti) whose identity terms exceed (and thus escape) the binary opposition of black and white and (2) a master–slave culture (the antebellum American South) whose identity terms are suffocatingly inscribed on a black–white opposition. Eulalia Bon "is" one kind of person in the former culture, another kind in the latter, and Saldívar adroitly discusses *Absalom, Absalom!* as a text that discloses subjectivity to be multiply constructed even as it tells the story of a man (Sutpen) incapable of this awareness. Finally, Saldívar juxtaposes this Faulkner commentary against a continuously pertinent reading of conflicted identity formation in Paredes's Chicano novel *George Washington Gómez*, concluding that the antirealistic forms of modernism allow both texts – through the suggestively different but equally failed life histories they narrate – to debunk any totalizing myth of origin or end.

The three essays in Part II – "The World in the Texts" – focus, respectively, on *The Sound and the Fury, Light in August,* and *Absalom, Absalom!* – canonical masterpieces according to virtually any account of Faulkner's work. But Cheryl Lester's scrutiny of *The Sound and the Fury* proceeds outside the terms of canonical reverence. Not that Lester is urging us to revoke *The Sound and the Fury*'s canonical status. Rather, she wants to bring into visibility an ongoing historical event that Faulkner's novel simultaneously registers and represses: the Great Migration of blacks from the South that began around 1915 and continued into the 1960s (i.e., throughout Faulkner's career). Lester focuses on *The Sound and the Fury*'s self-conflicted engagement with a historical phenomenon its author could neither ignore nor understand. The white South's emotional and economic "purchase" on Southern blacks was irreparably self-conflicted; white subject formation depended intricately on black silhouettes and reciprocities. Systemic violence against blacks lived side by side with intimate transferential projections on them. Lester argues that Faulkner – like some of his memorable protagonists (e.g., Horace, Quentin) – could not compass, emotionally and intellectually, the phenomenon staring him in the face. He could narrate this steady exodus of blacks from their home-land only by inverting both its direction and its racial focus. On this reading, Quentin Compson (alert throughout his deathday to every nuance of black behavior in Cambridge) experiences an exile displaced detail by detail from its black origin. Lester goes on to collect the various other "absences" in the text around the overdetermined figure of Caddy – sister, mistress, mother, mammy – concluding that *The Sound and the Fury* (like its writer) could encounter this historical event only in the form of loss and dispossession. A text usually celebrated for its achieved psychological intensity is here seen as shaped decisively by its racial positioning, and the histori-cal testimony it offers becomes eloquent in its very evasions.

Race equally determines Judith Bryant Wittenberg's tho-rough discussion of *Light in August*, but not in the form of a historical event that white Southerners were determined not to see. Rather, Wittenberg demonstrates race to be invisible in another sense. That is, and this is searingly true of *Light in August*, race may function as a wholly constructed, concep-tual phenomenon; melanin may have nothing to do with it. In this most race-obsessed of Faulkner's novels there are vir-tually no "black" blacks, only whites tormented by the thought that they may be, or be involved with, blacks un-aware. Pursuing her analysis through a Lacanian understand-ing of the symbolic order (the word world we pass our lives within) as *prior to* the "things themselves" to which words ostensibly refer, Wittenberg reveals the gossamer but inde-structible fabric of lies, rumors, beliefs, and sayings – of *words* – that cushion every character's thought and action in this novel. "Wordsymbols" do irreparable damage in *Light in August*, and Wittenberg argues that the novel is intricately complicit with the verbally generated acts of misprision and violence that it simultaneously analyzes – and in analyzing indicts. In making this latter argument she joins those other critics in the *Companion* who propose a Faulkner inescapably invested in, even though critical of, his culture's most disturbing racial and gendered practices.

Carolyn Porter's commentary on *Absalom, Absalom!* joins Ramón Saldívar's in providing some of the most provocative analysis of subject formation this much discussed text has yet received. Porter notes that Faulkner's early work is maternity-obsessed (especially *The Sound and the Fury* and *As I Lay Dying*), whereas *Light in August* is the transitional text about the fathers (McEachern, Hines, Burden) that heralds the meditation on the institution of patriarchy itself in *Absalom, Absalom!*. Pressing hard on those pages that narrate the child Sutpen's passage from being turned away at the planter's door to his accession to a "design," Porter identifies an intricate structure of speech and silence, of self-interrogation and intercession of the Other. The damaged child, potentially revolutionary, makes his way past his psychic wound and eventually "hears" the voice he requires – objective, impersonal, final – to sanction his design. Drawing on Lacan's model of subject formation, Porter argues that the negotiation of the Oedipal crisis supports not only patriarchy but Western theories of kingship and Christian theology as well. That is, the rebellious subject/son, seeking acknowledgment and hearing only the divine father's silence, finds his way into the mediated law (spoken by others) on the other side of that paternal silence. He joins the father rather than slaying him, ensuring that, even though actual sons and fathers succeed each other and die off in time, the *structure* of the father – what Lacan calls the "Symbolic Father" – retains its privileged authority. It is this authority, in the form of an alienated discourse, that modulates the son's accession into the symbolic order of the father. *Absalom, Absalom!* attests powerfully to the racial and gender-caused carnage that accompanies this accession. Indeed, the title of Porter's essay – "(Un)Making the Father" – points to the diagnostic energy Faulkner mounted in deconstructing, detail by detail, the "becoming" of patriarchy.

Warwick Wadlington's concluding essay recapitulates many of the dominant concerns already discussed. Like Moreland's opening essay, this last one is unusually informal and candid in its manner of engaging its reader. Wadlington sees Faulkner addressing (both as achieved diagnosis and as unwitting complicity) one of the cardinal ills of our century: the unshakable desire to think of the private sphere as radically different from the public sphere. He interrogates this desire on several levels, beginning with a reader's conviction that one's own private reading of Faulkner has little in common with the "institution" of Faulkner (the range of transactions – this *Companion* being a good example – that attend to Faulkner in public ways). Wadlington shows that the private act of reading is inevitably inflected by the stance of others: none of us is born knowing how to read, each of us enacts a scene of sustained cultural training when we unselfconsciously attend to or disregard certain aspects of a text as we go about the moment-by-moment business of reading. Likewise, the domain of the private marks our experience of the public. We do not encounter "some monolithic phantom abstraction like The Public, The Economic System, or The Culture." Rather, we absorb these realities through the agencies of particular people, filtered by their particular subjectivities. Wadlington draws on this fusion of the private and the public not only to launch a theory of "discerning reading" but also to claim that Faulkner's texts enact the same dynamic in their encounter with difference, their temptation to demonize difference (racial difference, gender difference) as inalterably Other. He then reads *Go Down, Moses* as about Ike McCaslin's doomed attempt to transcend private ownership without incurring indebtedness to others. For the most important projects we conceive are unrealizable without the troublemaking yet empowering participation of others. I might well close this portion of the Introduction by reminding you, the reader, that only by depending on my fellow contributors have I been able to access my own thought here, just as you may find your way into your richest Faulknerian thoughts and feelings through the mediation of these gathered and offered essays.

How might a reader most profit from this *Companion to William Faulkner?* If the volume is successful, its uses will exceed my predictions. Nevertheless, a certain number of Faulknerian inquiries are here explicitly enabled, and these may be identified at the outset.

Foremost, this is a volume that interrogates Faulkner's modernist practice as a phenomenon simultaneously sociological and aesthetic. Bleikasten masterfully sketches in the contours of European modernism, drawing on Italo Calvino's memorable claim that "what takes shape in the great novels of the 20th century is the idea of an *open* encyclopedia. . . . Nowadays it has become impossible to conceive a totality that is not potential, conjectural, and plural" (184). An open encyclopedia: the phrase finely captures the two dimensions – experimentation and monumentality – so characteristic of European modernism, and Faulkner's contribution to this enterprise is indisputable.

Yet a number of the *Companion*'s essays probe either modernism's discontents or Faulkner's discontent with modernism. He is surely the supreme American novelist to write himself out of modernism in the 1940s as decisively as he had written himself into it in the 1920s. Moreland and O'Donnell both pursue the limitations implicit in a modernist aesthetic, as well as aspects of Faulkner's work that seem to escape modernist tenets. We tend (with unavoidable imprecision) to call postmodern those writers who are creatively suspicious of modernism, and several contributors open up the possibilities of a postmodernist practice. In this regard Matthew's congenial analysis of *Barton Fink* (a 1990s film that playfully and frighteningly rehearses the plight of a Faulknerlike writer caught up in Hollywood insistences) interrogates explicitly the relation of modernist high culture to popular culture. "Both [modernist art and mass culture] bear the scars of capitalism," Adorno has tersely written, "both contain elements of change. Both are torn halves of freedom to which, however, they do not add up" (Huyssen 58). Matthews works to reconnect these "torn halves," to bring – as Wadlington wants to bring – the high individualist art of modernism back into relation to the broader culture and economy of twentieth-century modernization from which it sprang and in terms of which it has its deepest resonance.

In a related vein, several essays in the *Companion* press Faulkner's work against phenomena it is not normally made to confront. Saldívar shows *Absalom, Absalom!* to have a different face when juxtaposed against Paredes's *George Washington Gómez*, and he uses this juxtaposition to launch a broader exploration of American possibilities of subject formation. Lester and Porter likewise insert Faulkner within larger social dynamics than the writer himself is likely to have contemplated: racial/historical processes (the Great Migration) and political arrangements (the dynamics of patriarchy) that his work does not so much choose to represent as it is, so to speak, chosen by them. For a writer's choices coexist exquisitely with his involuntary enactments: the ratio between these discloses both his individual autonomy and his cultural situatedness.

It is difficult not to oppose these terms – autonomy and situatedness – yet many essays in this volume suggest that subjectivity itself is but a reaccenting of culturally proffered (or imposed) models of being. "Identity is the primal form of ideology," claims Adorno (*Negative Dialectics* 143), and so many arguments in the *Companion* bear down on the dynamics of interior subject formation precisely because the authors are intent on an exterior mapping of the larger culture's ideological resources – both as limitation and as possibility.

Finally, race emerges in these essays as an unpacifiable marker of difference in Faulkner's practice and in our commentary on that practice. Whether the focus on race be a comparative study of U.S. and Haitian identity models, or the indirect impact of the Great Migration on his texts, or a psychological probing of the conceptual core of white racism, or a structural inquiry into the role of race within a patriarchal dynamic, or a meditation on the broadly cultural need to think of difference and sameness as continuously interrelated – in all of these discussions the phenomenon of race is at the heart of Faulkner's present-day significance. More than his white male peers, he seems to have been wounded by race, and he risked his work more than they did on the representation of racial turmoil. It was a wager he knew to be unwinnable, one whose parameters exceeded his self-knowledge and whose pursuit would necessarily deprive him of mastery. Perhaps it is his acceptance of his own nonmastery – his inextricable situatedness in what Wadlington calls his culture's "tragic turbulence" – that best accounts for his ongoing and far from innocent vitality, even now, more than thirty years after his death, near the end of a century he never ceased to view with amazement.

I   The Texts in the World

1   Faulkner and Modernism

When I think Faulkner, I'm usually reading, writing, or teaching (and learning) about his work, or performing some combination of these three activities, and perhaps it is these activities that suggest the three things I think of Faulkner's work as doing and enabling others to do, the things I think literature and other cultural work can do at its best. First, his work reflects or *represents* certain realities (as in much *reading*, especially of "readerly" texts). It never does so directly, but it often does urge readers' attentions on past a relatively transparent medium toward the apparently solid message, past questions of how we are seeing toward questions of what we are seeing, in ways that tend to reinforce or articulate (or rearticulate) what seems natural, what seems like common sense. However, Faulkner's work, at other places and times in it, or in the reading, writing about, or teaching of it, also pointedly *criticizes* those same realities it represents, calling readers' attention back from what they see to how they see it, to the "nature" of reality and to "common sense" as constructions and questions for discussion (as in much *writing*, especially of "writerly" texts). And in still other ways, Faulkner's work *participates* in the ongoing social construction of those realities insofar as readers, writers, teachers, and students more or less consciously respond to such questions of nature and common sense as important cultural works in progress,

17

an ongoing process of social negotiation and change (as in much *teaching and learning*, for example).

What does all this have to do with modernism? The three functions I have suggested for literature assume different relations to one another in different social and historical contexts and in different kinds of texts. The American literature of the later nineteenth century that is often called *realist* literature seems to emphasize most the task of representing reality, although certainly it does also criticize and take part in those realities it represents (not least by rearticulating – as it restates – common sense). I think *modernist* literature tends to adopt a more emphatically and self-consciously critical role. And much of the literature called *postmodernist, contemporary, postwar, multicultural,* or *postcolonial* tends to place more stress on the ongoing, problematic relationship between the work and the social contexts of its production, reception, and circulation. Faulkner's work is usually considered modernist and correspondingly critical in its relationship to the social contexts in which and about which Faulkner wrote. But the social criticism elaborated in his work becomes more interesting if we consider how this critical function and modernist periodization remain closely related to a more representational function and realist discourse, and also to a more participatory function of transference, negotiation, and change, in a more obviously multicultural, multitemporal (or nonsynchronous) social context.

Faulkner's work does suggest trenchant criticisms of powerful cultural and psychological currents in his society, by articulating and especially by accenting disturbing motivations and effects that those discourses more often obscure, minimize, or ignore. For example, Joe Christmas's efforts in *Light in August* to become a man on the model of his adopted family's and his society's assumptions about masculinity reproduce those rites of manhood in several of their least flattering, most defensive and violent forms. At fourteen and fifteen, Joe and neighboring boys his age can "plow and milk and chop

wood like grown men"; however, to avoid "the paramount
sin" of being "publicly convicted of virginity," one boy arranges for five of them to take turns in a deserted shed with an
unnamed young black woman (*LA* 156). Instead of simply
emerging from the shed confirmed as a (white) man, however,
Joe enters the dark shed and feels his own confusion and fear
as "a terrible haste. . . . something in him trying to get out,"
something he is more accustomed to associate with the situation of the young woman here as part of her more general
social situation as feminine and black, "smelling the woman,
smelling the negro all at once," sensing only vaguely "something, prone, abject" (156). His reaction is unexpected and
desperate, but it recalls and focuses the larger social dynamic:
"He kicked her hard, kicking into and through a choked wail
of surprise and fear" (156–7). Joe's and the other boys' attempt
to overcome their own confusion and fear have violently assigned that confusion and fear to her, to be overcome by domi-
nating her. Their white manhood depends on that domination.

Joe reacts in much the same way to his adopted mother's
kindness to him, a kindness tempting enough that he wants
to lower his guard and cry, but for that very reason hated and
considered distinctly feminine: "It was the woman: that soft
kindness which he believed himself doomed to be forever victim of and which he hated worse than he did the hard and
ruthless justice of men. 'She is trying to make me cry'" (168–
9). And at his first news of "the temporary and abject helplessness" suggested to him by menstruation, the idea that "the
smooth and superior shape in which volition dwelled" could
be "doomed to be at stated and inescapable intervals victims
of periodical filth," Christmas only "got over it, recovered" by
going out and shooting a sheep: "he knelt, his hands in the yet
warm blood of the dying beast, trembling, drymouthed, back-
glaring," as if to reassure himself, "illogical and desperately
calm *All right. It is so, then. But not to me. Not in my life and
my love*" (185–6).

In a predominantly realist mode, this would be bizarre behavior indeed (and I would be rushing to agree with other readers that it is indeed bizarre), since it would tend to be viewed from the subject positions realism usually offers its readers, those of either an innocent social insider or a superior, moralistic social critic as the voice of reason, nature, or common sense (perhaps a non-Southern common sense). We would condemn this behavior as easily as most of Twain's audience in the 1880s and since have condemned the behavior of the 1830s slave society represented in *Huckleberry Finn*. In a more modernist novel like *Light in August*, however, such behavior begins to function less as an odd exception than as a critically articulated example of the social rule, with that rule viewed here from the (therefore) more alienated subject position of a disenchanted artist or impotently ironic social critic. It becomes an apparently grotesque but more profoundly representative example of the entire society's thought and behavior with regard to almost all its weaknesses and doubts. Thus even the spectacular near beheading and fire at Joanna Burden's house will figure as a crisis that begins to reflect on everything else, "as if the very initial outrage of the murder carried in its wake and made of all subsequent actions something monstrous and paradoxical and wrong, in themselves against both reason and nature" (296). Not just the occasional outrage but the entire culture – even its language – begins to seem "monstrous and paradoxical and wrong": the very extent of such cultural criticism forces it to speak not from the culture's own heart or conscience, which has begun to seem itself degraded and corrupt, but from a profoundly uneasy exile, detached from and probably unheeded by the culture it observes.

This is one way of explaining the apparently grotesque disturbances and distortions that also mark Faulkner's writing style. It is a style that dramatizes the strain and repeated failure by received reason, nature, and common sense to repress or at least grammatically to subordinate persistently outrageous horrors, stubborn doubts, endless qualifications. Some have attributed such cultural self-doubts in the early twentieth century in the United States and Western Europe to a widespread disillusionment with the idea of Progress after the world's most "civilized" nations conducted the apparently meaningless slaughter of World War I; others point to a threatened loss of masculine privilege, colonial power, religious belief, a presumed cultural consensus. Or, more specifically in the case of Faulkner as a white Southerner, to a history of defeat, poverty, and disillusionment. Or, as Joe says vaguely, "something," which may suggest a more accurate sense of the depressive, uncommunicative, atomized tendency of much modernist thought, as if that "something" cannot be named or thought without the most wrenching dislocations and fragmentations, as suggested in many modernist styles. Like Christmas with the sheep, the town in *Light in August* finally reacts to such apparently unthinkable, unnameable disturbances with an archaic ritual violence toward Christmas himself, "in whose crucifixion they too will raise a cross. 'And they will do it gladly,'" Gail Hightower says to himself. "He feels his mouth and jaw muscles tauten with something premonitory, something more terrible than laughing even. 'Since to pity him would be to admit selfdoubt and to hope for and need pity themselves'" (368). One problem, however, accented here in Faulkner's text, is that such reactions in defense of (a usually nostalgic or archaic) "nature" or "common sense" are never quite successful or final, either in their consequences or in the specificity or grammar of their narration. They are symptoms of a nostalgia or archaism patently out of sync with the modernist present. Another problem, suggested by Hightower's own ritualized isolation and impotence, is that the social criticism Hightower manages to articulate to himself in this passage expands to include Hightower, he himself as reluctant as the rest are "to admit selfdoubt and to hope for and need pity themselves." His criticism of his community implicates him, too, and thus his

criticism remains unspoken, unheard, and unacknowledged.
The cultural currents he criticizes are too pervasive for him to
challenge effectively, too pervasive even for him to escape.

In performing this profoundly *critical* function, then, Faulkner's work also inhabits and *represents* much of the force,
extent, and subtlety of the very same cultural and psychological currents it criticizes. It thereby represents the difficulties
and limitations of its critique, the difficulty, for example, of
militarily, legally, or moralistically eliminating such cultural
currents either from the human subjects these currents allow
to dominate others or from the human subjects these currents
not only dominate but also largely constitute in their own
subjectivities. Furthermore, this realist dimension of Faulkner's work also represents the limitations of critique by regis-
tering the power of dominant cultural currents to circumscribe, to shape, and even to motivate such cultural
criticisms. Such critique, then, cannot simply replace, out-
flank, undercut, or frame representation. Patrick O'Donnell's
essay in this volume, for example, describes the various imagined new "world orders" in which modernist artists have attempted to enact "a break with the dead past"; these imagined
worlds, however, turn out to be "haunted by – if not deeply
rooted in – some version of the cultural past that defies renovation, that insists on repeating itself as the 'return of the
repressed.'" That past may well be dead to belief, but it retains
its haunting power. The problem addressed in John Matthews's essay, also in this volume, is less the power of a persistent cultural past than the more organized powers of the modern American "culture industry," to which almost the only
effective resistance appears to be the "negation of social reality" in modern art. Modernist cultural activity is described
both as a resistance confined to the formal properties of modern art and as a resistance based on a modernist artist's attempt (and failure) to create a cosmos that would somehow
break free of a tragically repetitive past. It is not hard to see
how either activity might lead to an ironic sense of social

helplessness as well as to the charges of political complacency or conservatism associated with many modernist writers. Matthews has elsewhere identified the historical and economic process of modernization as "the sedimented empirical reality" to be found even in the "most private formulations of personal identity" in Faulkner's most successfully autonomous modernist text, *As I Lay Dying* (Matthews 79, 72). Faulkner's work thus shares the predominant impulse of modernism toward criticism, but it is also candid about the difficulties and limitations of critique. One might say that this work is realistic about critique, or critical of critique (in much the same way that realism is most effectively critical of romanticism), whether in literary or literary critical discourse. Ralph Ellison has appreciated Faulkner's continuing to address social issues, such as race and democracy, that Ellison sees as the peculiar strength of American literature, especially in the nineteenth century. Ellison sees other modernist writers like Hemingway evading such social issues by means of a "superstitious" attention to literary experimentation and technique. Faulkner himself was certainly interested in formal experimentation and technique, but the effect of his experiments tends less to control than to provoke disturbances of whatever perspective tries to control his subject matter. Perhaps this is one way to describe the modernist associations with cosmopolitan literary exile that Faulkner's work both addresses and in many ways refuses to endorse. This realist dimension of Faulkner's modernism ensures that its ironic, critical distance remains a problematic, unstable, and perhaps more promising social position.

The achievement of Christmas's crucifixion in the novel's antepenultimate chapter, for example, might suggest a modernistically aesthetic, ritual, tragic, mythic, perhaps religious or ironic resolution and transcendence of the merely personal, local, modern, or merely social problems detailed in the rest of the novel (compare other modernists' appeals to Byzantium, ancient Ireland, classical Greece, Jacobean England, or the Holy Grail for at least ironic perspective and comment on the present). Faulkner's novel continues beyond that apparently transcendent ending, however, as previous versions of a similar ritual violence have already suggested that such a redeeming or ironic tragic vision will not and cannot hold. After sacrificing the sheep, and after striking and leaving Bobbie and vomiting the first time he learns she is menstruating, Joe does manage to approach her again and to talk with her in bed "about her body as if no one had ever done this before, with her or with anyone else" (*LA* 196). "With her" reminds the reader of the possible irony that Joe is unaware of her social status as a prostitute, but Joe's and many readers' implicit hope here is that he and she might somehow be able to escape or transcend such considerations and come to their own preideological, precultural, or utopian understanding independent of their society's discredited thinking about virginity, prostitution, or race (cf. Weinstein, 130–1). "So he told her in turn what he knew to tell," casually: "I got some nigger blood in me" (196). Bobbie does not, however, hear this statement critically or differently or as if for the first time, its meaning to be considered and discussed between these two relative outsiders to this society. Instead, she freezes. She can only think of it as a fact, an identity to be either recognized as true or denied as false: "You're what? . . . I dont believe it" (196–7). Later she will consider this a confession of guilt on Christmas's part. Prevailing social constructions of race and prostitution will continue to prove almost irresistible for their thinking both about each other and even about themselves as two victims of that same thinking.

As for the way these dominant cultural currents not only circumscribe but also inform and motivate modernist cultural criticism, I am coming to that, but I stress again that these recognitions of the force of accepted representations and common sense do not mean Faulkner's work simply retreats before such difficulties and limitations of critique back to representation, or from modernism to realism. The world of his work does not feel natural, comfortable, or recognizable in the way that realist work feels to many readers. It does not effectively contain its society's self-criticisms and discontents, or reduce those conflicts to terms an individual character, narrator, or reader can resolve. There are profound social and psychological problems here, problems that disturb the flow of almost every sentence, and there is no comfortable position from which to view these problems, or not for long. Judgment here is not enough; it is not social change, it is not even pure. Faulkner's work focuses on the alienation and hysteria not just of single characters or types, but of whole communities and of their apparently most trustworthy critics as well. The subject positions of innocent social insider or moralistic social judge usually offered by realism to its readers, for example, as well as the more modernist subject positions of disenchanted artistic or ironic social critic, are all pulled into the social and historical soup. They are shown to be largely circumscribed and constituted by that social context, whether as insider or outsider, but this impasse, this contradiction between critique and complicity, may at the same time be what leads some modernist work toward a renewed sense of being engaged in and moved by that same increasingly complex and changing context. This social background begins to function more clearly neither as a stable foundation of social customs or moral beliefs – certainly not one to which we might realistically yearn for a return – nor as an oppressive or meaningless social context acting systematically and independently of our own critical positions and yearnings for escape. It is a context instead in which characters, narrators, readers, writers, teachers, and students are already inevitably and even movingly engaged, an ongoing cultural conversation and activity, marked by powerful currents but also by persistent disturbances, differences, transferences, renegotiations, reconfigurations, and change.

This postmodern-sounding dimension of Faulkner's work grows out of the failures, impasses, and emotional dryness of modernism when it is put to a social test, as Faulkner's work usually insists that it is. The disenchanted artistic or ironic social critic in Faulkner is never quite allowed to leave – nor ever quite wants to leave – the social field of the action. He (it is usually a he) becomes an embroiled character, like Hightower in *Light in August* or Mr. Compson, Shreve, or Quentin in *Absalom Absalom!*, not just judged for being removed but, as well, emotionally unable to remain removed. As a character he learns not only that this modernist disenchantment and irony are of limited social power and usefulness, but also that his own disenchantment and irony are much less impersonal and disinterested than he has wanted to think. As a character he is less determined and more emotionally affected than he has wanted to think. He recognizes the patterns of ritual violence, the failures of domination, but he is also learning to recognize his own hands on his ears, his own obsession with an ironic pattern, and his own defensive deafness to a persistently tempting difference and potential for social change – a difference and a potential often suspected if not quite heard in the histories of poor whites, blacks, women, children, or in certain moments of humor or in the work of mourning (histories of identities described in O'Donnell's essay as "aggregate, mixed," or what Weinstein in *Faulkner's Subject* describes as "the subject in process, the subject in contestation" [10]). What this character tends to think virtually unthinkable, others are somehow able to think, act, even sometimes to say. Whereas his own history threatens to fly apart, other strange and different histories seem somehow to be still actively under way. Whereas the modernist focus of Faulkner's work is on centers that cannot hold, a more postmodernist dimension of that same work listens fitfully for other stories as signs of life in a culture differently conceived. From a modernist perspective, this latter tendency may risk the loss of a certain critical rigor or edge (or perhaps a tempting illusion of purity), may degenerate from "an aesthetics of shock to a more traditional one of recognition" and ideological recuperation (Weinstein 10). There are other reasons, however, to take that risk.

Gail Hightower, for instance, whose analysis of the town's scapegoating behavior toward Christmas I have just cited, *learns* in the course of the novel that his preoccupation with this pattern in the town's behavior toward both Christmas and himself has served all too conveniently to distract him from his own similar thinking and behavior toward the members of his church and especially toward his wife. '"I came here where faces full of bafflement and hunger and eagerness waited for me, waiting to believe; I did not see them" (*LA* 487). Focusing on the death of his grandfather in the Civil War, he has offered his congregation, "instead of the crucified shape of pity and love, a swaggering and unchastened bravo killed with a shotgun in a peaceful henhouse" (488). He has focused on the recurring moment of his grandfather's, his own, and now Christmas's bravado and ironic defeat, but he is still affected by the faces and the voices of "bafflement and hunger and eagerness" that do continue no less than before to "hope for and need pity themselves." He has not allowed himself to see the face or hear the voice of his (unnamed) wife. Nor has he stopped warning his friend Byron Bunch against disaster long enough to recognize and respect the resourcefulness and vitality of Byron's desire, his love for Lena Grove, even when that love takes a form significantly different from the fateful pattern Hightower has come to know and expect. But he is also slowly learning from Byron's unexpectedly different story.

In *Absalom, Absalom!* Mr. Compson, Shreve, and Quentin also attempt to assume distant, ironic postures toward the inevitable defeat of their own and (they tend to think) all others' hopes and desires, yet they are moved despite themselves by those who have not abandoned hope, or whose hopes take different shapes as parts of different histories. Mr. Compson accepts the decline of his own family, but he also eventually, reluctantly admits he cannot quite understand in those same terms either Charles Bon or Henry or Judith Sutpen. Shreve and Quentin similarly confront the failure of their ironic explanations to account for the strength of these characters' feelings for each other or for the strength of Shreve and Quentin's feelings for these same characters. Apparently, the failure of one prevailing story or history, even canonized stories that have come to seem natural, timeless, and universal, does not eliminate the existence of, or the desire for, other people's unexpectedly, irreducibly different stories. We, too, may well read such stories with "bafflement and hunger and eagerness . . . waiting to believe" and wanting to learn from stories other than our own.

Something like this postmodern sense of involvement and participation in the ongoing social construction and exchange of the stories that make up our social reality, our nature, our common sense, is implied by the final chapter of *Light in August*, coming after the dubious transcendence promised by Christmas's crucifixion and then Hightower's ironic reflections on his own compulsive deafness to the people around him, particularly to his own wife and his friend Byron Bunch. Byron's courtship of Lena Grove continues in this last chapter, despite Byron's obvious virginity and Lena's having just delivered a child without being married. Byron is drawn not away from Lena, nor to scapegoat or dominate Lena as a threat to his sense of his own masculinity, but toward Lena, as if to learn how she thinks and acts what so many like himself have thought unthinkable, unbearable, unacceptable. What such conditions as virginity and unwed motherhood mean is never allowed here to resolve itself into unquestionable social judgment and fact, however, nor does the narration undercut or frame such representations in favor of a coherent criticism. This last chapter is narrated between an entirely new character and his wife as the two of them make love in bed. The accent here is on the production, reception, and circulation of Byron and Lena's story as much as it is on the story "itself." Why?

The furniture repairer and dealer who gave Byron and Lena a
ride in his truck has watched Byron as he "got himself desper-
ated up to risking all" and as he then met a gentle but firm
rejection by Lena: "Why Mr. Bunch, Aint you ashamed" (*LA*
501, 503). The furniture dealer could not see Byron, he says,
"but I knew about how I would have been standing and feeling
if I was him. And that would have been with my head bowed,
waiting for the Judge to say, 'Take him out of here and hang
him quick'" (504). The possibility of a compulsive, ritual violence toward weakness is not forgotten here, but the furniture
dealer's humor emphasizes that such ritual violence is not the
only or finally inevitable tragic frame for Byron and Lena's
story. Perhaps Byron remembers what Mrs. Beard at the
boardinghouse has told him earlier about what he assumed
was the townswomen's judgment of Lena's position, that "if
you had more than mansense you would know that women
dont mean anything when they talk. It's menfolks that take
talking serious" (419). With some humor, Mrs. Beard over-
states her case, but it is true that women and men have both
been kinder to Lena throughout the novel than anything in
their often tight-lipped talk would have suggested they would
be. Even the woman who is hearing this story in bed has asked
her husband at the first oblique mention of sex, "*Aint you
shamed? . . . Talking that way before a lady*" (496). She does,
however, successfully communicate her interest in sex and
love despite this talk, as Lena also does to Byron, as if she
knew in turn, before her first and second rejections send him
"blind through the woods," that "whatever he done, he wasn't
going to mean it." As she reminds him, "Aint nobody never
said for you to quit" (504, 506).

By a kind of transference as they consider and adapt Byron
and Lena's story to their situation in bed, the furniture dealer
and his wife are able to communicate and act on what neither
of them quite knows how to say, something beyond or beneath
or between the lines of what they do say, what the prevailing
talk allows them to say. They are able to communicate and act

on a different, perhaps less systematically or canonically articulated, more mediated body of knowledge, traces of which they recognize (as Hightower finally did) in their humor, their inconsistencies, their desire, their love, something they cannot quite say but still both fear and want to articulate, stories they do not quite understand but still both fear and want to hear. (And this is another force shaping Faulkner's style.)

When I think Faulkner I think of this condition of "bafflement and hunger and eagerness" for something just past what Faulkner the writer quite knows how to say, what the Faulkner character, narrator, reader, teacher, or student knows how to say, what their overlapping and changing cultures know how to say, so that each of us keeps coming back, one to another. It is a hunger that suggests a critical dissatisfaction with what the culture in general or any of us as individuals alone already know how to say in the terms of our public or private common sense. It is a recognition of our "bafflement and hunger and eagerness" to hear and discuss and adapt each other's different, changing stories to each of our different, changing situations. And never quite knowing how.

2   Faulkner and Postmodernism

Faulkner's "modernism" has often been the subject of spirited discussion about the author's intrusion on, or complicity with, the monumental literature of the twentieth century. To think of Faulkner within the terms of "postmodernism," then, necessarily involves an attempt to define the relation of modernism to postmodernism.[1] This relation can only be seen coming in the wake of Faulkner's fiction, as a kind of critical aftermath that allows us to see it as differentiated from the contexts in which it was written and by which it is constrained. In essence, discussing Faulkner in postmodernist terms means accepting the assumption that what makes his fiction powerful and timely is its capacity to resist, disrupt, or exceed both Modernism (with a capital "M") and Faulkner's own modernism – his intended response to the perceived literary, cultural, and historical contexts of his writing. Within the discussion of Faulkner and postmodernism, Faulkner stands not as the "author" or progenitor of texts but, to employ the famous metaphor articulated by Quentin Compson in *Absalom, Absalom!*, as the unseen drop that falls into a pool of water, giving rise to a series of ripples that move outward to another connected pool: "let this second pool contain a different temperature of water, a different molecularity of having seen, felt, remembered, reflect in a different tone the infinite unchanging sky, it doesn't matter: that pebble's watery echo whose fall it did not even see moves across its sur-

31

face too at the original ripple-space" (210). These ripples can be seen as the movement of Faulkner's text through modern and postmodern culture, through the different molecularities of historical transformations. Here, "Faulkner" figuratively exists as the "original ripple-space," as a spacing or ellipsis that suggests the text he writes is to be known not by its self-authored intentions but by his procession through shifting contexts. Paradoxically, the "original ripple-space" is preserved, suggesting that there is a tension or contradiction in Faulkner's work between a recognition of historical and subjective processes and a desire to halt their progression, a yearning after the atemporality and stasis of origins.[2] This tension is the sign of struggle in Faulkner between modernity and postmodernity. The revisionary capacity of his work opens its essential contradictions to our eyes, forcing us to recall its spaced (out), erased origins, allowing us to view its truly radical nature in the critical and cultural aftermath that follows its writing. In seeking out manifestations of these contradictions in Faulkner, I focus on some passages from the latter sections of *Go Down, Moses*. This fictional assemblage is, arguably, Faulkner's most transitional work, as it oscillates between tragic nostalgia for a lost past of certain, integral origins and the parodic embracing of an indeterminate future in which identity is aggregate, mixed. In *Go Down, Moses*, Faulkner put his writing on the line in such a way that the truths he had discovered and revealed are questioned and rearticulated in the aftermath of the production of his major novels.

Viewed solely from the perspective of modernism itself, the monumental works of high modernism embody two, seemingly opposed, tendencies. On the one hand, the works of Joyce, Woolf, Yeats, Pound, Proust, and Faulkner often reflect the authorial attempt to construct a self-contained, imagined "world" that vies to replace the lost world of political, cultural, and theological order that vanished with Nietzsche's "disappearance of God." Joyce's Dublin, Woolf's Bloomsbury,

Yeats's Byzantium, Pound's Tempio Malatestiana, Faulkner's Yoknapatawpha – all might be seen as linguistic realms inhabited and dominated by the artist-god who makes and populates them. There are, of course, significant differences between the historical materiality of Joyce's Dublin, the palimpsestic compression of Pound's "eras," Yeats's systems and cosmologies, Woolf's impressionistic collages, and Faulkner's "South," made up of bits and pieces, "a few old mouth-to-mouth tales," scattered and fragmentary "letters without salutation or signature," as Mr. Compson puts it in *Absalom, Absalom!* (80). Yet it can be argued that each author engages in constructing a "geography of the imagination" that bears some mediated, formalistic relation to the messiness of "reality" and the deformations of time passing. Many of these authors attempt to erect "wor(l)d orders" that, within the mythos of modernism, enact a break with the dead past; their making signifies the successful generation of a new cosmos – however hedged by reflection on its fictionality – the largesse of which (whether manifested by means of Joycean detail or Poundian megalomania) manifests the power of the artist. Paradoxically, these linguistic worlds inevitably *replicate* the past even as they represent the ethereal attempt to break free of it. All of the realms I have mentioned are haunted by – if not deeply rooted in – some version of the cultural past that defies renovation, that insists on repeating itself as the "return of the repressed."[3] Proust's Combray can be viewed as the scene of narcissistic regression; from *Dubliners* through *Finnegans Wake*, Joyce's Dublin is the site of cultural and historical paralysis; and, as several of Faulkner's readers have powerfully argued, the characters who inhabit Faulkner's Yoknapatawpha are locked into the tragic repetitions of their personal pasts – repetitions that recur through the generations of the Sutpens and the Compsons and the Sartorises in a landscape cursed by the twin specters of slavery and the Civil War.[4] The modernity of these works, then, partially resides in the negotiation of an essential contradiction between a rejection of the past and the inevitable repetition of the past in that very rejection. This contradiction exists because modernism can be viewed as an attempt to replace outworn orders and old monuments with new, linguistic orders and imagined geographies that, necessarily, reproduce the structures which have preceded them. If one wishes to make a world – even one founded on aesthetic rather than mimetic prerogatives – then that created realm will inevitably stand in a homologous relation to *the* world as it is perceived with its timeworn orders, syntaxes, and disciplines.

Another way of putting this is to say that modernist works are bound over to a formalism that both promotes and subverts the attempt to create a linguistic universe. This is the double bind of modernism, the constant movement between the extremes of sheer repetition and "making it new"; yet, there are moments in the works of the high-modernist authors I have mentioned that work beyond this contradiction, that rupture its bonds. In Faulkner, to return to Quentin's metaphor of the interconnected pools, these "postmodern" moments frequently appear in the form of a ripple effect – a movement along the surface of the text far removed from the nascent occurrence that initiated the series, yet one that profoundly puts into question the fatality of events and their aftermath often seen as characteristic of Faulkner's fiction. For Faulkner, one crucial effect of such moments is to undo the, otherwise, inexorable connection – observable in single figures such as Thomas Sutpen – between attempting to transcend the past, and being condemned to repeat it.

Go Down, Moses was assembled in the aftermath of Faulkner's most monumental effort, *Absalom, Absalom!,* and there are many ways to see the former as an echo of the latter. The obsession with blood and genealogy, with inheritance and dispossession, and, above all, with the connection between race and identity permeates both novels. Both bear "biblical" titles, thus signaling their entry into the modernist sweepstakes of "cosmic" works with epic parallels: Joyce's *Ulysses*,

Pound's *Cantos*, Broch's *Death of Virgil*. *Absalom, Absalom!*
is the cry of King David for his rebellious son in the story of
betrayal and paternal succession recounted in 2 Samuel; *Go
Down, Moses* recalls the enslavement and liberation of the
chosen people related in Exodus and specifically cites the refrain of a well-known black American spiritual: "Go Down,
Moses / Way down into Egypt land / Tell old Pharaoh / 'Let
my people go!' "[5] Both novels portray a white protagonist who
rejects his heritage and who enacts a failed attempt to create a
new, "original" self that can live beyond or outside of cultural
and temporal boundaries; both novels also portray a black
protagonist who bears a proximate or distant relation to his
white counterpart, and who mirrors "through a glass, darkly"
the white quest for identity. In *Absalom, Absalom!* there is
Thomas Sutpen, who attempts to escape his "poor white
trash" origins and to establish a pharaohic dynasty in the
swamps of northern Mississippi as he plans for a white, racist
empire that, in his imagination, will stand for all time as long
as the lines of genealogical succession are properly purified
and maintained. And then there is Charles Bon, the son (supposedly "mulatto") of Sutpen's first marriage, who apparently
wants only his father's acknowledgment of his own presence
and identity, and who becomes both the sacrificial victim to
Sutpen's design and the catalyst of his empire's slow destruction. In *Go Down, Moses* there is Ike McCaslin, who forsakes
ownership of the land in the attempt to forge a primordial
relation to it, but who discovers that the land is a fiction
disappearing before his eyes even as his corporeal being with-
ers with advancing age. And then there is Lucas Beauchamp,
Ike's proximate relation by virtue of a tangled skein of kinship
bonds, whose rights of possession of the already dispossessed
land are as compelling as Ike's, and who is described as the
"composite of the two races which made him . . . the battleground and victim of the two strains, he was a vessel, durable,
ancestryless, nonconductive, in which the toxin and his anti
stalemated one another, seethless, unrumored in the outside

air" (*GDM* 101). Lucas and his descendants, both victims and survivors in this novel of tragic race relations, inherit the land or, rather, retain its wasted, capitalized vestige in the form of the surplus of Ike's self-dispossession.

That scrap of common wisdom, "Those who forget the past are condemned to repeat it," could stand as a synopsis of the comparison I have made thus far between *Absalom, Absalom!* and *Go Down, Moses*. Indeed, the latter novel *does* repeat the former in many respects, but it is the manner of the repetition – an echo in a minor key – that marks *Go Down, Moses* as a postmodern revision/reversal of Faulkner's masterwork (even as, internally, *Absalom, Absalom!* marks itself in this manner at certain moments). Both Thomas Sutpen and Ike McCaslin seek an intimate, originary relation to the land they inhabit: In the former's case, it is a racist relation, in that it involves an attempt to exclude and differentiate a cultural other; in the latter's, though it might be argued that McCaslin seeks to include blacks in his design of "inherited disinheritance," he mythologizes his grounding, and in so doing, participates in a mapping of binary differences between animal and human, primitive and civilized, black and white that articulate the content of racist stereotypes. By raising up an empire out of the black mud of the Mississippi swamps – an enterprise that invokes one of the cruel paradoxes of slavery, as Sutpen toils alongside his black slaves, even as they, together, build the white manor that will debar them – Sutpen hopes, in Quentin Compson's words, to erase a past in which he was victimized by cultural differences and to "'look ahead along the still undivulged light rays in which his descendants who might not even ever hear his . . . name, waited to be born without even having to know that they had once been riven forever free from brutehood'" (*AA* 210). Ike, too, wishes to erase a guilty past by rediscovering his innocence, but in *Go Down, Moses*, as we shall see, that desire is sundered by the material bodies of history, who give the lie to the dream/nightmare of a past redeemed.

In essence, Sutpen desires to make the land itself eternally "his" by virtue of a purified genealogical succession. In a contradictory reversal and repetition of this process, Ike McCaslin forsakes the legal ownership of the land, and the big house and subjugation of black bodies that goes along with it. He becomes the "trustee" of the legacy that has been transmitted to Beauchamp and his descendants. It is as if he has become Sutpen twice-removed – an ironic, bureaucratic Sutpen merely managing for those formerly excluded others the estate (now fully capitalized, made over into the grimy banknotes that Ike forces on James Beauchamp's granddaughter in "Delta Autumn") that Sutpen had sought to establish through sweat, blood, and semen. In the logic that issues from the intersecting stories of *Go Down, Moses*, Ike "relinquishes" his inheritance – what little there is left of it after the deficits of his ancestors' IOUs – as part of his gradual recognition that the land belongs to no one, that it was created "not to hold for himself and his descendants inviolable title forever, generation after generation, but to hold the earth mutual and intact in the communal anonymity of brotherhood" (*GDM* 246). Through Sam Fathers, "The Bear" leads us to believe, Ike has established a new relation to the land, one reflected in his viewing of Sam's grave mound, which is "no abode of death because there was no death, not Lion and not Sam: not held fast in earth but free in earth and not in earth but of earth, myriad yet undiffused of every myriad part, leaf and twig and particle, air and sun and rain and dew and night, acorn oak and leaf and acorn again, dark and dawn and dark and dawn again, in their immutable progression" (313). Apparently, Ike gives up legal ownership of the land in order to immerse himself in it – to become one with it – in its endless recycling and "the communal anonymity of brotherhood."

Yet this imaginary relation to the land bears a disturbing resemblance to what Sutpen attempts to establish through opposite means: here, there is "no death" but repetition without end; here, the earth (and all that is contained within it) is transcendent, homogenized, timeless; here, all differences – cultural, corporeal, historical – have been erased. This, I would argue, is a restatement of Sutpen's dream of a timeless empire founded on a genealogical repetition of the same, with the crucial difference that Ike's vision of Sam's grave is inclusive, whereas Sutpen's design is exclusive. But both can be viewed as eerie repetitions of each other: their primary components – the erasure of difference through purification (*Absalom, Absalom!*) or assimilation (*Go Down, Moses*), and endless repetition of the same through genealogical succession (*Absalom, Absalom!*) or the recirculations of nature (*Go Down, Moses*) – are disturbingly similar. Does Ike then repeat Sutpen's mistake? In Faulkner's cursed South, are all whites, whether of goodwill or fascistic intent, condemned to repeat the past by enacting the same fantasies of assimilation and control in relation to the "other" – whether this be "nature" or "the land" or "blacks," collapsed into a mystified hegemony?

Were Faulkner to have concluded *Go Down, Moses* with "The Bear" (by itself, in the versions published separately from this "conspicuously fragmentary and cryptic" narrative collage, one of Faulkner's most widely read works), then it would be possible to respond affirmatively to these questions and, thus, to underscore the combined nostalgia and fatality often thought of as hallmarks of Faulkner's modernism and humanism.[6] Faulkner, however, chose to conclude *Go Down, Moses* not with the centerpiece novella of Ike McCaslin's narcissistic despair over the disappearance of the wilderness (and, hence, of himself, since he becomes more and more closely identified with "the big woods" as the work progresses) but with two stories in a minor key. Like most of the stories of *Go Down, Moses*, "Delta Autumn" and "Go Down, Moses" were published separately in earlier versions; in a work that continually skews chronology, Faulkner's placing of them at the end makes "chronological" sense as they tell the tales of Lucas Beauchamp's descendants. More importantly, these two stories that serve as postmortems of the monumental quests of "The Bear" reflect back on the genealogical tangles and successions of the McCaslin–Beauchamp line. They offer, I argue, a commentary on the imaginary transumption of identity in "The Bear" figured by "old Carothers' doomed and fatal blood" (*GDM* 280), as well as on the fatalism of "race relations" inextricably tied to the land by "threads frail as truth and impalpable as equators yet cable-strong to bind for life them who made the cotton to the land their sweat fell on" (281).

In terms of tone, "Delta Autumn" is certainly one of Faulkner's most cynical fictions, replete as it is with comparisons between a specious, threatening, "political" present and a lost, mythic past where the eternal verities of the unpossessable land prevailed. The story depicts Ike McCaslin's last hunt in the disappearing woods and swamps of northern Mississippi, and his disturbing encounter with a distant relative – an unnamed woman – of the Beauchamp line. In the following conversation between Ike and the younger hunters, the "old man" serves as a sorry replacement for Sam Fathers as he attempts to uphold the values instilled in him by his mentor:

"I'm going in," the other said harshly. "Don't worry. Because this will be the last of it."

"The last of the deer hunting, or of doe hunting?" Legate said. This time the old man paid no attention to him even by speech. He still watched the young man's savage and brooding face.

"Why?" he said.

"After Hitler gets through with it? Or Smith or Jones or Roosevelt or Willkie or whatever he will call himself in this country?"

"We'll stop him in this country," Legate said. "Even if he calls himself George Washington."

"How?" Edmonds said. "By singing God Bless America in bars at midnight and wearing dime-store flags in our lapels?"

"So that's what's worrying you," the old man said. "I aint noticed this country being short of defenders yet, when it needed them. . . . I reckon, when the time comes and some of you have done got tired of hollering we are whipped if we don't go to war and some more are hollering we are whipped if we do, it will cope with one Austrian paper-hanger, no matter what he will be calling himself. My pappy and some other better men than any of them you named tried once to tear it in two with a war, and they failed."

"And what have you got left?" the other said. "Half the people without jobs and half the factories closed by strikes. The country full of people to tell a man how to raise his own cotton whether he will or wont, and Sally Rand with a sergeant's stripes and not even the fan couldn't fill the army rolls." . . .

"We got a deer camp — if we ever get to it," Legate said. "Not to mention does."

"It's a good time to mention does," the old man said. "Does and fawns both. The only fighting anywhere that ever had anything of God's blessing on it has been when men fought to protect does and fawns" (*GDM* 322–3).

In this conversation between men, against the contemporary vicissitudes of the Great Depression, Hitler's rise to power, America's hesitancy over entering World War II, Roosevelt's presidency, and the erosion of patriotism (symbolized in the reference to Sally Rand, a popular stripper and "fan dancer" of the time, who, supposedly, even in uniform and without her fan couldn't attract enlistments), Ike holds up the durability of the land itself — outside wars and politics — as that which will predominate. Moreover, he argues that the ritualistic rules of the hunt, instituted to protect "does and fawns" (an interestingly gendered reference in light of the prurient comments about Sally Rand), will outlast governments and dictators, presumably because these rules — part and parcel of "the wilderness" — have been in place from the beginning of time. In essence, Ike argues "outside history" that there is a transcendent realm of rules, actions, and subject positions that guarantee the continuance of a world that, ironically, he comes to visit in this story for the last time. The poignancy of his claim is enhanced in his own eyes with the understanding that the world of "the big woods" is literally disappearing: "He had

watched it, not being conquered, destroyed, so much as retreating since its purpose was served now and its time an
outmoded time, retreating southward through this inverted-
apex, this ∇-shaped section of earth between hills and River
until what was left of it seemed now to be gathered and for the
time arrested in one tremendous density of brooding and inscrutable impenetrability at the ultimate funneling tip" (326-
7). Ike here imagines a "clearing" that, even while vanishing
on the map, manages to retain its original, imaginative shape
and impenetrability, but it is a space – analogous to the imaginative scene of Faulkner's own writing – increasingly troubled by his own diminishing, its contamination by history, its
isolationism. The sign of origins, the "delta" Faulkner typo-
graphically places in the text and includes in the story's title,
is a cipher, a form surrounding an emptiness, hemmed in on
all sides by temporality, change, difference. As I have suggested, one fantasy of high modernism is to carve out such an
imagined, timeless space, as well as to mourn its passing. In
"Delta Autumn," Faulkner allows Ike to articulate this imaginary locale, only, in the postmodern revisions of his own
writing, to disown it.

For Ike is certain it is a doe that is shot in these woods, the
ultimate and final violation of this feminized space in which
"does and fawns" are to be protected. For him, this is the final
traducement of the romance of undefiled origins and protected space in a downward progress that began with the discovery that the "holy grail" of the inherited trophy is full of
IOUs. It points toward a land and a future where, in his racist
projections, *Chinese and African and Aryan and Jew, all
breed and spawn together until no man has time to say
which one is which nor cares"* (347; Faulkner's italics). Such a
statement, coming from Ike McCaslin, is problematic and
complex: How are we to regard it? Is this "Faulkner" speaking
through Ike? Or is this Faulkner suggesting that Ike's values –
values in which segregation, ahistoricity, anticapitalism, and
identity formation are so twisted up together that it is impos-

sible to separate them – are as "outmoded" as the time and space represented by Ike's imagined delta? Nostalgia and critique are equally entertwined in such passages, but it is toward the latter that the gravity of this penultimate story in *Go Down, Moses* pulls us. How, with a conversation about "the Austrian paper-hanger" ringing in our ears – even if it is one articulated by agrarian isolationists – could we not read an attack, between the lines, on Ike's racial paranoia? "Delta Autumn" clearly takes place on the eve of America's entry into World War II, but most of *Go Down, Moses* was written between 1940 and 1942, the completed work being published in 1942, when America was well into the war and Hitler's "plans" for racial purification were quite apparent in the pogroms of Warsaw. While Faulkner could not have known of the holocaust taking place even as he was writing "Delta Autumn," we can observe in Ike's fear of racial assimilation – a fear mapped on to his sense of a lost, homogeneous "homeland" where the purified, ritualized self is born – Faulkner's critique of an idea that he had earlier figured in all of the vessels and urns, all of the hamlets, ghettos, and black abysses of his previous work. The idea subverted in *Go Down, Moses* is that the formation of identity is a matter of closing out and separating oneself from the "other," that the formation of the "authentic" self can only take place outside history, within a boundaried, segregated space. This space is always feminized in Faulkner's fiction because it is regressively associated with stereotypes of woman as virginal womb. This "innocent," modern version of identity has played itself out in *Go Down, Moses* as it played itself out in modern Western history with disastrous consequences. The rise of Hitler to power, the disappearance of the "virginal" wilderness, Ike's fear of assimilationism, his insistence on rituals that both protect and segregate the feminine other, and his anxiety concerning his own extinction – all are conflated in this story's autumnal.

In *Go Down, Moses*, Faulkner posits modern identity and its discontents only to undermine them by pointing the way

toward another, postmodern version of identity as "aggregate." For Ike's apprehension of a world where "all breed and
spawn together," expressed in terms of an apocalyptic potential that would clearly require his own extinction, takes visible shape in the character of the woman who has just left him.
James Beauchamp's granddaughter enters Ike's tent — now,
with a doe about to be shot in what remains of the "wilderness," the last retreat of ritualized, male identity — wearing "a
man's hat and a man's slicker and rubber boots, carrying the
blanket-swaddled bundle on one arm and holding the edge of
the unbuttoned raincoat over it with the other hand" (*GDM*
340). She is carrying, swaddled, her son, the son of Roth Edmonds and thus the last child of the assimilated McCaslin–
Beauchamp lines, crossed and recrossed by blacks and whites
in the history Ike has gathered from the family ledgers. The
scene is one of passionate rebuke and ironic traversals. The
woman, madonna-like, is bearing a child in her arms, yet she
is wearing a man's clothes; upon discovering her ancestry, Ike
screams at her, "You're a nigger!" (344), yet she is described as
"queerly colorless" (340), and Ike remarks to her, "You are
young, handsome, almost white" (346) in urging her to marry
a man of her "own race." Ike's racist imperative and, initially
at least, the guilt money Edmonds conveys to her through Ike
are rejected by the woman with the simple question "Old
man . . . have you lived so long and forgotten so much that
you don't remember anything you ever knew or felt or even
heard about love?" (346). She accepts the hunting horn bound
in silver that Ike offers her — originally, inherited from General Compson — but it is clear that this vestigial trophy is as
meaningless to her as the empty cup of Ike's familial inheritance. In this scene, she is a figure of youth, strength, and
continuance who momentarily touches "the gnarled, blood-
less, bone-dry old man's fingers" (345) after admonishing him
about spoiling Roth Edmonds with the transfer of inheritance: "I would have made a man of him. He's not a man yet.
You spoiled him. You, and Uncle Lucas — and Aunt Mollie.

But mostly you" (343). This is a stinging condemnation, for it is spoken in the very space (or what is left of it) of Ike's own initiation into manhood; moreover, the failure of "manhood" is here attributed to the transmission of inheritance – a failed transmission owing to the entanglements of genealogy and Ike's egotism regarding his capacity to purify himself and the land of the guilt of slavery by manumission. The granddaughter of Tennie's Jim stands as a walking rebuke to everything Ike fears and purports to be; she is a figure of transgression and "crossing" – black and white, male and female, disowned and legatee – who walks out of this story and into the open space of the future that Ike dreads as he shrivels up in his tent, his shrinking space doubly violated by the intrusion of the woman and the killing of the doe. As a figure for an alternative identity to that represented by Ike's separatist white male demesne, she seems to know more about love and "manhood" than Ike has ever learned, or ever forgotten.

Yet, however much he may critique Ike's separatist idealism and compounded racism in "Delta Autumn," Faulkner does not idealize its opposite: here, at least, he is no romantic proponent of a mystified "otherness" that would figuratively replace boundaries with "effluvia" (the term Ike uses to describe the presence of the granddaughter of Tennie's Jim), or modernist hierarchies of self and space with postmodernist "indifferences." Faulkner's postmodernism takes a specific form that moves beyond a mere rejection of the ritualized identity formation that bears the name of Ike McCaslin in *Go Down, Moses* and that I have termed "modern," even as this rejection is cast in the form of Ike's unnamed niece's rebukes. *Go Down, Moses* concludes with the title story, the tale of Samuel Worsham Beauchamp, the grandson of Lucas Beauchamp, about to face execution for murdering a Chicago policeman. Here, Faulkner takes the very iconography he had fronted in "Delta Autumn" with its references to the swaddled Christ child and the coming of a new age and stands it on its head. As if to "prove" Ike's miscegenist fears and predictions in self-fulfilling prophecy, Samuel Beauchamp, the last of Lucas's line, appears to fit all of the racist stereotypes Ike would attribute to the illegitimate offspring of, in this case, the McCaslin patriarch, Lucius Quintus Carothers McCaslin and his black female slaves. Like Jim Bond, the last of the "mixed" Sutpen–Bon line in *Absalom, Absalom!*, Samuel Beauchamp disappears into the banality of "underclass" criminality or madness.

How, then, to read this anticlimactic conclusion to *Go Down, Moses*? In terms of its placement, we may regard this disturbing story precisely *as* an anticlimax, and thus as yet another form of commentary both on Ike's pretenses and on any false optimism that may ensue from a black woman's rejection of these after she walks out of his tent and into history and a future that, for her, is equally open and desperately uncertain. Ike's apocalyptic attitude at the end of "Delta Autumn" is, finally, absurdly self-aggrandizing. He takes the stance of "après moi le déluge" (a "deluge" of miscegenated others), suggesting that, in his mind, he is the last bastion of purified identity and ritualistic codes; after his death and the disappearance of the sacred woods, all hell will break loose.

The progression from "Delta Autumn" to "Go Down, Moses" urges a connection between the unnamed infant of the former story and the adult criminal of the latter, as if, to follow Ike's trajectory, Samuel's fate *must* fulfill the ignoble fate of the child brought into the old man's tent.[7] But what "arrives" from infancy in "Go Down, Moses" is not the final evolution of some "rough beast" slouching "toward Bethlehem to be born"; rather, the subject of the story is arranging for the transportation of Samuel Worsham Beauchamp's dead black corpse to Mississippi. All that is left "after" Ike is dead bodies – one white and one black – just as all that remains of Thomas Sutpen's machinations are the bodies of Charles Bon, Charles Etienne St. Velery Bon, and Jim Bond – two dead, one living and deranged. These bodies are the historical fallout of the racist imaginary, represented in quite different ways by Sutpen and McCaslin. Heaven and earth do not consume themselves when Sutpen's dynasty falls or when Ike's world collapses, there is only a literal embodiment of the consequences of their projects. There is, at the end of *Go Down, Moses*, only the poor body of Samuel Beauchamp, who, like his ancestors, according to Aunt Mollie Beauchamp, has been "sold . . . in Egypt, sold . . . to Pharaoh" (362). And there is the white body of the policeman he has slain: the mystery as to why Samuel – a numbers racketeer working under an alias in Chicago – shot him in the back remains unexplained and unpublished; it is shrugged off verbally by Gavin Stevens as the act of a " 'bad son of a bad father' " (357). These two bodies, black and white, separate in death yet whose dust will commingle in that metaphoric "earth" Ike McCaslin holds so dear, are the signs and remnants of the violence that separates black from white in a world that fears and stereotypes the other. This result is not the apocalypse or transformation that causes Ike such anxiety in the final moments of "Delta Autumn," but repetitions of the same: the Civil War and its aftermath, fought all over again in miniature in Chicago; the selling of Benjamin unto Egypt transacted in modern times.

Yet this is not merely another version of the fatalism often attributed to Faulkner, the past *merely* repeating itself. Instead, in *Go Down, Moses*, the past is brought into the present and realized, not mythicized, in the violence that precedes the title story's eulogistic events. The story works *against* Ike McCaslin's and Gavin Stevens's stereotypes – the fated child of "mixed blood," "the bad son of a bad father" – precisely because its subject is the transfer of a black corpse that must be returned home. It is not metaphorical bad luck, "mixed blood," or fate that is at issue here, but Samuel Worsham Beauchamp's literal body lying in its coffin. This singular, named body enters the story as irrevocably present, even in death a specific agent in and of history, not an amorphous, anonymous element of cyclic, tragic historical progressions. Indeed, one might argue that only as a corpse does Samuel

Worsham Beauchamp attain historical agency, suggesting that, for Faulkner, the very bodies tortured and subjugated under slavery are all that is visible of black subjectivity in slavery's aftermath. In this anametaphoric story, the prose is flat, spare, "realistic," stylistically implying that this stark violence, these stark bodies, proceed from the prosaically rendered rituals of initiation and identity formation we read in "The Bear."

Against this backdrop, Gavin Stevens and the editor of the newspaper conduct the last in a series of payoffs and exchanges that occur throughout *Go Down, Moses:* when they agree to contribute the lion's share to the cost of the funeral and the transportation of Beauchamp's body. This is the white, liberal response to the tragedy of slavery, the guilt money that Ike McCaslin attempted to pay in a different coin. Remarking on this act of generosity, the editor responds to Gavin Stevens's question, "'All right?': 'No it aint all right . . . But it don't look like I can help myself. By Jupiter . . . even if I could help myself, the novelty will be almost worth it. It will be the first time in my life I ever paid money for copy I had already promised before hand I won't print'" (360). The editor is referring to the fact that he will not print the story of Beauchamp's death for Aunt Mollie Beauchamp's sake, although, in a final, viciously ironic twist, Mollie asks him to publicize the story of her grandson's death even though she can't read, as if seeing the mere shape of the letters will provide a vestigial substitute in black and white for Samuel's living body ("'Miss Belle will show me whar to look and I can look at hit. You put hit in de paper. All of hit'"[365]). Faulkner's critique of the making of Yoknapatawpha, actually a form of authorial self-critique, is sharpest at such moments: Samuel Worsham Beauchamp's life and death cannot be written; his acts and being cannot be comprehended as part of the "story of the South" or the Yoknapatawpha saga. Ultimately, he cannot be narrativized, either by Ike McCaslin, who would wish to place his multiple body (black/white; perpetrator/victim) within the "white" fiction of identity's origins and ends, or by Faulkner, who concludes *Go Down, Moses* with the lawyer Stevens's declaration that he needs to get back to his desk. The realm of law and writing is, in this instance, a retreat from the presence of Beauchamp's body. His body is a historical "disturbance" that cannot be negotiated within fictive patterns, be they those of McCaslin's apocalyptic imagination or the fragmentary cosmos of Yoknapatawpha.

Faulkner's postmodernism in *Go Down, Moses* is thus manifested materially, as a refusal to write (off) Samuel Worsham Beauchamp, to provide a "satisfying" climax to his novel, or to indulge in a remystification of the "other" as somehow survived or transcendent − a tactic he deploys elsewhere in, for example, *Light in August*, where the slaying of Joe Christmas is portrayed in spectacularly apocalyptic terms, and where the "corrupted" materiality of his indeterminate body is wrought into an antimyth transmitted unto generations. Beauchamp is a corpse in the final moments of *Go Down, Moses*, nothing more and nothing less, his story unpublished and unreadable. There are other, similar moments scattered throughout Faulkner's fiction, when the quest for origins and the attempted limning and inscription of identity is sundered by corporeal materiality. Whatever Addie Bundren may have been in life, however she may have been viewed by the members of her family, each of whom "reads" her differently, there is no discounting the presence of her decaying body in the coffin: just the opposite of being ineffable, "a word to fill a lack," her body is all too scandalously real to the offended passerby who smells it in *As I Lay Dying*. In *The Hamlet*, the very prodigality of Eula Varner's body belies her mythification by the community of Frenchmen's Bend, and serves as a revelation of what Ratliff and the others really "make" of her in that she is implicitly compared to Isaac Snopes's cow, a body bestialized and consumed by an idiot. In *Absalom, Absalom!*, the intermingling and mutability of bodies both black and white are counterweights to Sutpen's desire for a genetic succession that will supposedly guarantee the incorporated permanence of his identity – his "character" through lasting generations. *Go Down, Moses* recalls these instances and assembles them into a narrative whose purpose is to unravel the knot between identity and writing, to portray the bodily basis of human suffering and desire, and to represent the contradictory iterability and singularity of a nontranscendent version of history. The novel accomplishes this by reversing and critiquing several of Faulkner's long-held narrative ideas: the quest for origins; the inscription of identity in letter, tale, gravestone; the idealization of nature; the allegorization of the "other," feminine or black, as "present absences" in the rhetorically ornamented vessels, urns, liquids, atmospheres, and abysses of his fiction. The postmodernism of *Go Down, Moses*, and in less concentrated ways of Faulkner's fiction at large, comes about as a result of Faulkner's revisionary capacities, which enabled him to scrutinize and put under question the constituent elements of the modern, mythologized "world" he had erected across the Yoknapatawpha novels. In this way, he allowed himself to see the limitations of his own art and understanding, and to force a confrontation between his writing and the irrefutable materiality of history.

NOTES

1 The most revealing work to date on Faulkner's modernism is that of Moreland, who views Faulkner as both inscribing and resisting – through repetition – modernist fascinations with hierarchy, genealogy, and the categorizing of the "Other."
2 See Matthews ("Elliptical") for an illuminating discussion of how ellipses works in Faulkner's fiction as a rhetorical and epistemological device.
3 See Schneidau's discussion in *Waking Giants* of the repressive presence of "history" and monumentalism in canonical modernist texts.
4 Irwin, from a psychoanalytic perspective, and Sundquist (*House*), from a historicist perspective, have written compellingly of the tragic repetitions of Faulkner's fiction.
5 The refrain of this sad and ironic slaves' lament anticipates the circularity and differential repetitions of Faulkner's novel. It begins and ends with

the word "go," but in the first instance, the word is a command from the supreme paternal authority, Yahweh, telling Moses to go into Egypt and free the Jewish people; in the second instance, the "go" of "let my people go" is both part of the command and a sign of *release* from a temporal paternal authority, that of pharaoh.

6 According to Minter, 187. Minter goes on to suggest that *Go Down, Moses* "defines every text as an ur-text and pre-text, and then requires us to begin making connections and patterns that we must then revise or even repudiate" (189). Although Minter does not label it as such, this is as incisive a statement as one can find concerning the "postmodern" qualities of Faulkner's work.

7 Actually, the infant and Samuel Worsham Beauchamp *are* related as descendants of the Beauchamp line: James Beauchamp's granddaughter is, as far as one can ascertain, Samuel Worsham Beauchamp's second cousin.

3   Faulkner and the Culture Industry

"Thanks for your heart, Bart." – *Barton Fink*

Boy meets girl.
Boy sues girl.
Boy meets girl.
Boy sues girl. – William Faulkner

"Sometimes I think if I do one more treatment or screenplay," Faulkner complained in 1944, after a decade of intermittent screenwriting in Hollywood, "I'll lose whatever power I have as a writer" (Wilde 309). The myth of the artist corrupted by newly dominant commercial media like the movies and magazines has become the modern counterpart to the nineteenth century's myth of the serious writer condemned to popular neglect (H. N. Smith 3–15). Rather than Hawthorne's fury at the "damned mob of scribbling women" or Melville's lapse into obscurity and eventual silence, the 1920s and 1930s produced legends about Faulkner and Fitzgerald squandering years hack writing in California's Babylon.[1]

Two reflections on the new market conditions for writing after World War I – one imaginative, the other theoretical – may help us understand what the mass media were to mean to Faulkner's generation. In their 1991 film *Barton Fink*, Joel and Ethan Coen illustrate the destructive effect of Hollywood on the serious writers who sought to make fortunes there while

51

preserving their artistic integrity. Barton Fink, launched by the triumph of his first Broadway play in 1941, agrees hesitantly to his agent's offer of a lucrative screenwriting contract with "Capital Pictures." A week of writer's block on his first assignment drives Fink to consult another writer, who chances to be a famous Southern novelist – America's greatest living novelist, according to Fink's startled salutation of Bill Mayhew in the studio men's room.

Fink comes to know a once great artist now lost to cynicism and alcohol, the drink standing, as Mayhew's mistress puts it, as a "levee" against the "manure" of Hollywood. Between rounds of violent delirium tremens, Mayhew inscribes a copy of his latest novel to Fink; he wishes that this book, *Nebuchadnezzar*, may "divert" Fink in his "stay among the Philistines." Despite the assurances of Capital's head, Jack Lipnik, that the writer is "KING!" at his studio (a promise sealed when Lipnik kisses the sole of the terrified Fink's shoe), it is the mogul who commands the writer's imagination. "Right now the contents of your head is the property of Capital Pictures," Lipnik's assistant warns Fink early in the film. After both Mayhew and his mistress, who admits to Fink that she has ghosted her lover's last two novels and several screenplays, are shot to death and then decapitated, Barton is left doubting if any writer can practice "the life of the mind" at Capital Pictures. As he sits beside the Pacific in the film's last scene, a young woman asks if the box beside him is his. Because he has been entrusted with the parcel by the murderer, we may suspect that it contains a victim's head, but Fink won't look and can't say:

"What's in the box?"
"I don't know."
"Isn't it yours?"
"I don't know."

After Lipnik has wrathfully rejected his "arty" screenplay, Fink is told that he will remain under contract, everything he writes belonging to Capital, but that the studio will use nothing until he learns to turn out what is wanted. Fink must decide if he's been handed his head in a box, if the studio has indeed taken his heart.

Barton Fink conducts a narrative of initiation, complete with human sacrifice, through which the serious writer learns what it means to become a commercial writer. The Coen brothers care about historical specificity, populating their film with caricatures of recognizable figures from the studio decades, because they wish to identify a pivotal moment in modern American culture. To the extent the film satirizes moviemakers' pandering to consumers with mass-produced pulp under the direction of craven investors and assorted delusionaries, it exposes the emergence of what has been called "the culture industry." During those same years, two German Jews, Max Horkheimer and Theodor Adorno, took refuge in Hollywood from Nazism, and resumed their critical investigations of art in modern culture by writing a series of essays on the relation between enlightenment and artistic expression. "The Culture Industry: Enlightenment as Mass Deception" argues that a singular transformation has occurred in contemporary art's admission that it is a commodity and that "a change in the character of the art commodity itself is coming about. What is new is not that it is a commodity, but that today it deliberately admits it is one; that art renounces its own autonomy and proudly takes its place among consumption goods" (*DE* 157).

For Horkheimer and Adorno, what the culture industry produces violates art's essential purposelessness, its expression of individuality through style, its insistence on beauty and pleasure in their pure uselessness, and hence its fundamentally negative function in society. Art ought to resist – impassively, through its willful beauty – the social and economic practices in which it is embedded. However much I may have to simplify their position (elaborated individually and collaboratively over a number of other works),[2] I do so to avail myself of a critique that probes mass culture much more deeply than the shallow complaint that it lacks aesthetic merit. Horkheimer and Adorno let us ask what such debased art *does*.[3]

There is little doubt about what such art *is*, and how it got to be. Horkheimer and Adorno inveigh against the unremitting uniformity and predictability of art designed by the culture industry:

A constant sameness governs the relationship to the past as well. What is new about the phase of mass culture compared with the late liberal stage is the exclusion of the new. The machine rotates on the same spot. While determining consumption it excludes the untried as a risk. The movie-makers distrust any manuscript which is not reassuringly backed by a bestseller. . . . For only the universal triumph of the rhythm of mechanical production and reproduction promises that nothing changes, and nothing unsuitable will appear. Any additions to the well-proven culture inventory are too much of a speculation. The ossified forms – such as the sketch, short story, problem film, or hit song – are the standardized average of later liberal taste, dictated with threats from above. (*DE* 134)

When Jack Lipnik (the Coen brothers' version of Jack Warner, head of Warner Bros.) cries out to Fink to "tell a story. . . . Make us laugh, make us cry" and tries to explain to his new writer that his assignment involves writing to genre – "it's a *wrestling* picture" – he illustrates this point exactly. Only Mayhew's secretary-mistress, Audrey Taylor, knows how to teach the aspiring scriptwriter this lesson; she instructs him about "formulas," and as he embraces his new muse, the camera leads us into the bathroom and down the waste pipe of the toilet.

Horkheimer and Adorno see the emergence of the culture industry as a historical event, the product of the massive infusion of capital into the cultural sphere. Perhaps earlier the popular arts possessed more potential for originality, but once the "unleashed entrepreneurial system" (*DE* 120) gained control, "films, radio and magazines [came to] make up a system which is uniform as a whole and in every part (*DE* 120)." Fink arrives in 1941 to find this system firmly entrenched. But the

historical Faulkner arrived in 1932, when a Hollywood figure
like Sam Marx (head of the Story Department for Metro-
Goldwyn-Mayer) was hoping to recruit serious writers to the
movies because "he was clearly interested in the possibility of
their making an original and creative contribution rather than
bent on turning them into formulaic 'hacks'" (*FMS* xxiii). The
attitude was shared by early studio pioneers, including the
intellectually accomplished Irving Thalberg, who headed
MGM, and by Howard Hawks, who grew to be Faulkner's
sponsor in Hollywood, but who admired him first as a reader
of his fiction.

It would be tempting (but finally simplistic) to blame technology itself for the changes in mass culture that Horkheimer
and Adorno find most deplorable. Walter Benjamin risks such
a view in "The Work of Art in the Age of Mechanical Reproduction," an essay remarkable for its grasp of how mass-
production techniques govern distinctively modern art forms
like photography, musical recordings, and film. But the force
that determines the industrialization of art must be traced,
according to Horkheimer and Adorno, to the interests of monopoly capitalism:

The basis on which technology acquires power over society is the
power of those whose economic hold over society is greatest. A
technological rationale is the rationale of domination itself. It is the
coercive nature of society alienated from itself. Automobiles,
bombs, and movies keep the whole thing together until their level-
ing element shows its strength in the very wrong which it furthered.
It has made the technology of the culture industry no more than the
achievement of standardization and mass production, sacrificing
whatever involved a distinction between the logic of the work and
that of the social system. This is the result not of a law of movement
in technology as such but of its function in today's economy. The
need which might resist central control has already been suppressed
by the control of the individual consciousness. (*DE* 121)

What makes the culture industry so pernicious is its hijack-
ing of art's capacity to resist the social order (including the
dominant economic practice). Because mass culture in the

1930s and 1940s came to rely on centrally and complexly organized systems that oversaw national production, distribution, and advertisement functions, mass culture's own interests lined up with those of liberal monopoly capitalism, the prevailing social and economic order. As a result, the mass-produced cultural work delivered experiences that were socially "useful" to the status quo. Horkheimer and Adorno identify the way the culture industry produces false satisfactions for legitimate desires. If art ought to usher us into the realm of pure pleasure, industrial art disciplines pleasure to serve the narrative and moralistic ends of formulaic plot ("every kiss in the revue film has to contribute to the career of the boxer" [DE 142]); if popular art promises purposeless amusement, the movies or magazines insist that we consume cultural fare for self-improvement or cultural prestige, thereby rationalizing purposelessness under purposeful entertainment; if art lives as the sublimation of desire, the culture industry promises only to prolong and defer desire (it "does not sublimate; it represses" [DE 14]); if art ought to stimulate the audience's powers of imagination and reflection, the movie instead controls the direction and speed of response and robs the consumer of spontaneity (DE 126); if the greatest art expresses its dense negation of the stratified social order, mass culture superficially synthesizes serious and "light" art into harmless universality by pretending that elite and working-class interests may be aligned.

This last charge constitutes the severest failure of the culture industry for Horkheimer and Adorno, and it will carry us back to *Barton Fink* for a moment before we proceed to Faulkner's trials as a commercial writer. Because contemporary mass culture, as a debased form of bourgeois art, seems to absorb proletarian materials, it masks the conditions under which it comes into existence: the exclusion of the lower class, of the disfranchised under capitalism.

The purity of bourgeois art, which hypostasized itself as a world of freedom in contrast to what was happening in the material world, was from the beginning bought with the exclusion of the lower classes – with whose cause, the real universality, art keeps faith precisely by its freedom from the ends of the false universality. Serious art has been withheld from those for whom the hardship and oppression of life make a mockery of seriousness, and who must be glad if they can use time not spent at the production line just to keep going. (*DE* 135)

Serious bourgeois art can be faithful to its nature only by *admitting* it is founded on social exclusions and by *refusing* to pretend that "high" art belongs to all. Bourgeois art thus expresses an implicit negativity toward the social order responsible for class divisions by displaying the contradiction between claimed universality and the practice of elitist retreat from the material world.

Barton Fink offers up a deliberately cliché-ridden version of Faulkner–Mayhew as the suffering artist in Hollywood, the once kingly writer grazing madly like Nebuchadnezzar outside Babylon. But the Coens also assign some of Faulkner's experiences to Barton Fink in order to examine the unwitting complicity of the serious writer with the culture industry, even as he anticipates resisting it. Like Faulkner, who arrived for his first interview with a studio official bleeding from a head wound, Fink suffers mosquito bites that disfigure his face and prefigure his bloody path through Hollywood. (Fink later slaps a mosquito on Audrey's back and discovers she's dead in his bed.) His first assignment is a Wallace Beery wrestling film, as it was for Faulkner, although Fink lasts through the nightmarishly repetitive screening of an earlier Beery success ("I will destroy you," the wrestler promises to the viewer), whereas Faulkner left after twenty minutes ("Can you stop this thing? I know how it's going to end," he told the startled projectionist). Col. Jack Warner tricks Faulkner into a seven-year contract at the end of his Hollywood career, a biblically resonant number taken by the Coens for the length of Fink's bondage, too. Fink is the latest avatar of the innocent writer, Faulkner's youth, the doubling signaled by having aspirant and mentor share the Hollywood muse Audrey.

Fink's aspirations in 1941, however, have been shaped by

the 1930s, the very decade so many of modernism's masters partially sat out in the studios of California. Fink tries to explain to his agent why he might not want to abandon the New York stage; he's on the verge of real success, "the creation of a new living theatre, of and about the common man." "I guess I try to make a difference," he professes. These are the very hopes he transplants to Hollywood, where they are given their comeuppance brutally. Fink's neighbor and apparent soulmate at the Earle Hotel is an insurance salesman named Charlie Meadows. Charlie sympathizes with Fink's struggles to write for the pictures, offers to tell him stories about a real salesman's adventures and to explain wrestling, and listens politely to Fink's description of himself as one who writes "about you – the average working stiff, the common man."

Not only will such writing fail to satisfy Lipnik, it finally enrages the common man himself. For it turns out that Fink's working stiff is a homicidal psychotic known as "Madman Mundt" to the Los Angeles Police Department detectives who solve the murders. In a moment of apocalyptic fury, Mundt sets fire to the hotel, guns down the two detectives, and releases Fink from the bed to which he's been handcuffed. Fink's fatuous presumption that he can be the Shakespeare of the common man (his Broadway success is called *Bare Ruined Choirs*, a phrase from Sonnet 73) vanishes into Mundt's roaring accusation "YOU DON'T LISTEN." Like the doctor who charges Charlie ten dollars to tell him he has an ear infection he already knows he has, Fink looks into the face of the disciplined and abused common man and discovers his murderous rage at being kept from everything beyond what he knows. Consumer, product, and victim of the culture industry, Mundt exposes its covert complicity with fascistic oppression. As he runs down the hotel corridor firing his submachine gun, he screams, "I'll show you the life of the mind," and executes one of the detectives with a "Heil Hitler." The 1930s turned bourgeois writers into "tourists with typewriters" (in Mundt's words), and they contributed to the taming of the masses through the dissemination of industrial culture. "The masses, demoralized by their life under the pressure of the system, and who show signs of civilization only in modes of behavior which have been forced on them and through which fury and recalcitrance show everywhere, are to be kept in order by the sight of an inexorable life and exemplary behavior. Culture has always played its part in taming revolutionary and barbaric instincts. Industrial culture adds its contribution" (*DE* 152).

With the recognition that the life of the mind is the practice of violent repression, *Barton Fink* draws to a close its meditation on the emergence of the culture industry. At a time when the *Saturday Evening Post* might pay $2,000 for a single story, or MGM that much per week to its celebrity writers, few professionals could afford to ignore such "gold mine[s]" (*SL* 110). From 1929, when Faulkner married the recently divorced Estelle Oldham Franklin (and gained two stepchildren), through his father's death in 1932 (leaving him as oldest son responsible for his mother), a daughter's birth in 1933, his brother's death in 1935 (for the welfare of whose widow and children he took responsibility), and the steady acquisition of a house and property in Oxford, Mississippi, until 1948, when he sold the film rights to *Intruder in the Dust* for $50,000 to MGM, Faulkner struggled to remain solvent. Royalties from his novels rarely cleared three figures. What he could not raise in advances from his publishers, he earned by selling short stories or getting studio deals for six or seven months at a time. Complaining that writers ought to be free from such "bourgeois impediments" (*SL* 90), he submitted to these two forms of "orthodox prostitution" (*SL* 85).

Once we acknowledge the economic and social coordinates of all cultural expression, we may be tempted to simplify the nature of commercial work by seeing it as designed strictly to meet market requirements. But emphatically for a writer like Faulkner, even works aimed at the mass market possess reflective and resistant features that make their *relation* to the culture industry and the social order it endorses the very heart of the problem. In the cases of Faulkner's limited experimentation with popular forms for his longer fiction, he typically ends up extending the conventions and probing more deeply into the causes of their popularity. Leslie Fiedler's survey of the pop culture material in *Sanctuary* demonstrates superbly how Faulkner both avails himself of formulaic detective and horror fiction, comic strips, and pornography and also reflects on the morality of an aesthetics of debasement. Anne Goodwyn Jones likewise shows how Faulkner's incorporation and transformation of popular romance elements in *The Wild Palms* expresses alarm about the stability of gender positions and artistic authority in a social and cultural hierarchy threatened by mass culture. How may we locate the same sort of reflective resistances in Faulkner's writing for screen and short-story markets?

The first piece of fiction Faulkner sold to Hollywood was a story called "Turnabout," originally published in the *Saturday Evening Post* (March 5, 1932). MGM paid him $2,250 for the rights. Faulkner had already begun preparing scripts under his first studio contract at MGM when Howard Hawks suggested he work on an adaptation of his own story. Hawks was familiar with Faulkner's fiction and had entertained a project to film *Sanctuary*, but he despaired of getting anything resembling it past the censors. The director's brother William (later Faulkner's agent in Hollywood) called his attention to the *Post* story. Faulkner produced a script in a scant five days; it was so good that Thalberg gave Hawks permission to shoot it as it was.

In "Turnabout" an American aviator (a captain named Bogard) discovers a drunken British sailor asleep on the street in a port town during the war. Thinking to scare the apparently callow and underemployed boatman into a more professional attitude toward combat, Bogard takes Claude Hope on a bombing run over Germany. The naval gunner surprises with his mettle under fire and, on landing, lavishes praise on his

American colleagues for their skillful descent despite a dangling unreleased bomb under the right wing. Bogard blanches when he realizes the disaster they have unknowingly averted, and agrees to accompany Hope on the British sailors' next mission (which all the involved Americans suppose is mostly domestic harbor-tag).

Hope and his captain, taciturn but almost equally boyish, take Bogard on a terrifying, nerveless torpedo escapade, during which they, too, deal with an unreleased explosive; in this case, however, the crew winches the suspended torpedo back into place, drops it again from its backward-facing tube, and, as prescribed, outraces the launched missile before swerving from its course. Profoundly impressed by this display of fearless skill and high-spirited modesty, Bogard arranges for a case of Scotch to be delivered to Hope as he sleeps in the street. (Unlike other sailors, Bogard learns, torpedo boat crews had to leave their ships when they were stored under docks at night.) The story closes with Bogard's reading a subsequent notice of the crew's disappearance in action, in tribute to his English comrades, Bogard undertakes a particularly foolhardy and independent aerial raid on a château headquartering the enemy command. Although he survives to be decorated, Bogard's frustrated rage at war's destruction of the common man constitutes the story's last sentence. As he bears down on his target, he snarls, "God! God! If they were all there – all the generals, the admirals, the presidents and the kings – theirs, ours – all of them" (CS 509).

Faulkner's story of wartime adventure, with its celebration of individual courage and its warm discovery of Anglo-Saxon brotherhood beneath national suspicions, makes the kind of yarn popular between the wars. Hemingway included it in an anthology of war stories, and the studios made lots of pictures from such fiction. But "Turnabout" exceeds its mold at critical points, and in doing so reflects on the social and cultural formations responsible for its own commercial appeal.

We might begin by noting that Bogard's condemnation of

the political and military leaders responsible for war vastly widens the story's aperture of dissent. This pacifistic jolt may surprise a reader more familiar with Faulkner's portraits of gallant, foolhardy Sartorises and his own fascinated posturing about his (fictitious) military experiences in World War I. But the prospect of another war deeply depressed Faulkner, who later tried to enlist at age forty-five to help stop Hitler, and who wrote a monumental antiwar epic, *A Fable*, during the Cold War. "Turnabout" subtly identifies the forms under which capitalism has empowered certain social institutions to administer its interests. In the war's extreme "solution" to the crisis of monopoly capitalism in the modern era, however, such institutions betray their arbitrariness, fail to cover the behavior or desires they seek to control. "Turnabout" suggests three spheres in which the war allows glimpses of a shaken ideology: in the misplaced heterosexuality of the soldiers' intimacy, in the antiauthoritarianism of the rank and file, and in the underrationalized technology of warfare that endangers self and enemy alike.

Bogard's first look at Claude produces an odd impression: "He was quite drunk, and in contrast with the heavy-jawed policeman who held him erect on his long, slim, boneless legs, he looked like a masquerading girl. He was possibly eighteen, tall, with a pink-and-white face and blue eyes, and a mouth like a girl's mouth" (*CS* 475). It would be possible – mistakenly, in my judgment – to interpret this characterization of the "girlish" (476) Claude as evidence of soldierly "homoeroticism." Paul Fussell uses this term to distinguish "a sublimated (i.e., 'chaste') form of temporary homosexuality" (Fussell 272). Fussell contends that there was little active homosexual behavior among troops during World War I, but that the trenches prompted "something more like the 'idealistic', passionate but non-physical 'crushes' which most of the officers had experienced at public school" (272). One need not grant Fussell's total spiritualization of the homoerotic to take his point. The kind of tender fellow-feeling soldiers permit binds them as a fighting unit; their fraternity – physically intimate yet generally nonsexual – resembles what Eve Sedgwick has called "homosocial" behavior. "'Homosocial' describes social bonds between persons of the same sex" (Sedgwick 1). In our society men vigorously police the border between the homosocial and homosexual, interposing homophobia and "normative" heterosexuality. But this is a historical asymmetry typical of our society and not all others. (Sedgwick claims that the ancient Greeks interwove homosocial and homosexual behavior under their form of patriarchy. Doubtless the present panic of the U.S. military over lifting bans against gays stems from an arbitrary opposition between "acceptable" unacknowledged homoeroticism bonding soldiers and "unnatural" homosexuality.)

In "Turnabout," however, Claude draws Bogard's heterosexual notice, at once promising and precluding a relation. Faulkner's excessive figurative language endangers the "chaste" order of men without women under service. In the girlish Claude, Faulkner poses an irreconcilable hint of the sexualities (within and with others) repressed in defense of the dominant social order. In the story's figural register, Claude carries the disruptive mark of the drag queen, the carnival ("masquerading") transvestite. His valence actually contradicts the light air of predictable homoeroticism in all the other relations – particularly the public school game Claude and Ronnie carry on and the touching care the combatants take to furnish one another with shelter, raiment, and drink. Given the antiwar sentiment of Bogard's final line, one might say that "Turnabout" understands war and capitalism to be practices by which patriarchy exercises its power, enacts order as a matter between men.

The combatants in "Turnabout" conflict with authority openly and behave with remarkable independence. The "King's Regulations" turn into a subject for mockery early in the story, and Bogard is amazed to learn that the boat pilot determines the destination for each mission entirely on his own: "It's Ronnie's show," Claude boasts (*CS* 499). Such free-dom inspires Bogard to disregard his own orders when he at-tacks the château after completing his appointed mission; the narrator stipulates that had the exploit failed, Bogard "would have been immediately and thoroughly court-martialed" (*CS* 509). The antic, incorrigible nature of the sailors makes them seem childlike; Bogard tells the delivery man how to recog-nize the recipient of the Scotch: "He'll be in the gutter. You'll know him. A child about six feet long" (508). Claude violates military order in laying claim to the street as bedroom and getting in the way. The M.P. decides he "must think he's a one-man team" (478), a phrase that nicely summarizes the refusal to subordinate individuality to administered efficien-cy. The war machine echoes capitalism's contempt for devi-ant, disorderly, playful, useless behavior, but "Turnabout" stubbornly includes it without finding a place for it.

As the double escapade with balked explosives suggests, technology also proves to elude total administration. The makeshift windlass the sailors use to retrieve mislaunched torpedoes is the result of an initial disaster: "Made first boat; whole thing blew up one day" (507). Claude wonders why "clever chaps like engineers" cannot find a less "clumsy" so-lution, but the limitations of modern technology actually pro-duce old-fashioned pride in manual work: "Every cobbler to his last, what?" (505). Both war vehicles, the bomber and the torpedo boat, require inhuman accommodation: the gunner pod resembles a dog cage; the shallow boat has no seats and makes everyone sick at first; it has a "vicious shape," the machine gun looking through a screen "with its single empty forward-staring eye" (493). The crew's eventual loss confirms the suicidal derangement of such technology, just as the fol-lowing description of the airplane registers the more general incoherence of the machine age: "It looked like a Pullman coach run upslanted aground into the skeleton of the first floor of an incomplete skyscraper" (486–7).

One peacetime sphere for high-technology products requiring the advantages of total administration and heavy capital investment turned out to be the movies. "Turnabout" seems prescient about its own appeal to the movies when it pictures combat scenes. As the torpedo boat approaches its target, for instance, Bogard notices on its side "the painted flag increase like a moving picture of a locomotive taken from between the rails" (503). A moment later, a similar effect: "High above them the freighter seemed to be spinning on her heel like a trick picture in the movies" (504). One wonders if that "single empty forward-staring eye" behind the "screen" might not be a camera already filming. The coordination of so many specialized groups in planning, shooting, cutting, and releasing a movie might recall recent war efforts, both of them faces of the administered capitalist state.[4] (See Benjamin.)

But as Horkheimer and Adorno observe, movies wage war in the deeper sense of training the masses to accept their conscription into an army of exploited laborers. The budding scriptwriter Barton Fink intuits this when he finds himself at a USO dance during the war and needs to defend his civilian status against the hostility of the soldiers. Pointing to his head, he says, "This is my uniform. This is how I serve my country." Faulkner senses this affinity between war and the culture industry; his war story was already thinking self-critically about itself as a movie.

MGM insisted on one drastic change in Faulkner's story; I think we can detect how it provoked him to a still further reflection on the ways of the culture industry. Irving Thalberg as head of the studio had urged his director (and brother-in-law) Howard Hawks to use Faulkner's original script as written: "You're not going to muddy it up by changing it?" (Kawin 1977, 76). Hawks reassured him, but soon learned that MGM had a complication on its hands; Joan Crawford needed a project immediately (since she was contracted to appear in several films a year), and the studio decided "Turnabout" might be made to accommodate her. Faulkner, then, was presented with the task of writing in a substantial role, with romantic subplot, for a female star.

The script Faulkner produced ingeniously made the problem of the woman's place in the movie the very question to be entertained.[5] The first scene shows three children at play, Ronnie, Claude, and Ann. Ronnie complains about the girl's tagging along, but Ann protests that "I have just as much right here as you have." Claude relents, but only if "she doesn't muddy the water."

In several important ways, Ann's presence does muddy the water. She needs to be related to the soldierly trio of "Turnabout," so Faulkner makes her Ronnie's sister and constructs a romance plot around her and Claude, who now lives with the Boyce Smiths as a ward. She must be made an object of desire, so Ann becomes Claude's fiancée, gathers in a stray kiss or two from her newly affectionate brother, Ronnie, and falls in love with Bogard, who marries her in the last scene after Ronnie and Claude have completed a suicide mission. Although one can feel Hollywood conventions reshaping Faulkner's story, one can also see his imagination resisting too slick a repackaging.

The simple presence of Ann may be read as the transformative force of the cinema itself in Faulkner's narrative. That is, Joan Crawford *is* the movie. I think Faulkner proved a quick study of the star-vehicle system; he must have understood that the female romantic lead exists to be desired as object by the male audience, and to be identified with as desiring subject by female spectators. Since movies require mass audiences comprised of both genders, the task of the successful commercial film involves satisfying both desires with the same narrative of images. For those occupying the masculine position among the viewers, the pleasure of the movie arises from experiencing the desire to know, to see. Given the West's cultural preconstructions, as Teresa de Lauretis has put it, this position may be related to the quest of Oedipus. The

Oedipal narrative solves the Sphinx's riddle with the answer "man"; it rests on the social reality of patriarchy in which woman functions as sign and value of exchange according to the incest prohibition that founds social relations.

In cinema as well, then, woman properly represents the fulfillment of the narrative promise (made, as we know, to the little boy), and that representation works to support the male status of the mythical subject. The female position, produced as the end result of narrativization, is the figure of narrative closure, the narrative image in which the film . . . "comes together." (142)

For the female spectator, however, identification must be doubled. The viewer's engaged subjectivity cannot identify herself as object, and so must occupy the "masculine" position simultaneously. It is the distinctive formal opportunity of cinema that it offers these simultaneous positions for the spectator: "the look of the camera and the image on the screen, the subject and the object of the gaze" (142).

Because we are still dealing with writing and not the movie itself, we cannot follow the camera's gaze, but Faulkner's script does suggest Ann's constitution as the product and intersection of these contrary forces. Ann as object materializes within the semi-incest plot Faulkner imports from *The Sound and the Fury*. As Sedgwick might predict, Ann mediates the bonds between Ronnie and Claude. They're constantly tussling in childhood, playing "Beaver" (the same lookout game they play in the short story), and generally discharging homosocial current through Ann. Her lack of a proper place occasions a relentless exercise of male property rights; the two, quite daftly, keep entrusting her to each other for safekeeping (because "girls have no sense").

Faulkner's script, then, locates the place of woman in film as the image of exchange and value within the Oedipal logic of patriarchal narrative. There really is no place for Ann in the story, but when asked to, Faulkner found her as the repressed subject of patriarchy. (When Faulkner was told there was to be a part for Joan Crawford in the film, he reportedly said, "I don't seem to remember a girl in the story" [Blotner 1984, 307].) The echoes of *The Sound and the Fury* remind us of Caddy's exclusion from the scopic tyranny of that other Oedipal narrative, and we might recall that that "lost woman" was (according to Faulkner's 1946 Appendix to the book) first to marry a motion picture magnate in Hollywood, and then to find her way to a Nazi staff sergeant's arms. Joan Crawford understood she was intruding, moreover; she tearfully regretted that Hawks could not talk the studio out of defacing Faulkner's great story.

Good soldiers both, however, director and star agreed to make the best of it. So Crawford asked that at least Faulkner write some of that "clipped" dialogue for her. Did. Joan got to talk like the boys, and her stylistic enfranchisement marks the other valence of her doubleness in the script. For Ann defies her objectification in the Oedipal narrative – at least until the script's final images of resolution. Scandalously, and indispensably from the standpoint of the movie's need to activate female desire, Ann decides to sleep with Claude despite not loving him and without expecting to marry him. Claude and Ann agree that "weddings are as dead as peace" (*FMS* 193), but that does not stop Ann from taking Claude to her bedroom, all the while insisting that what they are doing is "not love" (190). At one point, she explains to her brother why she will not marry Claude: "But not yet. Ronnie. Not right now. Let me wait until I . . . until I can . . . until I can stop" (178). This is as far as Ann can go, but the moment amounts to a successful negation of male plans for her.

Ann muddies the clarity of patriarchal privilege over her body and affections: Claude cheerfully explains that Ronnie is "the same as my brother. I'm going to marry his sister, that is" (139). A landlady for the three cadets' menage (Ann has joined the Wacs and lives with them) observes that "they was like one family. You couldn't hardly have knowed which were the brother and which the fiancey" (173). Faulkner's brilliant solution to making a place for Ann involves capacitating her to strike a blow at the masculine frame. When she withholds her love from Claude, or later dissembles to him about her love for Bogard, Ann is refusing to comply with the Oedipal logic of narrative itself. The questor Claude ends blinded like Oedipus, but emphatically not in possession of tragic insight: "He couldn't even see it when it came to kill him. He couldn't even say, now I've got one second more!" (254).

Feminist cinema ought "to enact the contradiction of female desire, and of women as social subjects, in the terms of narrative; to perform its figures of movement and closure, image and gaze" (de Lauretis 156). Faulkner's screenplay does not manage this effect; instead, it illustrates, albeit with some self-consciousness, the will to closure and coming together demanded of the Hollywood formula romance. The script closes with a series of one-shot dissolves, from newspaper notices of the boat crew's death, to Bogard's military citation, to hospital, travel, and wedding scenes. All of these cauterize the injuries inflicted throughout by Ann's presence. They lead to the final shot, in which Bogard now utters his antiwar lines to the cooing Ann, who "draws his head down to her breast" and murmurs "Hush – hush" (FMS 255). Only when woman refinds her place in marriage may she reassume the mantle of Sphinx/Jocasta and hush criticism of the social order, the fate this film succumbs to as it makes its way through the assembly line of the culture industry.

By reading so closely one of Faulkner's contributions to both the commercial short-story market and commercial cinema, I have tried to suggest the capacities for reflection and resistance he brought to his work. In a number of isolated pieces of scholarship, Faulkner critics have begun to appreciate the impingements of commercialization on his writing.[6] My approach means to distinguish Faulkner's productive engagement with mass cultural forms from reductionist dismissals of his pandering to market expectations in order to make money. To segregate any writer's serious art fiction totally from his or her writing for commercial uses, or even from an awareness of market pressures, is to participate un-critically in a myth advanced by modernist aesthetics.

Andreas Huyssen points out that the legendary autonomy of the modernist work "is always the result of a resistance, an abstention, and a suppression – resistance to the seductive lure of mass culture, abstention from the pleasure of trying to please a larger audience, suppression of everything that might be threatening to the rigorous demands of being modern and at the edge of time" (55). Such a modernist aesthetic betrays itself as a "theory of modernization displaced to the aesthetic realm" (57). To be at "the edge of time," to repel a modernized world, is to confront the "revolt of the masses" as a prime force of social transformation. Huyssen observes that in "the age of nascent socialism *and* the first major women's move-ment in Europe, the masses knocking at the gate were also women, knocking at the gate of a male-dominated culture" (47). The expression of liberatory aspirations in mass cultural forms like popular romance, short fiction, theater, and ulti-mately the movies leads high culture to associate mass cul-ture with the feminine, to try to subordinate it as woman, according to Huyssen. We might link Charlie Meadows's rage, Ann's amoral indulgence, Faulkner's critique of militarism, even Horkheimer and Adorno's identification of socially re-pressive qualities in bourgeois art all as allied indications of the threats posed by the masses – women, working stiffs, maverick soldiers.

If we valorize only the elite works (or portions of works) that suppress mass culture, we fail to maintain sufficient ana-lytical purchase upon the ideology of modernist autonomy. Huyssen argues that Adorno well knew the *dialectical* rela-tion between modernism and mass culture; he quotes Adorno in a letter to Benjamin: "Both [modernist art and mass cul-ture] bear the scars of capitalism, both contain elements of change. Both are torn halves of freedom to which, however, they do not add up" (58). As for mass culture, the longings for enfranchisement and respect apparent in our examples of worker and woman ultimately collapse under the weight of suicidal rage or submissive acceptance. Capitalist interests come to saturate mass culture. For its part, elitist modernism retreats in the cultural sphere from the specter of social transformation inherent in the emancipatory advances of modernization. At the same time, the uncompromising modernist work does attempt a salutary negation of modernization's ills: rampant and brutal authoritarianism, the commodification and debasement endemic to the culture industry.[7]

In concluding, I call attention to a story Faulkner wrote in 1931 that explicitly considers the relation between high and low culture, between modernist and commercial writing. "Artist at Home," which appeared in Story (August 1933), irreverently debunks such literary segregation and predicts Faulkner's own more complex negotiation of mutually dependent spheres. A novelist, Roger Howes, and his wife, Anne, move to the Virginia countryside from New York City after he sells his first book. Secluding himself in order to write, Howes lets his mail pile up in town but suffers a stream of starving Greenwich Village artist friends who want to consult him about their work. Anne disapprovingly tolerates these invasions until she falls in love with one especially forlorn young poet, John Blair. With Roger's apparent permission, the two pursue their relation, until Howes finally reasserts his mastery at about the same time Blair renounces homewrecking.

"Artist at Home" comically deflates the pretensions and hypocrisy of professional writers. Roger proves a cold-blooded exploiter of his own domestic complications; he passively encourages his wife's dalliance because he sees it will provide him with material for the story he's had trouble writing. The rustic narrator observes ironically that Roger's retreat to his study leads to a "bull market in typewriting, you might say" (CS 639). Since Roger has begun his career as "an advertisement writer" (627), commercial savvy directs his writing. Even the narrator notices that a simple affair is pretty ordinary stuff – which "can be seen in any movie" (636). What makes the story really "good" is Blair's effort to secure Howes's consent to a socially advanced solution to their problem.

Blair affiliates himself with the literary and moral avant-garde. He is a struggling poet, so fine and deprived a sensibility that, as Anne reports to her husband: "He's had nothing, nothing. The only thing he remembers of his mother is the taste of sherbet on Sunday afternoon. He says my mouth tastes like that. He says my mouth is his mother" (640). Fortunately, our narrator does not have to figure out what to make of this; the three prove too much for him, to whom this all looks like a much simpler question of fornication and adultery. Blair tries to spur Anne's exploration of new moralities, but at first she complains that he patronizes her: "Freedom. Equality. In words of one syllable, because it seems that, being a woman, I don't want freedom and don't know what equality means" (634). When the sad poet renounces his love, standing in the rain outside her house all night, and later dies of consumption, the myth of the scandalous, suffering, antibourgeois avant-garde poet is complete.

Such high-minded artists make their pilgrimages to Howes, paradoxically, because they want the key to the market. Anne notices that Blair never asks whether a poem is good, only "Will this sell?" The poet shows his work to the successful novelist as if he is "flinging caviar at an elephant" (633). But Howes believes that a little more success in the literary marketplace might be just what the elitist poet needs – to make him proud enough or mad enough to write something with "entrail" in it (632). Blair's alienated submission to the market leads to modest success when he derives a love poem from his affair with Anne and sells it to "the magazines that don't have any pictures" (643). Howes's own artistic use of the affair leads to a dispute with Anne, to whom he tries to present a fur coat bought on the proceeds, and who denounces her husband's pillaging of life "to dress me in the skins of little slain beasts" (645).

In "Artist at Home" Faulkner pays back Sherwood Anderson for his fictionalization of the young Mississippi poet in "A Meeting South," and also for Anderson's begrudging advocacy of Faulkner's first novel at his publisher's. (Anderson supposedly agreed to recommend it if he did not have to read it.) So Faulkner wittily constructs a story about the cannibalization of life out of his own experiences with Anderson and his wife (Elizabeth Prall, whom Faulkner had worked with in New York City). More important, however, the story invents a third position for the writer. Beside the market-wise and parasitical novelist and the pretentious elitist poet, between mass culture and high modernism, if you will, Faulkner opens up the position of the narrator. That narrator is characterized by his voice, unmistakably Southern and rural, and by his tone, bemused and skeptical. In the force of its colloquial irony, in its devotion to the acceptance of local ways and the community's indigenous vitality, it assumes a perspective from which both modernization and modernism might be criticized. I close with the merest suggestion that such a position grows increasingly central to the Faulkner of the 1930s. In the voices of Cash and Darl Bundren, Quentin Compson and his father, V. K. Ratliff, even the narrator of *Absalom, Absalom!* – voices otherwise so various and distinct, the modernist of Yoknapatawpha via Hollywood positions his fiction between the forces of modernization and modernism.

NOTES

1 Blotner (1974) reports that when an associate cleaned out Faulkner's desk after his last extended stay in Hollywood he found several empty bottles and "one of the legal-size lined yellow pads Faulkner used. The top sheet was filled with characters in Faulkner's tiny hand. It was the beginning of a whole series of formula phrases – 'Boy meets girl . . . Boy sues girl' – which went on for pages" (1175–6). Besides mocking the monotonous predictability of studio romance films, Faulkner's pad also gibes at Hollywood's subjection of love stories to commercial, contractual rule.

2 Besides the other essays in *Dialectic of Enlightenment* (hereafter *DE*), see especially Adorno's *Aesthetic Theory* for a consideration of the relation between the work of art and the social reality framing it.

3 Horkheimer and Adorno do not consider all popular art to fall under the rubric of mass culture. Folk art, in being various and local, opposes standardized products of the culture industry.

4 In Anita Loos's *Gentlemen Prefer Blondes* (1925), a female veteran of ambulance service during the war finally finds on a Hollywood lot what she's been missing: "And Henry's sister has never been so happy since Verdun, because she has six trucks and 15 horses to look after and she says that the motion picture profession is the nearest thing to war that she has struck since the Armistice" (216).

5 This version of the screenplay, the second, contains the greater part of what Faulkner contributed to the adaptation project. For a third version, he was assigned an assistant scriptwriter, Dwight Taylor; subsequent major additions were made by two other writers. Faulkner eventually received credit for "Story and Dialogue." With Hawks, too, there were always significant departures even from the shooting script because he encouraged actors to improvise lines. I want to make it clear that I am not discussing the film itself as produced, which appeared as *Today We Live* (MGM 1933).

6 See Donaldson regarding Faulkner's reflection on the expectations of the *Saturday Evening Post* reader; Porter (1981) on Faulkner's general efforts to convert the "reified" consumer of fiction into an active, critical participant; Lester on the pressure to neaten and better commodify *The Sound and the Fury* in the Appendix; Urgo on cinematic technique in *Absalom, Absalom!*; Matthews on Faulkner's critical reflection on the short story market; the articles by Fiedler and Jones already mentioned; Godden and Rhodes on Faulkner's awareness of popular works like Horace McCoy's *They Shoot Horses, Don't They?*; and portions of all the contributions to Fowler and Abadie's *Faulkner and Popular Culture*.

7 In substantially different ways, Kenner and Bleikasten offer defenses of the modernist work's autonomy.

4   Faulkner from a European Perspective

From Cleanth Brooks, the champion of the New Criticism, to the present New Historians, Faulkner's Southernness has been a permanent and central concern of American criticism. Much has been written too about Joyce's Irishness, but today it is certainly no longer a priority for Joyceans, and to dwell at length on Proust's Frenchness would strike most Proustians as utterly incongruous. Admittedly, Faulkner's fiction is more patently grounded in a specific geographic area and a specific historical experience than that of any of his contemporaries, yet some thought should perhaps be given to the troubling fact that, year after year, his novels are read with excitement by thousands of people all over the world, most of whom will never know another South than his – a world within words.

Faulkner was American and Southern, through and through; his literary ancestry can easily be traced back to Poe, Hawthorne, Melville, Twain, and Sherwood Anderson; his indebtedness to the popular traditions of Southern oratory and Southwestern humor has been established beyond dispute. Like all major American novelists, however, Faulkner is nonetheless a novelist of European descent. His many fathers include Cervantes, Scott, Balzac, Dickens, Flaubert, Dostoevsky, Hardy, Conrad, Mann, Joyce, and Proust, to mention only the novelists.[1] Faulkner's intertext is just as thick as that of any of his peers, and just as heedless of national and regional boundaries. Reading a great Faulkner novel like *Absalom, Ab-*

75

salom! is reading the entire palimpsest of Western culture, even as looking at a Picasso is confronting the whole history of Western painting. To read his fiction only as Southern fiction, to interpret it exclusively as a sociohistorical document or even, less positivistically, as a kind of fictional meditation on Southern history, Southern myth, and Southern manners, is therefore to leave out much of what makes it unique and interesting. And the true nature of his reputation is likewise misunderstood if it is only seen as an accidental effect of the Cold War.[2] Granted, Faulkner's American reputation was established in the 1950s by an odd coalition of conservative New Critics and ex-Marxist New York intellectuals, and their motivations were probably far from innocent, but it should not be forgotten that his reputation in Europe was already fairly high in the late 1930s.

Did Faulkner's novels not somehow exceed the occasion of their birth, how could they have won recognition in France and be admired by Malraux and Sartre (two writers on the left, neither of whom was an expert on the South) long before they were taken seriously in Faulkner's own country? And what does it mean that today they matter much more to a Colombian writer like Gabriel García Márquez, a Urugayan writer like Juan Carlos Onetti, or a Peruvian writer like Mario Vargas Llosa than to a postmodern American author like John Barth? There are surely cultural and historical reasons for Faulkner's remarkably strong impact on Third World writers, but that he has also been a decisive influence on French novelists as diverse as Louis-René des Fôrets, Claude Simon, Pierre Guyotat, and, more recently, Pierre Michon, on Germans like Uwe Johnson and Wolfgang Koeppen, and on many other European writers, is clear evidence that his appeal is not limited to specific cultural areas.

Over more than six decades now novelists from everywhere have publicly acknowledged their debt to Faulkner, and so many tributes from so many authors seem to indicate that he is most likely to keep his high rank among modern classics.

Granted, not all of his novels have achieved international status, and it seems improbable that the recent rehabilitations by American critics of *A Fable* and other later works will alter or extend the Faulkner canon that has come to establish itself outside the United States. But *The Sound and the Fury, As I Lay Dying, Sanctuary, Light in August, Absalom, Absalom!*, and *The Wild Palms* belong as much to the history of the European novel as to that of American fiction.

Faulkner the writer was no more a gentleman farmer from Mississippi than the writer Proust was a Parisian snob of the Belle Epoque or the writer Kafka a German-speaking Jewish insurance man from the declining Austro-Hungarian empire.

The very universality of his appeal points intriguingly to the singularity of his achievement. Admittedly, to emphasize a writer's universality may be an easy way to remove his work from the untidy tangles of history. Yet how and why, every now and then, a writer escapes the limitation of his or her time and place, crosses regional and national boundaries, and comes to establish himself or herself as a world classic is a question worth asking. To allege that works survive only because they continue to serve powerful group or class interests that have a stake in their survival, or to argue that there are no "eternal masterpieces" because each new generation of readers invests the *Iliad* with new significances, is not to answer it.[3] If Emily Dickinson's poems and Robert Walser's fiction are still read today, it is certainly not because they are, as the Foucauldian phrase goes, continually "reinscribed" in relations of power. And while it is true that interpretations have changed and keep changing, the intriguing question remains why and how, over time, a number of books could outlast a succession of widely different contexts and readerships. What is found valuable in a literary work is surely not an immutable essence, and there is no final proof that canonical texts have acquired a safe transcultural and transhistorical status, but historicist denials of something like aesthetic transcendence lack likewise validating evidence. Knowledge of the social and historical conditions under which a novel was written is indispensable for a proper understanding of its cultural environment; a novel's relationship to its environment, however, is never simply representational, nor does it account in any way for the way the novel affects its readers.

Faulkner's novels possess an enduring power beyond the culture out of which they arose and even beyond the language in which they were written, since most of their non-American readers know them only through translations. So, instead of endlessly reading Faulkner *into* American contexts, why not read him out of them for a change? If Faulkner was not a provincialist, many of his American critics are. Comparative studies about him and other writers usually focus either on his kinship with some fellow Southerner or on his connection with modernist writers of the English-speaking world. From time to time, one will no doubt come across a fleeting allusion to Mann or Proust, but the overall impression one gets in reading Faulkner criticism is that nearly all the major novelists of the twentieth century wrote in English. Such a parochial approach hardly furthers our understanding of Faulkner's contribution to world literature, and anyway, by now we probably have more articles on Faulkner's debt to Joyce or T. S. Eliot and more essays on his impact on Southern fiction than we need. The time has come, I think, for a broader and more distant perspective, allowing us to relate him, beyond regional and national boundaries – and through informed comparison rather than pious clichés – to twentieth-century novelists of equal rank on both sides of the Atlantic.

This is, of course, no easy matter. Literary canons are revisable; literary hierarchies never stop shifting, so that a writer's rank, his supposed "greatness," can never be taken for definitively granted. To give just one instructive example: for the educated French public, after World War II, the five "giants" of American fiction were Faulkner, Dos Passos, Hemingway, Steinbeck, and Caldwell. Today neither Caldwell nor even Steinbeck would be on the list, and, for various (ideological rather than aesthetic) reasons, the reputations of Dos Passos and Hemingway are obviously no longer as high and secure as they looked in the 1950s.

Tomorrow most of today's "giants" will have dwindled to dwarfs, whereas, conversely, some obscure writer not even published in his lifetime may have risen to posthumous fame. And even the greatest classics usually had to spend a season in purgatory before they ascended to heaven. Faulkner's international reputation (as distinct from his national reputation), however, remains as undisputed thirty years after his death as it was at the climax of his literary career, when he was awarded the Nobel Prize, and in the early 1990s, at least, he is still read, admired, and studied as one of the great novelists of our century.

Who are the others? Who are his peers? My own list consists of two Frenchmen, a German, two Austrians, two Irishmen, an Italian, an Englishwoman, a Russian émigré, and a Jew from Prague. In chronological order: Marcel Proust, Thomas Mann, Robert Musil, James Joyce, Virginia Woolf, Franz Kafka, Hermann Broch, Carlo Emilio Gadda, Louis-Ferdinand Céline, Vladimir Nabokov, and Samuel Beckett. With Faulkner, they are a dozen. Needless to say that other writers – Gide, Svevo, Döblin, D. H. Lawrence, Hemingway, Dos Passos, Lowry – might have been considered for admission into my pantheon, and that my selection has all the precariousness and arbitrariness of personal value judgments, even if, for the time being, several of my choices are likely to be ratified by current critical opinion.

My speculations, then, rest on nothing but the debatable claim that these twelve novelists are the major figures of Western fiction in the first half of our century, and that as such they have made more substantial contributions to the novel genre than all the others.

From what vantage point can they be considered together? Dissimilarities far outweigh resemblances. As soon as we take a closer look, their idiosyncrasies stand out so glaringly that the idea of treating them as a group of kindred spirits and of examining their works as part of the same configuration seems presumptuously silly. Imagine them together in the same room. What would they have to say to one another? What affinities are there between the exuberant language games of Joyce's and Gadda's fiction and the frugal prose of Kafka's? Between the opulent orchestrations of Proust and the bleak minimalism of Beckett? Between the hoarse ejaculations of Céline and the sophisticated playfulness of Nabokov? Whenever we think of the great realists of the nineteenth century, from Balzac to Tolstoy, we think of them as a big family, of writers having, for all their differences, much in common. Someday, presumably in a century or two, the novelists of our century will be likewise perceived as brothers and cousins, but for the time being we still lack the distance to identify them as members of the same tribe.

Modern fiction springs from such a variety of assumptions and offers such a bewildering multiplicity of practices that one may well wonder whether there is enough common ground to make comparison pertinent. For the only evident feature these novelists share is precisely – or, rather, imprecisely – their *modernity;* the only unifying concept available to us is "modernism," the magic notion under which they have been retrospectively lumped together by Anglo-American critics. Yet scarcely any of the distinctive features usually attributed to modernism applies to all of them. Not all of them were reckless experimentalists, not all of them had a passion for technical innovation, not all of them resorted to symbol and myth as unifying devices, and probably none of them thought that the primary subject of a novel should be the process of its own making. They assuredly wanted to "make it new," but their very desire for a fresh start points to an acute sense of belatedness, and Mann's *Doktor Faustus,* Proust's *Recherche,* Joyce's *Ulysses* (not to mention *Finnegans Wake*), as well as Faulkner's *Absalom, Absalom!* or Nabokov's *Ada* testify in various ways to the challenging and

potentially paralyzing awareness of an overripe tradition. Indeed, nearly all of the major novelists of this century, even the
most daringly experimental, were tradition-haunted, just as
Matisse and Picasso were in painting, Schoenberg and
Stravinsky in music, Pound and Eliot in poetry. Written in a
time of social change and cultural crisis, their works question, revise, recompose, and reevaluate the legacy of the past
without ever canceling it. For there is presumably no other
way to write *against* tradition than to write *through* it.

And in their search for new idioms of fiction, modern novelists kept caring about the relationship of word and world.
"What is reality?" Virginia Woolf asked in response to Arnold
Bennett's assertion that a novel's characters must be "real" if
the book is to survive. "And who are the judges of reality?"
(103). Woolf's questions reverberate throughout twentieth-
century fiction: modern novelists all knew that there was no
such thing as objective reality, only each individual's *sense* of
it. Hence their abiding fascination with consciousness, with
the flickerings of subjective perception and the eddies of subjective experience – with what philosophers at the turn of the
century like James, Bergson, and Bradley identified as "stream
of consciousness," "real duration," or "immediate experience." That much, at least, our dozen have in common: from
Proust to Beckett, from Mann to Musil, they all bear witness
to the increasing acceleration and complexification of the "in-
ward turn" taken by the novel since the late nineteenth century. Whether they adopted autobiographical modes or resorted
to polymodal or polyphonic arrangements, they all created
sharply interiorized fictional spaces, in which the reader was
made to feel individual psyches at work.

Compared to Balzac's, Dickens's, or Tolstoy's, theirs is
therefore a smaller, less solid, more fragmented world, and
one much less self-confidently charted. Following the pioneer-
ing work of Flaubert, James, and Conrad, their novels tend to
relate whatever is described to a perceiving mind. The gener-
alization of perspectivism does not imply, however, that real-

ism was discarded. The focus of attention shifted from the common ground of a shared concept of reality to the manifold shades of "immediate experience," but the introverted or "impressionistic" mimesis of the modern novel redefined and displaced the realistic code without giving up its referential claims, and it took pains to establish its own kind of plausibility. In its disregard for logic and grammar, the "interior monologue" was after all a mimetic device meant to capture as truthfully as possible the uncontrolled flow of half-articulate mental processes. Overhearing Molly Bloom's oceanic night thoughts, Clarissa Dalloway's musings, or Quentin Compson's fevered rememberings rests on the assumption that the inevitable screen of language separating reader from character is not really there. The emphasis of recent criticism on Joyce's language experiments should not obscure the fact that not only *Dubliners* and *Portrait of the Artist as a Young Man* but also *Ulysses* owe as much to the meticulous realism of the nineteenth-century novel as to the poetic devices of the Symbolists (Robert Musil called *Ulysses* "spiritualized naturalism"). The shifting patterns and pulsations of Virginia Woolf's fictional prose are a deliberate attempt to approximate what she conceived to be the nature of consciousness itself. And within their own technical and stylistic conventions the first three sections of *The Sound and the Fury* aim at the immediacy of the mimetic. It is probably not fortuitous that the best practitioners of "stream of consciousness" were Irish, English, and American. Whereas the French penchant for psychological analysis culminates in Proust's *Recherche*, and the brooding, burrowing *Innerlichkeit* of the Germans triumphs in Musil's arcane essay-novel, it is the probing, testing spirit of Anglo-American empiricism we see at work in Joyce, Woolf, and Faulkner. If nearly all modernists have been interested in depth psychology, Proust and Musil shunned interior monologues.[4] Among the major practitioners of fiction of their time, Joyce, Woolf, and Faulkner were the only ones to attempt *psychograms*, the only ones to conjure up the illusion

of minds caught, as it were, in the act. And no one has been
better at rendering the raw intensities of extreme emotion
than Faulkner; no one before Faulkner ventured into the benighted brain of an idiot.

Where the French and German modernists intellectualized,
analyzed, or philosophized, their English and American coun-
terparts attempted to come as close as possible to the actual
processes of the experiencing consciousness and to make
words enact what they enunciate. In turning language into a
seismograph of the mind, these modernists were doing for
fiction what William James, Bergson, Bradley, and Husserl
were doing for philosophy. Indeed, their objectives strikingly
resemble those of phenomenology, as defined by Merleau-
Ponty: "All its efforts are concentrated upon re-achieving a
direct and primitive contact with the world . . . it tries to give
a direct description of our experience as it is . . . being apparent in our desire, in our evaluations, and in the landscape we
see, more clearly than in objective knowledge" (vii, xviii).
Joyce, Woolf, and Faulkner were not more modern than their
homologues on the Continent, but among the latter, only Céline and the half-French, half-Irish Beckett have matched them
in the invention of a new idiom, suited to the *petite musique*
of our drifting selves.

One might argue that one realism gave way to another, and
yet we are reluctant to call these writers realists. An innovative technique like interior monologue pulled in two directions at once. Although originally intended as a realistic device, it was bound to have antirealistic, antiillusionist effects;
its very newness drew attention to the artificial patterns of
language itself. Benjy's monologue in *The Sound and the Fury*
is sleight of hand; in reading it we gasp and wonder but don't
weep. The effect is more distancing yet when several voices
take turns telling or untelling the story, as they do in *As I Lay
Dying*. Extreme psychomimesis digs its own grave.

Besides, even for those who used it abundantly, interior
monologue was just one tool among others. Joyce's many-

leveled strategy required a distinct structure and style for each of the chapters of *Ulysses*, and in the late ones, little is left of the realistic context elaborated earlier on. In Woolf's novels, the reaching out after "life" is likewise counteracted by the need for high stylization and controlled aesthetic design. *The Waves*, for instance, reads like a prose poem rather than a novel. And with Beckett, the last great modernist (or the first postmodernist?), mimetic representation turns out to be as minimal and problematic as everything else; from the early stories of *More Pricks than Kicks* to the thin trickle of his late texts, it keeps constantly shrinking, so that in the end nothing is left but the wan whisper of a dying voice.

Early modern novels such as Mann's *Buddenbrooks* or even Faulkner's *Flags in the Dust* still aim at the full and faithful rendering of large areas of individual and social experience in the panoramic and documentary spirit of nineteenth-century realism; late ones – Beckett's as well as Nabokov's or Gadda's – declare more willingly their impatience with mimetic constraints and flaunt more provocatively their contrivedness. Yet what characterizes modernist fiction by and large is neither naive realism nor systematic antirealism, but the ever renewed tension between *mimesis* (foregrounding of the referent) and *poesis* (foregrounding of the medium and the writing process). This tension also occurs over and over again in Faulkner, and can be very easily traced from *Soldiers' Pay*, his aggressively modernistic first novel, to *The Reivers*, his mellowly recapitulative last. To argue that his work developed from "stream of consciousness" neorealism to freewheeling pre-postmodern fabulation would be a crude oversimplification. True, in *The Sound and the Fury* and *As I Lay Dying* interior monologues figure more prominently than in any of his later work. Yet Benjy's soliloquy can hardly fail to strike the reader as a linguistic artifact, and we do not have to wait for *The Hamlet* to find sudden ruptures in style, sharp tonal switches, and breaches in verisimilitude: In the conspicuously fragmented *As I Lay Dying* stylistic homogeneity, mim-

etic plausibility, and narrative coherence are already undermined by all sorts of microtransgressions of novelistic
decorum.[5] Faulkner's compositional strategies have widely
varied from one book to another; and in the later novels,
building as they do on the earlier ones, Faulkner's fiction
tends to refer back to itself as a self-generating process, shifting emphasis from the immediacies of felt experience to the
hazards of telling and retelling. But no matter how far it re-
cedes, the referential horizon is always there. Even *Absalom,
Absalom!*, despite its ceaseless exposure and questioning of
narrative practices, implies a realistic frame of reference, and
its ultimate stake is nothing less than History.

Faulkner's has been from start to finish a duplicitous discourse, drawing on many resources and resorting to many
ruses just to keep moving along. Whatever the technical devices used, the sheer foregrounding of language through stylistic oddities and rhetorical heightening in all of his novels
prevents his prose from ever functioning as the transparent
medium of realistic make-believe. Reading Faulkner is in fact
like interpreting the pictures used by Gestalt psychologists to
illustrate their figure—ground paradoxes: looked at one way,
his novels seem to represent a preexisting reality; looked at
another way, they present themselves as autonomous and au-
totelic verbal structures. We can never look one way without
being somehow aware of the other.

The modernists' self-conscious concern with the novel as a
demanding art form was obviously just as deep as their need to
articulate a doubt-ridden sense of reality. Take any of our
twelve writers: not one who was not passionately dedicated to
his or her craft; not one who did not choose his or her vocation as a form of heroic priesthood. Nearly all the major novelists of this century have been overreachers — alike in their
high bets on writing, alike in attempting the impossible.
What we have come to admire as their accomplishments are
in fact the splendid ruins of extremely ambitious enterprises,
as ambitious, in their own day and their own way, as those of

Balzac or Melville had been a century earlier. *A la recherche du temps perdu, Ulysses, Der Zauberberg* and *Doktor Faustus, Der Mann ohne Eigenschaften,* Broch's "polyhistoric" novels, and Gadda's *Quer pasticciaccio brutto de, via Merulana (That Awful Mess on Via Merulana)* are all novelistic *summae* trying to encompass the culture and recapitulate the accumulated knowledge of an entire society. As Italo Calvino has pointed out: "What takes shape in the great novels of the twentieth century is the idea of an *open* encyclopedia, an adjective plainly at odds with the noun *encyclopaedia,* whose etymology indicates an original claim to exhaust the knowledge of the world by confining it within a circle. Nowadays, it has become impossible to conceive a totality that is not potential, conjectural, and plural" (184). Indeed, conceived in a time of fast social change and deep cultural crisis, beset by many uncertainties and by an ironical sense of contingency, fragmentariness, and uncompletedness (Proust died before having completed his *Recherche,* and neither Musil nor Gadda finished his magnum opus), "the great novels of the twentieth century" all mock their own pretensions. The history of the modern novel is one of diminishing expectations. In Mann, something no doubt persists of the sturdiness of the nineteenth-century bourgeoisie (Georg Lukacs still saw him as one of the great "epic realists"). With Nabokov, the disenchanted enchanter, literature both celebrates and derides itself in the virtuoso performances of a master parodist, and with Beckett, its quest for totality collapses into a sardonic comedy of nothingness.

Faulkner was closer to Balzac than to Beckett in his demiurgic desire to create "a cosmos of his own." Yet in its own way his oeuvre, too, exemplifies the high hopes and fine failures of the modern novel. Is *Absalom, Absalom!* not also a "potential, conjectural, and plural" totality? And yet, once we start thinking of Faulkner as a neighbor of his European contemporaries, we begin at once to sense how much he differs from them. Is it, as has been often said, because he was not a standard "man of letters" and wrote most of his work in the rustic reclusion of his backward home state? In his slightly patronizing essay on "Faulkner and the Avant-Garde," Hugh Kenner remarks that "no other major twentieth-century writer was so isolated from his peers" (182). Maybe he was. But isolation has been the novelist's lot from the beginning: "The birthplace of the novel," Walter Benjamin wrote, "is the solitary individual" (Benjamin 1955, 413). None of the great twentieth-century novelists was gregarious, none was comfortably at home in his or her social milieu, and it is perhaps also worth remembering that if Faulkner was an "exile-in-residence" (Grimwood 23), for more than half of his peers expatriation was a literal fact. Significant, too, is that unlike some of the great poets of their time, none of these novelists (apart from Virginia Woolf) belonged to an organized literary group, and few even showed real interest in the militant avant-gardes of their day. Proust was interested neither in cubism nor in futurism, and his taste in music did not go beyond Wagner, Debussy, and Fauré. The dadaists did not care about Joyce nor did Joyce care about them. Musil and Broch had little in common with expressionism. Céline and Nabokov were both men of "strong opinions" with little more than scorn for their contemporaries. A measure of aloofness, withdrawal from the bustle of the social scene, and distrust of both mass culture and vanguard illusions, were probably prerequisites for the fulfillment of their self-set tasks. And Faulkner's sense of isolation can hardly have been deeper than Kafka's, Gadda's, Céline's, or Beckett's.

Yet it developed in different circumstances. The most obvious, though generally overstressed and oversimplified, difference between Faulkner and his fellow writers in Europe is, of course, that he was born and spent most of his lifetime in the rural environment of the Deep South. His European confreres all lived in cities if not metropolises, and were novelists writing from within a distinctly urban culture. Proust's work is associated with Paris, Joyce's with Dublin, Kafka's with

Prague, Woolf's with London, Musil's and Broch's with Vienna, and Gadda's with Milan. It was in Paris and Vienna, the two nerve centers of European culture and European art between the turn of the century and World War I, that modernism started. And when it reached America in the early 1920s, T. S. Eliot, Ezra Pound, Scott Fitzgerald, and Ernest Hemingway, unable to identify themselves and their work with their native country, fled to Europe, as Henry James and Gertrude Stein had done earlier on. The young Faulkner made, as we know, a different choice: after a short tour of Italy, Switzerland, France, and England, he went back to Oxford, Mississippi, discovered that his "own little postage stamp of native soil was worth writing about," and set out to turn it into the matrix of his fictional "cosmos" (*LG* 255).

Faulkner's choice had far-reaching consequences for his career and work. It not only made him a Southern novelist; it also made him a most singular modernist – not a lesser one, but one unmistakably different from the others. For while providing him with abundant material for his fiction, the South was also instrumental in shaping his language. The impact of the Southern oral tradition on his dialogues and on his rhetoric has often been noted. It is not limited, however, to his use of the Southern vernacular and to his debt to Southern oratory. According to students of orality, thought and speech, in oral cultures, are cumulative rather than subordinative, aggregative rather than analytic, and reveal a strong propensity for what rhetoricians used to call "copia."[6] Accumulation and copiousness are also hallmarks of Faulkner's prose. The natural movement of his writing and, it seems, the spontaneous thrust of his very thinking are toward arborescent expansion and patterned repetition, and interestingly, the prevalence of parataxis, the tireless adding on of narrative and descriptive statements, is even more conspicuous in his manuscripts than in his published texts. The "voiced" quality of this prose, its breathless, never-ending rush and rustle, does not imply, however, that Faulkner's novels are less "written" than those coming directly out of an urban tradition of print-conscious literacy.[7] Faulkner's writing grew out of a young man's avid reading, and as a writer with a sharp sense for visual patterns and even a real graphic gift, he was as alert to the possibilities of typographic space as any of his contemporaries, and he well knew that when we read a novel only the eye listens.

It would be wrong, too, to think that Faulkner's attempts to energize the written word with the inflections and rhythms of living speech and thus to relate his fiction to a local oral tradition, remove him from the mainstream of modernism. Faulkner was certainly not the only modernist to care about voice and the spoken word. *Ulysses* is a book of many voices, and one of Céline's major innovations as a French writer was that in the snarling slangy (yet insidiously rhythmic) soliloquies of his *Voyage au bout de la nuit*, he broke away from a mandarin tradition in which orality had been repressed for at least three centuries. So let us beware of sweeping statements and small extrapolations. It is not enough to say, as Kenner does, that "What we have in Faulkner . . . is a way of being intensely local which profits from a range of expressive devices not local but all developed by several great contemporary innovators whose intention was to see their native region from afar, with cosmopolitan eyes" (193–4). Faulkner did not use modernistic tricks just to intensify and universalize his fictional rendering of Southern experience. In weaving them into the vibrant texture of his own discourse, he charged them with fresh energies and made them answer his own pressing needs.

First among these needs came the need to tell: "I'm a storyteller. I'm telling a story, introducing comic and tragic elements as I like. I'm telling a story – to be repeated and retold" (*LG* 277). In his early years, Faulkner belonged to a community in which the telling and retelling of stories was still a major mode of social exchange and cultural transmission, the more cherished as after the Civil War recounting the Southern past had become the nostalgic memory-keeping and myth-making of a defeated people. Oral narratives are performative utterances intended for a palpable audience. Faulkner's tales were written, printed, and meant to be read in silence and solitude, but at their most compelling – as, for example, in Rosa Coldfield's discourse in *Absalom, Absalom!* or in the Tall Convict's tale in "Old Man" – they are indeed mesmerizing performances, with something of the force of what J. L. Austin calls illocutionary and perlocutionary acts.

Much nonsense has been written about Faulkner the shaman, Faulkner the bard. Faulkner was anything but an untutored, primitive singer of tales from the backwoods. It is true, nevertheless, that he is closer than any of his great contemporaries to the traditional *Erzähler* mourned over by Benjamin, and that his work possesses a popular and epic dimension not found to the same degree anywhere else.

Yet the epic tale, with Faulkner, is by no means incompatible with narrative sophistication, nor is his way of staging communal storytellers just an old-fashioned device. In foregrounding the teller, the telling, and the listening, his framed tales simulate the conditions of oral storytelling and attempt to reclaim something of the lost experience of living voices in their actual give-and-take context. In one sense they look wistfully back toward a lost paradise of narrative, and therefore may be said to betray the Flaubertian ideal of impersonality and aloofness to which many modernists, including Mann, Joyce, and Kafka, still subscribed. But at the same time, in throwing into relief what we now call the narrative enunciation, in pluralizing narrative voices and narrative codes, and in insisting on the conjectural nature of what is being told, they lead to a fictional practice in which the claims to truth of any narrative utterance appear highly problematic, and in which the authority of any narrative agency is brought under constant suspicion. *Absalom, Absalom!* is, of course, the paradigmatic text here: through its use of intradiagetic narrators and narratees, the novel clearly builds on

the tradition of oral storytelling, but simultaneously deconstructs it by using it in such a way as to make the successive
narratives cancel one another and leave the reader with the
diverse threads of a story yet to be told. The detour through
orality, the most archaic form of communication, thus allowed Faulkner to share the preoccupations of the most innovative novelists of his day and to raise fundamental questions
about *the epistemology of the narrative* – a prime concern, as
we know, not only in the modernistic novel but also in the
later fictions of writers as diverse as Barth, Pynchon, Fuentes,
Simon, Cortazar, or Calvino. Indeed, a case could be made for
reading Faulkner not as a modernist but, rather, as a forerun-
ner of those later slippery, hybrid, nondescript things we
loosely identify as "postmodernism" or "magic realism."

There is probably no other major novelist of the twentieth
century at once so eager to discover the new and so deeply
embroiled in the old, nor can I think of one whose work exhibits greater tension between the two. Throughout Faulkner's
novels we sense in varying degrees the same double pull or
double bind: the irrepressible urge to tell, to give remembered
experience narrative articulation, or at least to bring it somehow to the light of language, and the opposite impulse to
question and negate the validity of his own procedures. The
general thrust of modernism was away from narrative. In
Proust's *Recherche* there is little dramatic excitement, and
incidents dissolve into the quiet iridescence of remembered
time. Nor was telling stories a priority for Joyce and Woolf,
Musil and Broch. But it was still one for Faulkner.

His restless experimentalism was not Joyce's cool, deliberate play with forms. It was a way out of the tensions between
conflicting demands, an attempt to produce fictions that
would hold together and survive against crushing odds, or, as
Faulkner himself put it, trying to nail together a henhouse in a
hurricane. Faulkner was in such a hurry that he would use
whatever tool came in handy. He just had no time to wait for
the mot juste. Small wonder, then, in his reckless prodigality

his prose sometimes comes to resemble the "jumble of fragmentary Greek and Latin verse and American-Mississippi obscenity" attributed to Labove in *The Hamlet* (138). Apart from Joyce and Gadda, all the great modern novelists, even Céline, sought homogeneous stylization, what Proust called "le vernis des maîtres." With Faulkner, the varnish often cracks.

Not that his novels are ever disheveled monsters. Faulkner's craftsmanship differed from Hemingway's, yet his early masterpieces are admirably *durchkomponiert* and, on closer inspection, even the later, seemingly looser, more episodic novels – *Go Down, Moses*, the Snopes trilogy – reveal a firm sense of organization. But there are also gropings in the dark and moments of strain and disarray. And there are lapses into logorrhea, fits of rhetorical overkill, making the reader feel that there is just too much of everything. "If you manage to disassemble one of his pages," writes García Márquez, "you get the impression that there are springs and screws too many, and that it will be impossible to restore it to its original state" (15). In its explosive overcrowdedness, Faulkner's language departs from the standards of stern spareness and high finish the New Critics taught us to associate with Anglo-American modernism. But the New Critical concept of modernity has always been a narrow one, and there is no valid reason to reduce modernism to the slightly frigid formalism of the "well-wrought urn." There was room in it for baroque excess and exuberance as well for classical restraint and economy. To say that Faulkner wrote as he did because he lacked formal discipline is about as relevant as saying that Pollack dribbled because he could not draw.

What fascinates in novels like *The Sound and the Fury* and *Absalom, Absalom!* is not the polished perfection of the self-contained artifact but the sheer pulse and power of their language, its endlessly shifting patterns, and the sense of poignant urgency it conveys. Among Faulkner's peers, only Céline matches him in this uncanny ability to bring language to furious incandescence and to generate a nonstop text electrified by a constant influx of self-consuming intensities.

Novelists not only work with different assumptions and intentions, with different materials and tools; they also work with different tempers, at different temperatures. Some are cool, others tepid, and yet others are hot. Of the masters of twentieth-century fiction, Faulkner is probably the hottest, the most impetuous, the most passionate. And he is also, in the last resort, one of the most compassionate. For there is another trait that contributes to his uniqueness: a rare capacity to empathize with the dispossessed and the humiliated, a keen sense of evil and suffering, what his first French readers rightly identified as his *tragic* genius. True, all the prominent novelists of our horrendous century have been connoisseurs of chaos, and *La Cognizione del dolore,* the title of Gadda's last novel, could have served for many others. But the only true heirs of Dostoevsky were Faulkner and Kafka. It is difficult, I admit, to imagine two writers as profoundly dissimilar. "Faulkner is as American as Kafka is Judeo-German," Jean-Jacques Mayoux notes, "their symbolic and dreamlike reality is as different as it can be" (172). Apart from having birds nested in their names (*Kavka* means "jackdaw" in Czech), there seems to be very little indeed for them to share. Yet once Kafka has been stripped of his aura of saintliness and of the esoteric glosses of his pious exegetes, and once we begin to see through Faulkner's Southern legend, it appears that both were primarily writers of savage honesty, with a compelling and often wildly extravagant imagination and rare gifts for the grotesque and the bizarre. One invented chillingly distanced, eerily enigmatic parables, the other has left us intricate, tragicomic chronicles of the Deep South. One wrote with merciless clarity, the other with tropical luxuriance. But both told stories about stray sons and formidable fathers, both were obsessed with guilt, pain, and death, and both conjured up stark and powerful visions of extremity. Despite its Southern redneck background, *As I Lay Dying* is as zany as anything in Kafka, and in such stories as "The Metamorphosis," "In the Penal Colony," or "Jackals and Arabs," anguish and terror grip us with as much force as in *Sanctuary.*

Furthermore, Faulkner and Kafka were both writers for whom writing meant much more than literature. "Kafka's genius infinitely exceeds Joyce's," wrote Broch, "for in contrast to the latter, it does not give a damn about aesthetics and technique, and grasps at once the ethical by its irrational roots."[8] Faulkner did care about aesthetics and technique, but he, too, had an unfailing instinct for the "irrational roots" of man's behavior, he, too, often pushed explorations to what Kafka called "the limits of the human."[9]

Among modern novelists, Joyce has been admired as the most prodigious artificer, Mann as the most thoughtful ironist, Proust as the shrewdest analyst. For the graceful arabesques of lyrical prose and delicate glimpses into the dark, we have Virginia Woolf; for tense metaphysical speculation and flights into utopia, myth, and mysticism, we can turn to Musil and Broch, to Gadda for the convoluted splendors of the baroque, to Nabokov for the dizzying heaven of "aesthetic bliss," to Céline for the deafening nightmares of history; and for those who expect literature to take them to the threshold of silence, the supreme guide is still Beckett. In range of sensibility and depth of thought, in formal inventiveness and stylistic flexibility, all these writers differ, as might be expected, enormously, and it would be pointless to put one above the others, even though in terms of influence the Jovelike Joyce is undeniably the one who has left the most enduring mark. But Kafka and Faulkner, I would argue, occupy a place apart: They were neither novelist-poets nor novelist-dissectors nor novelist-essayists; they were above all startlingly original storytellers and fictionmakers, with a kind of imaginative density probably unmatched in the twentieth century by anyone else, and they are most intriguing storytellers because their tales are so mysteriously simple or so hopelessly entangled that they somehow fail to "make sense." In Kafka, the suspicion that this is a world beyond understanding in which no one can ever feel at home takes hold of the reader from the start; in Faulkner, it comes almost as an afterthought, once all the sound and fury have been spent. But both keep their readers in the dark and leave them at a loss; both imprison them, as they do their characters, in helpless wonder that is as likely to turn to anguish as to laughter.

Knowing that they had power only over words, Kafka and Faulkner used them – as masterfully as their peers, yet in denial of all mastery – neither to seduce us into the enchantments of an other world nor to teach us the ways of this world, but just to let us know how little we know, and how much we err in our innocence and guilt.

NOTES

1 For fuller discussions of Faulkner's indebtedness to European writers, see Richard P. Adams and Michael Millgate.
2 On this point, see Lawrence H. Schwartz.
3 See, for instance, Pierre Macherey's response to Marx's question "Where does the eternal charm of Greek art come from?" in *Literature, Society, and the Sociology of Literature.*
4 In *Le temps retrouvé,* Proust objects to what he calls "l'oblique discours intérieur" because he finds it unfit for the rendering of the depths of the psychic life. Musil likewise has strong reservations about Joyce's use of "stream of consciousness." See Proust, III, 890, and Musil, 584.
5 For a more detailed discussion of antirealistic devices in *As I Lay Dying,* see "A Tour de Force," one of my chapters on this novel in *The Ink of Melancholy,* 149–62.
6 See, for instance, Walter J. Ong's standard study *Orality and Literacy: The Technologizing of the Word,* 31–57.
7 For a recent and rigorous analysis of Faulkner's voices, see Stephen M. Ross.
8 "Kafkas Genie reicht freilich unendlich über das Joycesche hinaus, weil es im Gegensatz zu diesem sich einen Pfifferling über das Aesthetisch-Techniche kümmert, sondern das Ethische unmittelbar an der irrationalen Wurzel anpackt." *Briefe,* in *Gesammelte Werke,* VIII, 273.
9 "An den Grenzen des Menschlichen überhaupt" entry for March 26, 1911, *Tagebücher 1910–23,* 41.

5 Looking for a Master Plan: Faulkner, Paredes, and the Colonial and Postcolonial Subject

Much has been written about Faulkner's attitudes toward class and race and about his representations of these issues as the fundamental structures of his most successful fictions. Myra Jehlen, notably, argues for the determining role of the category of class in novels such as *Sartoris, The Unvanquished*, and especially *The Sound and the Fury* and *Absalom, Absalom!*. Although she does not ignore the centrality of race, Jehlen claims that the reigning problematic in Faulkner's account of Southern antebellum history is the internal class conflict between two sectors of white agrarian society – the lordly, cavalier plantation class versus the Jeffersonian, homesteading, working-class peasantry. In a deconstructive analysis of *Absalom, Absalom!* that raises questions of race and class in a related but divergent register, Richard C. Moreland shows how the various narrative strategies of Faulkner's novel are intended to avert the recognition of this struggle between classes and to disregard the insistent presence of other narratives that underscore the additional pressures of race and gender in Sutpen's story.[1]

As a classic instance of this paradigmatic structure of revelation and aversion in Faulkner's major works, *Absalom, Absalom!* reflects the ideologies of the historical era in which it was composed, the mid-Depression years of early-twentieth-century America. These ideologies underlie Faulkner's connection with the issues of coloniality and postcoloniality that

96

began to appear in much American, Latin American, and European literature of the immediate pre–World War II years. André Bleikasten's claims in the present volume that Faulkner is "a novelist of European descent" and that his work has had a "remarkably strong impact on Third World writers" might well be best understood in this light. Latin American writers in particular have noted that the link between historical narrative and social and racial ideology in Faulkner's fiction has made him an important forebear of their work.[2] Chief among the questions of ideology that Faulkner addresses and that make his fictions of such moment to Latin America are those having to do with subject formation in relation to racial and social ideologies and the frightening pressures emerging from the colonized world as it begins to throw off its colonial burden. Thomas Sutpen's story as filtered through the several narrators of *Absalom, Absalom!* is of special interest for Latin American and postcolonial writers, for it is the narrative of Faulkner's most enthralling encounter with the colonial and emerging postcolonial subject.

Perhaps nowhere more powerfully than in *Absalom* is Faulkner's focused analysis of subject formation in general articulated. By comparing Faulkner's vision of the process of ideological construction of the subject with a similar problematic in Américo Paredes's Chicano novel *George Washington Gómez*,[3] a text that is exactly contemporaneous with *Absalom* but narrates a history of American colonialism from the vantage point of the internally colonized Mexican-American subject, some of the parameters of twentieth-century American identity construction may come to the fore. Both Faulkner's and Paredes's novels are instructive in what they tell us about fiction itself and its role in the representation of America, American identity, and its relation to the consciousness of other emerging subjectivities.

To see how and why this is so, we need first recall briefly the story of Thomas Sutpen's origins as it is pieced together throughout *Absalom, Absalom!* by Rosa Coldfield, Mr.

Compson, Quentin Compson, Shreve McCannon, and Sutpen himself. Sutpen's autobiography, as told to Quentin's grandfather, General Compson, and passed along through Quentin's father to Quentin and Shreve, informs us how as a young boy Sutpen migrated with his "redneck" family in the early nineteenth century from the West Virginia Appalachian region to the Virginia Tidewater proper.[4] As the Sutpens descend from the mountains and trek southward, the young Thomas gradually comes to distinguish through a series of incidents the existence of class hierarchy and to discern the nature of his own class identity within that hierarchy, a position, as he sees it, below that of black people. Southern agrarian class structures, not the racially driven institution of slavery, thus inform the young Sutpen's initial sense of self-consciousness.

The incipient recognition of class identities crystallizes into a defining pattern for Sutpen one day (around 1823) in a celebrated scene when, sent by his father to deliver a message to the planter whose land they work as tenant farmers, he is prevented by a uniformed black butler from delivering the message. Ignominiously and unceremoniously directed aside by the imposing black figure, he is icily advised "never to come to that front door again but to go around to the back" (*AA* 188). This moment of searing affront and cold epiphany for the "eleven twelve or thirteen" (184) year old Sutpen becomes, as Sutpen himself through Mr. Compson's narrative later informs us, the crucial, determining moment around which his later "design" for the construction of a life is to be organized. His sudden recognition that there was a "difference not only between white men and black ones, but a difference between white men and white men not to be measured by lifting anvils or gouging eyes or how much whiskey you could drink then get up and walk out of a room" (183) was, Sutpen tells us, "like an explosion – a bright glare that vanished and left nothing, no ashes nor refuse just a limitless flat plain with the severe shape of his intact innocence rising from it like a monument" (192).

Moreland (10–11) notes that this primal scene severely contesting Sutpen's "intact innocence" is hardly primal at all but in fact extends the significance of earlier scenes describing the Sutpens' descent from the mountains into Virginia, as when his father is first bodily "carried or thrown out" of a "doggery" "like a sack of meal" by "the first black man, slave, they had ever seen" (AA 182), and later is "not even allowed to come in by the front door" of genteel taverns (183). That is, many years later Sutpen takes the incident at the front door of the plantation house in retrospect as the *unique* moment of subject formation, when in fact it is not unique but represents instead one in a *series* of social moments that together have shaped his life. There is nothing as fortuitous, metaphysical, or even mysterious about the incident at the plantation house door that causes Sutpen's epiphany as Sutpen's narrative later tries to claim. Instead, Faulkner shows that the script for that incident is not inscribed in Sutpen's destiny by the willed autonomous action of a masterful Subject but, rather, has been already underwritten by the historical circumstances in geopolitical space and the diachronic time of the region where Sutpen lives.

The several incidents leading up to the affront at the door of the big house do not induce him to understand something about the nature of his position in Southern antebellum agrarian society or early-nineteenth-century American labor markets, that is, between enslaved black people and lordly, slave-owning white ones. Instead, Sutpen hears in these incidents the summons of the ideological structure that sanctions this particular social hierarchy, and he embraces the position offered him within it. "Sutpen accepts and teaches himself once and for all this naturalization of a social act as a simple, even an unobjectionable fact" (Moreland 11). Molded by that event, to which Quentin's grandfather later ironically refers as "the boy-symbol at the door" (AA 210), Sutpen thus accedes to a master plan, "a design," by which he may rule his life: "I had a design," he says: "To accomplish it I should require money, a house, a plantation, slaves, a family– incidentally of course, a wife. I set out to acquire these, asking no favor of any man" (212).

As Jehlen notes, *Absalom, Absalom!* is part of the emergent literature of poor Southern whites of the 1930s. James Agee's *Let Us Now Praise Famous Men,* and reports like *Mississippi: A Guide to the Magnolia State* (1938), by the WPA's Federal Writers' Project, tell a story parallel to the one that Faulkner here narrates, emphasizing the devaluation of labor, white as well as black, wrought by the Southern land oligarchy (*AA* 62). This devaluation of labor's significance in the construction of the modern South stresses the question of the value of labor in the first place and reflects Faulkner's own ambivalent sympathy for Sutpen and real men like him who seem to represent the antebellum, Jeffersonian ideal of the independent, self-sufficient yeoman farmer.

Faulkner's depiction of Sutpen and his working-class origins in the antebellum period is, to be sure, critically sympathetic and hence diverges from an unproblematic repetition of either the cavalier myth of the Old South as being a harmonious, organic society benevolently guided by an elite, leisured, proprietory class or the ideologically loaded narrative of Jeffersonian self-reliance. The very strain in viewing Sutpen as a Jeffersonian yeoman no doubt comes from Faulkner's uneasy sense that the moral line dividing Southern aristocrat from yeoman is an uncomfortably ill-defined one. Hence, Carolyn Porter is surely correct when she notes in her contribution to this volume that "once Sutpen's dynastic aim is in place, the failed ambitions and thwarted pride of the peasant, the poor white, could be reinscribed within the figure of the rich white owner." Even Sutpen's father's incapacity to root himself and his determined besottedness could be seen as signs that from the beginning the ideal of self-reliance has already failed to take hold internally or has slipped away as an achievable goal before the boy Sutpen has even been able to formulate it as a

desire.[5] For all his assumed allegiance to the ethos of the
aristocratic proprietory class, Sutpen thus continues to be
traced, and ultimately undone, by the very desires and fears
born of his poor white origins that his acquired gentility attempts to hide.

In detailing the minutiae of the internal contradictions of
Sutpen's desire, Faulkner poses a very different narrative of
the racial and class-based contestations of Southern labor history. This other narrative paradigm remains, however, exclu-
sivist and reductive in its positing of Southern social history
predominantly in terms of the binary structures of white capitalism. It makes class struggle and the competing interests of
white farmers and plantation owners the central question of
Southern history: Should the region's economy be organized
around slave plantations or around Jeffersonian homesteads?
It suggests, moreover, that it was not American slavery and the
Civil War with its straining dislocations of the antebellum
social structure but, rather, the internal conflict between
white agrarians of different means that forms the true core of
Southern history (Jehlen 64).

From this perspective, then, the real threat to Sutpen's "design" is the very plantation itself (and the plantation system)
that is the object of his desires. To overcome the social trauma
experienced by "the boy-symbol at the door," he becomes a
gentleman farmer; but to become a gentleman, he sacrifices
his ethical manhood as an affronted "redneck" seeking to sublimate the indignities wreaked on his kind and kin by insensi-
tive gentlemen farmers. Sutpen's rise and fall, spanning the
years of the established plantation hegemony from the early
1820s to 1865, sketches, consequently, a radically different,
critical, picture of the antebellum South than the one imagined by the cavalier myth (Jehlen 64).

Moreland argues similarly that "Faulkner analyzes both
Sutpen's emotional readiness as an outsider to adopt a neatly
reductive, already culturally dominant ideology [the self-

sustained monumental image of the planter], and also Sutpen's representative Southern and American attraction to this
particular ideology [figured in Sutpen's life 'design']" (10).

Sutpen in his story is an innocent immigrant to the Southern plantation society, who adopts that society completely without apology,
with the effect that the society's contradictions are condensed, crys-
tallized, and made strange instead of being more gracefully displaced
through the social hierarchy or over the generations: the plantation
economy's lawless opportunism and lawful opportunity appear together, for example, in one person's story instead of in different
social classes or different generations of a more slowly established
family like the Compsons. (Moreland 100)

The narrative of Sutpen's "design," complex as it is, nevertheless includes one element other than the story of class
struggle between poor white farmers and rich white slave-
owners. Before Sutpen came to Yoknapatawpha to accomplish
his "design," he had already experienced plantation life, in
colonial Haiti, during the early decades of the nineteenth century and following the slave rebellions of 1791–3.[6] Having
understood after "the boy-symbol at the door" incident that
"if you were fixing to combat them that had fine rifles, the
first thing you would do would be to get yourself the nearest
thing to a fine rifle you could borrow or steal, or make," Sutpen also intuited that the acquisition of land and power is not
always "a question of rifles": "So to combat them you have
got to have what they have that made them do what he did.
You got to have land and niggers and a fine house to combat
them" (AA 192). And so as a fourteen-year-old boy "in 1823"
(193), remembering having heard in school that "there was a
place to which poor men went in ships and became rich, it
didn't matter how, so long as that man was clever and coura-
geous" (195), Sutpen "went to the West Indies" (192, 193, 194).
Looking toward the colonial Caribbean as a place where "poor
men went and became rich," Sutpen thus joins the ranks of
literary and historical figures for whom the colonial enterprise became the instrumental task in obtaining the object of

their desires and establishing themselves as agents of destiny and subjects of history.

To be a consequential subject, however, as Vivek Dhareshwar has noted, "is at the same time to undergo subjection." But being a colonial subject means "being formed by . . . 'la Relation' – a term that designates the several ways in which metropolitan culture dominates the colonies or the former colonies" (147–8). The effect of colonialism on the colonized is all-encompassing, but there is another relation at stake in colonial situations, and it is also a subject of Faulkner's novel. The colonial relation exhibits psychological subjection quite apart from the subjections fostered by class and race distinctions. This additional relation, a dynamism that, in Albert Memmi's words, "chained the colonizer and the colonized into an implacable dependence, molded their respective characters, dictated their conduct" (ix), functions by instructing both colonizer and colonized not only in the necessity but even in the desirability of their given relation so that the established hierarchies of colonial society come to be seen as freely conceived, chosen, and enacted. And equally, just as there is a logic in the reciprocal, mutually self-defining behavior of the two colonial partners, "another mechanism, proceeding from the first, would lead inexorably to the decomposition of this dependence" (ix). Shaped, then, by their mutual bonds in colonialism into a dialectical interrelation that configures the construction and enactment of character and moral agency, both colonizer and colonized subject will, according to Memmi, of necessity face an equally corrosive disruption of the identity formulated by their former relation of dependence at moments of revolt, revolution, or decolonization. In Sutpen's case, this double relation of dominance and dependence has special resonance not only during his Haitian experience but also later, in Yoknapatawpha County, where it will serve crucially as one of the determinants of his relations with white and black society and with the white and black members of his own immediate world.

The first motive that Sutpen espouses in his Haitian adventure is the wish to make economic profit: he "had decided to go to the West Indies and become rich" (*AA* 199). In pursuit of that motive, however, he meets a class of people unlike those of the antagonistic worlds of both his own Scottish mountain people (195) and the plantation owners of the Tidewater whom he has fled. He enters instead into a colonial social structure explicitly built upon suppressed relations of interlocking racial articulations.

The Haitian colonial world has rules and codes that share some features with the worlds of class and racial supremacy that Sutpen already knows, but it is also quite distinct in other ways. Structured in a pattern of mutual dependency that alters the ethical and social priorities of both colonizers and colonized, colonial societies in general tend to bring to the fore other subcultures "previously recessive or subordinate in the two confronting cultures" (Nandy 2). In Haiti, these subcultures form a mediating middle ground between the overwhelming polarities of the racially and economically supremacist white people and the dominated blacks.

Whereas it had been Sutpen's experience before his voyage to Haiti that both Virginian mountain and Tidewater cultures were awesomely static and dichotomized in their construction and enactment of categories of difference based on race and class, Haitian colonial society offered a more intricate expression of difference and the understanding of difference. The contingency of Caribbean history, with its succession of European dominant cultures, including those regarded as suspect from the Anglo-Saxon perspective – namely, the Mediterranean cultures of Spain and, to a lesser extent, of France – makes it possible for gradations of white and black to exist between the absolute poles of the racial chromograph. The category of the racially mixed mulatto and the many other gradations of mixed race *mestizaje,* problematic as it remains for both Afro- and Hispano-Caribbean colonial society, nevertheless represents historically a class of racialized identity

that is neither black nor white but distinct, even if determined in the last instance by its racial pedigree. No such
distinction holds in the context of American Southern racism,
where one drop of African blood makes one totally black, as,
later, Sutpen to his peril will decisively understand. American
slavery and class structures do effectively create identities
formed on the basis of the dividing lines between master and
slave or landlord and tenant, but Haitian colonial society acts
as if the division were precise, all the while living the experi-
ential blur between the two. At least in some instances, notably in the legitimation of the mixed-blood mulatto through
the legalisms of marriage and property rights, Haitian colonial
society, for all its limitations, allows for the complicated expe-
riential reality of racial difference.[7] To his lifelong chagrin,
Sutpen will experience the real effects of the long history of
English, French, Spanish, and African relations on the island,
relations that remove questions of class and race from the
simple binary configurations of black and white or rich and
poor on the mainland. These relations, experienced as processes of cultural transcoding and racial revaluation, constitute the core of the uniquely colonial ideology Sutpen encounters in Haiti. To his, and his family's, full misfortune, he
fails to respond to the features of this process in the colonial
Caribbean and is incapable of translating it to white supremacist Yoknapatawpha County, Mississippi. His formative so-
journ to Haiti thus crucially signals a missed possible colonial
alternative to his later American tragedy.

As a child before the incident at the plantation house door,
Sutpen had certainly known racial difference, experienced as
"a kind of speculative antagonism not because of any known
fact or reason but inherited by both white and black" (*AA*
186). After the incident, Sutpen begins to suspect that this
"speculative antagonism" on the part of poor white people
toward blacks might be misdirected against black people "because they were not it, not what you wanted to hit" (186). The
truer target of this antagonism was "*them*" (92), the unseen

aristocratic white men who owned both the grand plantation houses and the condescending black butlers who barred their doors. In Haiti, however, Sutpen experiences a social world where race does not constitute an absolute category of psychological identity or ethical performance, where one might indeed elect to identify, or act, as if race were not a constitutive category, or even a "speculative antagonism." Quentin's abject speculation in *The Sound and the Fury* that "a nigger is not so much a person as a form of behavior; a sort of obverse reflection of the white people he lives among" (*SF* 86) extravagantly voices a parallel intuitive insight into the social quality of apparently essential racial forms. In *Absalom, Absalom!*, Haiti serves as the site of the elusive possible insight that at issue in the elaboration of an identity is not the truth of race antagonism (or of class conflict, for that matter) but, rather, the transcription, by an act of ethical commitment and subjective assignment, of a strategic design on race and class difference.

From Sutpen's account of his Haitian adventure to Quentin's grandfather, General Compson, Quentin and Shreve later hypothesize that the clear and distinct dichotomy between racial and class motivations figured in the "boy-symbol at the door" episode is decisively shattered for Sutpen in Haiti when he is deceived into thinking that his first wife's mother "*had been a Spanish woman*" when in fact she "*was part negro*" (*AA* 283). The historical facticity of that distinction is one that Sutpen initially may not have been able to appreciate. After the disclosure, however, Sutpen is compelled with a vengeance to reformulate racial identity as a real, and no longer merely a "speculative," antagonism. In the aftermath of the discovery that his Haitian wife, Eulalia Bon, is a mulatta, and realizing that his own child by this woman, Charles Bon, links him to the butler barring his entry into the mansion rather than to the world of the masters within the mansion, Sutpen rejects the ideology of mutually imbricated racial and social identities underpinning aspects of colonial Haitian life. Instead, he embraces and accepts as real, with apparent equanimity, the very racial polarities and "speculative antagonisms" of the slave-owning South that will ultimately destroy him and his design.

Abandoning the authentic sympathies of a family a second time, Sutpen later admits that " 'I found that she was not and could never be, through no fault of her own, adjunctive or incremental to the design which I had in mind, so I provided for her and put her aside'" (194). And so, from "a little island set in a smiling and fury-lurked and incredible indigo sea, which was the halfway point between what we call the jungle and what we call civilization" (194), as General Compson describes Haiti, Sutpen returns to Mississippi with a master plan and the means to implement it. With this full acceptance of race as the determining category of identity, Sutpen now completely sets aside the contingencies of class difference as the motivation of his "design." Racism, no longer merely a "speculative antagonism," thus now becomes the consciously chosen and uncontested motive force behind Sutpen's "design." Perhaps, then, in the unfolding of this narrative of psychoracial consciousness we have the core of what Bleikasten has termed Faulkner's "contribution to world literature."

Moreland says of some other Faulkner narratives: "Old Southwestern and frontier tradition of horse-trading stories would become what Walter Benjamin discusses as an endangered and dangerous memory – a precapitalist or marginally capitalist social and economic tradition on which Faulkner would draw . . . for his own critical alternative to both the property-based capitalism of the Old South and the money based capitalism of the New" (19). These "usually humorous narratives of the Old Southwest" are significant because they offer a vision "of an ambivalently precapitalist frontier society that was more rudely confrontational, violent, heterogeneous, and unstable than that cultural and literary idea of the Southern plantation aristocracy which largely took its place – a supposedly noncapitalist, unambitious, leisured genteel culture whose contradictions were actually only more elaborately mediated by hierarchy or rationalization" (100).

In 1990, Américo Paredes published a novel, *George Washington Gómez*, composed during the Depression, that addresses the very issues Faulkner raises but from a different perspective of the Old Southwest. *George Washington Gómez* is set against the real history of Southwestern racial and cultural-political conflict. It takes as its moment the 1915 uprising in South Texas by Mexican-Americans attempting to create a Spanish-speaking republic of the Southwest. In the wake of this failed uprising, hundreds of innocent Mexican-American farm workers were slaughtered by Texas Rangers, summarily executed without trial, at even the smallest hint of possible alliance with or even sympathy for the seditionists.[8] The result was that South Texas was virtually cleared of landholding Mexican ranchers and farmers, making feasible the Anglo development of the region into its capitalist agribusiness formation in the 1920s. Paredes's novel situates us in the midst of this historical scenario, taking its tonal key from the pathos concerning the fates of those innocents from whom was exacted the cost of bitter defeat. My discussion of Paredes's remarkable novel starts with a passage from early in the text as Gumersindo and Maria Gómez discuss with Maria's mother and brother, Feliciano García, the naming of the child who has been born to them in the midst of the seditionist uprising and its bloody aftermath. In response to Maria's question as to a proper name for the child, the other characters offer a variety of names, each indicative of an alternative narrative within which the child's destiny might be played out: all are considered but, oddly, rejected. Finally, the child's mother speaks: " 'I would like my son . . .' she began. She faltered and reddened. 'I would like him to have a great man's name. Because he's going to grow up to be a great man who will help his people.' " Gumersindo, her husband, responds playfully, saying, " 'My son . . . is going to be a great man among the Gringos'" and then adds in sudden inspiration, "'A Gringo name he shall have! . . . Is he not as fair as any of them?'" (16). We might see this moment as an example of the process whereby an "individual" is "appointed as a subject in and by the specific familial ideological configuration in which it is 'expected' once it has been conceived" (Althusser 176). At issue immediately in the novel, then, are questions of "identity," "subjectivity," and "consciousness," especially as these concepts relate to culture.

Trying to recall what "great men" the Gringos have had, Gumersindo considers before exclaiming: "'I remember . . . Wachinton. Jorge Wachinton.'" The grandmother's attempt to say the strange name "Washington" comes out as: "'Gualinto. . . . Gualinto Gómez'" (17). . . . And so the name sticks. The clash of identities that is the substance of Gualinto Gómez's life is instantiated at this originary moment where the various discourses that might have ordered his life are signaled to us. The child is a "foreigner in his native land," and his story will follow out the implications of the ideologies unconsciously projected in his "very good name," ideologies that will position him as a subjected representation of the imaginary relations to the real conditions of existence in the early-twentieth-century borderlands of South Texas.

Each of the names, those considered and rejected, as well as the one chosen and immediately transformed into its dialectal equivalent, signals a different set of speech genres and promises to inscribe the child into a particular discursive history. Speech genres serve as normative restraints on our most intimate intentions; they form the legitimate borders of what we can say and not say (Bakhtin xv). The textual instance at hand represents two sets of such speech genres at work: on the one hand, the utopian hopes and dreams of the father and mother, who optimistically project a future of reconciled differences under the crossed references to the child's promised Mexican and American destinies; on the other hand, the historically validated misgivings of the child's uncle concerning these crossed destinies. As he leaves the scene of ritual naming, Feliciano, soon to be the child's surrogate father, sings some verses from one of the most famous of the *corridos* – ballads – of border conflict, *El Corrido de Jacinto Trevino*.[9] Prefiguring the violent murder of Gumersindo by Texas Rangers in the very next chapter, the song activates an entirely different speech genre to guide the interaction between the child's Mexican nurturing and American enculturing.

The instability of this opposition is signaled throughout the remainder of the novel by the continuing instability of the title character's name. In crucial early scenes, before he enters the American schools, the child is Gualinto Gómez, with a name he and his uncle like to explain is "Indian." These idyllic preschool years will later serve as the Edenic counterpoint, the largely untroubled duration of no time before the fall into history, that might ironically reemerge to save him for history. In the narrated present, however, once the child enters school, his heart and mind become the battleground for cultural control:

So [Gualinto] began to acquire an Angloamerican self, and as the years passed . . . he developed simultaneously in two widely divergent paths. In the schoolroom he was an American; at home and on the playground he was a Mexican. Throughout his early childhood these two selves grew within him without much conflict, each an exponent of a different tongue and a different way of living. The boy nurtured these two selves within him, each radically different and antagonistic to the other, without realizing their separate existences.

It would be several years before he fully realized that there was not one single Gualinto Gómez. That in fact there were many Gualinto Gómezes, each of them double like images reflected on two glass surfaces of a show window. The eternal conflict between two clashing forces within him produced a divided personality, made up of tight little cells independent and almost entirely ignorant of each other, spread out over his consciousness, mixed with one another like squares on a checkerboard. (147)

To raise the question of "identity" as this passage does is not to celebrate it or fix it as something that is essential, knowable, and known as an a priori. What follows instead in the course of the narrative of Gualinto's history is a systematic exploration of the attempted standardization of the notion of "identity," fully as much by the American school system, which attempts to pass off ideology in the guise of truth, as by the economic system that commodifies the complex differences of identity by reflecting it as a catachretic, specular image on the "glass surfaces of a show window" in the marketplace. Equally operative, even if repressed from the conscious levels of the manifest narrative, is the fixation of Mexican gender ideology that also identifies Gualinto as a belated heir to the tradition of armed resistance represented most starkly by his uncle Feliciano. Given this interplay of determining discourses, figured in this passage by the cubist image of the "checkerboard" of consciousness, from this point on, "identity" will not be available except in the form of a mediation, one that includes the existential materials of daily life along with those psychological ones in which the identity form is imprinted in the early versions of twentieth-century mass culture. The catoptric theater of reflecting showcase windows is not accidental but symbolic; a representational stratagem. The magic mirrors of the marketplace are contrived to confound identity and the subject's relation to commodities mingled with its reflected selves in the object world. Paredes's narrator later adds:

Consciously [Gualinto] considered himself a Mexican. He was ashamed of the name his dead father had given him, George Washington Gómez. He was grateful to his Uncle Feliciano for having registered him in school as "Gualinto" and having said that it was an Indian name. . . . The Mexican national hymn brought tears to his eyes, and when he said "we" he meant the Mexican people. . . . Of such matter were made the basic cells in the honeycomb that made up his personality. (147)

This initial characterization turns out to be romantically, not to say sentimentally, incomplete. It implies that we might be able later to read off the "real" identity of the subject by virtue of its relations to its experience of the Mexican object world that fills the private world of his affective life. From this view, to determine the position of the subject in the real is to recognize both the content of ideology and its source: the two are the same, as a particular experience of reality is taken to determine the content of ideology. Paredes denies, however, that the identity of the subject may be understood solely by virtue of its "conscious" positioning for, as we learn:

There was also George Washington Gómez, the American. He was secretly proud of the name his more conscious twin, Gualinto, was ashamed to avow publicly. George Washington Gómez secretly desired to be a full-fledged, complete American without the shameful encumberment of his Mexican race. He was the product of his Anglo teachers and the books he read in school, which were all in English. . . . Books had made him so. (148)

This passage furthers the point about "identity" and the constitution of the subject as a social construct. Still, Gualinto's American self is not to be read simply as a latent repression of the Other ready to break through from unconscious levels of the psyche to overwhelm the manifest Mexican identity of his conscious self. The mediation between the terms is infinitely more complex than the classical scenario of "true" and "false" consciousnesses might imagine.

Without the security of the knowledge or even of the feeling that he will encounter what he already knows, Gualinto, like other "Mexicotexan" children, does not have the advantage of his parents who, as combatants in a racial and class struggle against an invariable enemy, knew who they were. The narrative of the parents' identity, troubled and painful as it might be, is nonetheless a determinate one, available in all of the icons of Mexican material culture but encoded most starkly in the Spanish-language expressions of Mexican folklore: jokes, popular sayings, legends, and songs. In the traditional *corrido*, for example, the most formalized expression of the organic patriarchal discourse that names this identity, the fates of the individual and the community are not separate. Rather, they are bound together in an almost unitary structure as are the various stanzas of the song. For the parents, conceptions of identity and subjectivity imparted by the traditional social environment are contained, as Gramsci has noted, in "language itself," "common sense," "popular religion," and therefore also "in the entire system of beliefs, superstitions, opinions, ways of seeing things and of acting, which are collectively bundled under the name of 'folklore'" (323).

For the children, however, now "gently prodded toward complete Americanization" rather than violently repressed for being Mexican, subjected to the interpellative work of both traditional Mexican folklore and American ideological systems, represented here by the enculturating school and the objectifying economic system, identity both "is" and "is not" what "it" seems to be. The American and the Mexican enculturing networks each acquire causal status by seeming to produce the effect of a continuist, primary, active *subject*. Gualinto the American would thus be seen as the product of a pluralist American melting-pot ideology, while Gualinto the Mexican would be the shaped product of a sustaining traditional world. But as Paredes brilliantly shows, the apparently homogeneous, deliberative subject of borderland cultures emerges less as either a sovereign and causal, or dependent and effected, consciousness than as the doubly crossed "*subject-effect*" (Spivak 12) of both American ideological and Mexican folkloric systems. Rather than full subjective agency, we are given the simulation of fullness and agency.

These double Mexican and American culture systems both acquire within their own spheres a presumed priority by virtue of their apparent production of a formed subject. But this subject is then also taken to be an active causal agent, itself willfully capable of producing and reproducing the effects of both the American ideological and the Mexican folkloric configurations within which its own singular fate is said to evolve. Hence, what might initially have been conceived of as a double cultural systemic cause, must now be regarded as the dual effects of a (bifurcated) sovereign subject. Yet, simultaneously, the presumed sovereign subject remains the effected product of ideology and tradition. Within these doubly crossed negations the sovereign Chicano subject, initially conceived as a formed effect and then as a forming agent, now appears instead as "the effect of an effect, and its positing a metalepsis, or the substitution of an effect for a cause" (Spivak 13). This metaleptic ground demarcates the social space of the bordered subject, encompassing both the figural construction of willed behaviors and the elaboration of ideological processes of subjectification. Now, if in the wake of this double deconstruction the category of the subject is to remain a viable one, henceforth it must be seen as the marshaling of a category that is at once essential and provisional, sovereign and bifurcated, a compelling form of what Spivak terms the "strategic use of positivist essentialism in a scrupulously visible political interest" (13). Standing in the borderlands of culture, the Mexican-American subject exists on an unstable ground of double negations: "Hating the Gringo one moment with an unreasoning hatred, admiring his literature, his music, his material goods the next. Loving the Mexican with a blind fierceness, then almost despising him for his slow progress in the world" (Paredes 150). What it would take, materially and psychologically, to imagine a unitary identity, to imagine how one would go about conceptualizing what you can, by definition, not yet imagine since it has no equivalent in your current experience, that is the substance of the remainder of Gualinto's story. The conceptualization of identity that we are offered at novel's end is not a precritically ideal one; instead, it remains historically, dialectically problematic to a disturbing degree.

Straddling the multicultural ground proves to be too much for Gualinto Gómez, who, near the end of the novel, finally

changes his name legally, forsaking the bewildering unreality
of his former composite names, both the American "George
Washington," with all of its own now mixed ethnic signals,
and the Indian "Gualinto," with all of its associations with
familial and cultural history, for the simpler "George G.
Gómez." At novel's end, now an officer in army counterin-
telligence whose job is, ironically, "border security" (299),
Gualinto is curiously troubled by a recurring dream, which
itself is a return of repressed boyhood daydreams. In the
dream, he imagines himself leading a victorious counterat-
tack against Sam Houston's army at the decisive battle of San
Jacinto. With Santa Anna hanged and all traitors dispatched,
in the dream "Texas and the Southwest will remain forever
Mexican" (281):

He would imagine he was living in his great-grandfather's time,
when the Americans first began to encroach on the northern prov-
inces of the new Republic of Mexico. Reacting against the central
government's inefficiency and corruption, he would organize
rancheros into a fighting militia and train them by using them to
exterminate the Comanches. . . . In his daydreams he built a modern arms factory at Laredo, doing it all in great detail, until he had an
enormous, well trained army that included Irishmen and escaped
American Negro slaves. (282)

On the verge of quite self-consciously losing himself as a pre-
movement *mexicano* into the American melting pot, Gualinto's political unconscious in the form of the collective memory instantiated by the sense of self offered by his father's, his
uncle's, and his mother's lives, returns to offer an alternative
ideology and self-formation.

The discursive speech genres of birth certificates, educa-
tional degrees, career dossiers, service records, or legal court
records bind Gualinto institutionally to a formidable identity
discourse. As expressions of institutionally sanctioned ideologies of self-consciousness, these documents figure the discursive and sociopolitical power that defines Gualinto in racial
and class terms as an assimilated bourgeois subject. Songs,

jests, legends, stories, and dreams from everyday life seem no match as counterexpressions of another way of imagining one-self. But now the simpler structures of a precritical utopian dream emerge to trouble the stability of his newfound bourgeois self. Gualinto's self-formation is powerfully formed by the public American sphere he has chosen to embrace. He continues to be authored as well, however, by experiences and discourses of experience that by now have retreated into the unconscious fantasy structures of his life. At the point of complete denial of his Mexican past, Gualinto can thus, in the aftermath of his daydreams and fantasies,

end up with a feeling of emptiness, of futility. Somehow, he was not comfortable with the way things ended. There was something missing that made any kind of ending fail to satisfy. And he would stop there, to begin from the beginning a few days later. But he had outgrown those childish daydreams long ago. Lately, however, now that he was a grown man, married and with a successful career before him, scenes from the silly imaginings of his youth kept popping up when he was asleep. He always woke with a feeling of irritation. Why? he would ask himself. Why do I keep doing this? Why do I keep on fighting battles that were won and lost a long time ago? Lost by me and won by me too? They have no meaning now. (282)

Here, the issue concerns the configurations of identity put at stake by shifting relations of material and cultural production on the U.S.-Mexican border in the first decades of this century. This unmooring of the subject position from the bonds of institutional ideology could explain why Gualinto's present "childish daydreams" and "silly imaginings" leave him "with a feeling of emptiness, of futility." It is for good reason that Adorno has claimed that "identity is the primal form of ideology" (1973, 143). Situated in the sphere of intimacy, these "daydreams" fuel a decidedly discomfiting "primal," utopian self-formation that stands against the one he has consciously "chosen" under the various signs of his interpellation. That is to say, the fantasy structures of the unconscious return bringing a historical memory that has the practical function of designating an alternative, even if deeply latent, content to the formed subject of history. As Jameson has noted, "Fantasy," in this sense, "is no longer felt to be a private and compensatory reaction against public situations, but rather a way of reading those situations, of thinking and mapping them, of intervening in them, albeit in a very different form from the abstract reflections of traditional philosophy or politics" (Jameson 171). These alternative public spheres remain potential for Gualinto, situated as they are as knowledges formed by the anxiety of the clash between the everyday real and utopian fantasy. In *George Washington Gómez*, this potential remains precariously fragile. Fantasy might as easily serve to dissipate practice and undermine its intent; and the immense factor of gender remains latent and repressed, the traces of its course deferred and displaced. Still, the sublimation of the possibility of historical agency into the political unconscious at novel's end is only a first expression of the present reconsideration of the contradictory complexities of contemporary Latino identity.

That white children are caught equally in the dialectical bond formed by the repressive apparatus of white supremacy is an issue Paredes understandably skirts because his subject is Mexican enculturation to that white world. Faulkner is more acutely conscious of the double bind of white supremacist ideology in *Absalom, Absalom!* and other novels, such as *Light in August*. In *Light in August*, as in *Absalom*, the racial subject is formed explicitly in a reactive structure of mutual codependence. Joe Christmas and Joanna Burden, especially, in their ambiguous relations to each other and to the Mexican racialized subject that figures in their respective histories, perhaps represent Faulkner's own undecided attitudes toward racial hybridity. Thus, in *Light in August*, Joanna Burden – whose namesake, Juana, her father's first wife, was a Mexican – accedes to her father's view that the black race is the "white race's doom and curse for its sins" (*LA* 252). Describing the merciless image of this doom to Joe Christmas, Joanna says:

I thought of all the children coming forever and ever into the world, white, with the black shadow already falling upon them before they drew breath. And I seemed to see the black shadow in the shape of a cross. And it seemed like the white babies were struggling, even before they drew breath, to escape from the shadow that was not only upon them but beneath them too, flung out like their arms were flung out, as if they were nailed to the cross. I saw all the little babies that would ever be in the world, the ones not yet even born – a long line of them with their arms spread, on the black crosses. (LA 253)

As in the image of the infant Gualinto Gómez in his mother's arms at the beginning of George Washington Gómez being called to a determinative racial identity, the babies envisioned here by Joanna bear the marks of their own defining fate. This is particularly true of the sacrificial figure, Joe Christmas. His father, unnamed but identified by his mother, Milly Hines, as "a Mexican" (LA 374), bequeaths to Joe Christmas the mestizo double ambiguity of being neither black nor white, essentially. In fact, Joe Christmas's identity as a "white nigger" (LA 344), that is, as someone who to his peril obscurely inhabits the border between white and black, stands on the far side of Sutpen's refusal to acknowledge his own mixed-race son, Charles Bon, by his Haitian wife, Eulalia. Like Gualinto Gómez, these figures challenge the absolutist rule of white supremacy and the constructed nature of racial and class identity as they live and suffer their consequences.

Significantly, then, both Faulkner's and Paredes's protagonists are involved in a modernist project of situating American identities within the local and hemispheric economies of personal and social praxis. If Sutpen can stand as a figure of the internally conflicted nature of class and racial relations in the antebellum South, so too does Gualinto Gómez represent the contradictions and limitations of attempting to construct a singularly authentic ethnicity. The impasse reached by both characters in their respective narratives produces a sense of closure that can scarcely be circumvented: Sutpen dies at the hands of a representative of the class he has forsaken, while Gualinto is poised to disappear into the very white society that has murdered his father and attempted to eradicate his history. At the same time, however, both figures are exemplary instances of how American culture operates broadly to imagine the possibility of subjective self-verification. For Sutpen, this verification occurs at the expense of his family and loved ones, in particular of his Haitian and American wives, his daughter and his mistress, and their children, who bear their lives and deaths in response to Sutpen's "design." Gualinto's verification of identity occurs to the extent that he forswears his Mexican family for an American one. Yet, in both instances, the fashioning of this identity takes place within the political framework of reclaiming and reconstructing a master plan, a design of absolute self-consciousness that might be inviolate by any context.

Ultimately, what we get in both narratives is not verification and inviolate reconstructions of self-consciousness but overt exposures of the limitations of disillusioned subjectivity. This can best be explained by the modernist project that underpins the writing of each story. Quentin repeats Sutpen's story, attempting to make the "trouble" (AA 178) Sutpen's and not society's by reducing the story to one of innocence versus reality. Paredes, too, shows the constructed quality of universal and ethnocentric consciousness and indicates how personal identity can be made to bolster repressive and limiting ideologies. Yet, in both cases of contact with the colonial and the internal colonial subject, and whether representing "boy-symbols at the door" or failed "leaders of his people," Faulkner and Paredes also show what is at stake in repressive cultural symptoms and habits that lead to social exclusions. In both instances, we are made to ponder productively the effects of such exclusion in local and global terms. Linked to problematic notions of national ideology, and failed American identity patterns inherently linked to class and racial categories, *Absalom, Absalom!* and *George Washington*

Gómez both stand as archetypal modern American fictions, debunking coercive, totalizing myths of unproblematic origin and end.

NOTES

1 Moreland notes, particularly, that "[Faulkner] repeated certain dominant structures of thought in the post–Civil War American South and the post–World War I United States and Europe, first to explore and understand their motivations and consequences, then critically to revise certain structural contradictions and impasses that were shared by both these post-war cultures, and that were elaborated in Faulkner's own and others' literary modernism" (4).
2 For recent discussions of Faulkner's influence on Latin American writers, see especially Díaz-Diocaretz, Edwards, Frisch, and Martin.
3 Paredes's novel, currently in its second printing, was published in 1990 but was composed between 1936 and 1940. Paredes insisted that the story appear exactly as it stood when he finished it in 1940. Hence, its sentiments are those of its Depression-era origin rather than its postmodern publication date. References are to the first printing of the novel.
4 The word "redneck" is Rosa Coldfield's (*AA* 97). All references to *Absalom, Absalom!* are hereafter identified in the body of the text.
5 My thanks to Philip Weinstein for this observation.
6 Jehlen inexplicably claims in her otherwise brilliant class analysis of *Absalom* that Sutpen arrives in Haiti "just before the slave rebellions of 1791–93 which haunted American slavers forever after" (66). Sutpen, who is said variously to have been "born in 1808" (*AA* 179) or to have been "now getting on toward fifty-five" (63) in 1861, could not have been present in Haiti during the black Jacobin revolts of the late eighteenth century.
7 The compelling accounts of colonial and revolutionary Haitian culture are those of C. L. R. James. See especially *The Black Jacobins* and "Dialectical Materialism and the Fate of Humanity."
8 See Harris and Sadler, 381–408, and Montejano.
9 The classic study of the ballads of border conflict is Américo Paredes's "*With His Pistol in His Hand.*"

II The World in the Texts

6 Racial Awareness and Arrested Development: *The Sound and the Fury* and the Great Migration (1915–1928)

Nothing in William Faulkner's large body of writings has received more critical attention than his fourth novel, *The Sound and the Fury*, which marks the conclusion of the author's apprenticeship and the beginning of the so-called major period of his literary career. The novel's stunning technical innovations partially account for this attention, particularly because the difficulty of reading and understanding this text is somehow compatible with being moved by it. Although a solid portion of the critical commentary has been devoted to explications of the experimental form of the novel, the real mystery of the text (and, I think, the reason we return to it again and again) resides in its power to move us. This power is characteristic of the writings Faulkner produced from the end of the 1920s to the early 1940s, that is, from *The Sound and The Fury* (1929) to *Go Down, Moses* (1942), writings in which Faulkner grappled with forces of major psychic and social significance.

As the commencement of this trajectory, *The Sound and the Fury* occupies an ambiguous place, and recent critics have accused it of being too private, too mired in the psychic realm, and too inarticulate about social forces that are more clearly revealed in his later works (cf. Sundquist 1983, Morris). John Matthews, however, has argued that the novel's cautious articulation of these social forces reflects the "rhetoric of containment" that dominated modernist aesthetics and the New/Jim

123

Crow South (Matthews 1987). Like Matthews, I shall argue here that the novel both flees the material and ideological conditions of its production and seeks to disclose them.

By examining these conditions from the "interior" perspective of a single Southern household, *The Sound and the Fury* reveals its broader social context primarily through indirection, inference, and analogy. Set primarily in northern Mississippi in 1928, the year in which it was composed, the novel makes few general assertions about its social or geographic milieu, leaving readers to decide how the private history and life of the Compson household illuminate or are illuminated by their broader context. In fact, Faulkner's career as a writer can be described as a gradual and self-conflicted struggle to map out, negotiate, and critique the contours of this relation between the private and the public, and thus to disclose the family as an ideological apparatus that sustains residual social relations and obstructs social change.[1] It is – his own resistances notwithstanding — this persistent exploration and critique that has made his name synonymous with Yoknapatawpha County, his most fully developed fictional milieu.

Faulkner's articulation of this informing context – the historical narrative of Yoknapatawpha County – is what readers must debate and contest. No more than any other historical narratives of the South can the historical narrative of Yoknapatawpha County be understood as objectively given, as "a priori . . . a totality, a unity, or a grand story whose plot and hero we already know" (Jay 270). Such totalizations and grand stories have always been informed by and sustained particular interests such as those of the Southern planter class, the Southern Agrarians, the social realists, the New Critics.[2] Although Faulkner himself accessed this larger history not simply as materials to explore and document but as a social reality to be opposed and transformed, his critics have not always shared these oppositional goals. Many of Faulkner's earliest and most influential critics, for example, were Southern

Agrarians who had vested interests in the narrative of a
racialized and patriarchal agrarian South, a narrative that sustained their privileged position as white male subjects within
it. As the vested interests of Faulkner's readers have changed,
new questions and interpretive methods have been brought to
bear on the interpretation of his historical narrative of Yoknapatawpha County. As a result, although a large body of
criticism is devoted to Faulkner, it is important to offer contestatory views of the writer's relation to his world, not only
of his treatment of history and the South, but also of the ways
in which memory, representation, race, gender, sexuality,
modernism and modernity, and domination traverse his work.
The question of Faulkner's historical context – namely, the
history, legacy, and identity of the South and its peoples –
remains an acute point of cultural contestation. Far from
seeking to place Faulkner's writings in a pregiven context,
then – as if this context could provide a simple background or
solution to the texts – I hope to characterize the political and
cultural motivations of Faulkner's and our own struggle over
the very determination of this context.

Although Faulkner wrote *The Sound and the Fury* in 1928,
and died in Mississippi the day before I turned ten years old in
Detroit, I have always felt close to the problematic history he
sought to negotiate and I seek to negotiate in turn. After having watched the flight of my white friends and neighbors from
"inner city" Detroit in the 1960s; having participated in the
early 1970s, with countless others, in the migration to a
booming and rapidly changing California against the backdrop
of Detroit's collapsing automobile industry; and having arrived, a graduate student in Buffalo, to witness the massive
layoffs that accompanied the closing of the Bethlehem Steel
Plant, I was deeply responsive to the following passage from
Faulkner's *Light in August* when I read it in 1981.

All the men in the village worked in the mill or for it. It was cutting
pine. It had been there seven years and in seven years more it would
destroy all the timber within its reach. Then some of the machinery

and most of the men who ran it and existed because of and for it would be loaded onto freight cars and moved away. *But some of the machinery would be left . . . – gaunt, staring, motionless wheels.* (4, my emphasis)

I was immediately struck by this vivid critique of capitalism's myth of progress and sole motive of profit, by this footnote on the rapidity of change and the exploitation of people implicit in the logic of capitalism, and perhaps most of all by its description of the industrial and commercial ruins this process has contributed to the twentieth-century landscape. Like the sculptor Mark di Suvero, I developed a libidinal attraction to the corroded, crumbling, and demolished steel, brick, asphalt, and concrete I grew up with in Detroit, Los Angeles, and Buffalo. For these ruins are monuments to the disorientingly rapid shifts in the constitution of place characteristic of American industrial and postindustrial culture.

The disorienting experience of change is fundamental to *The Sound and the Fury,* where the body of the black mammy Dilsey herself serves for Faulkner as a sort of twentieth-century ruin or landmark in a South shifting from an agrarian to an industrial economy and from a rural to an urban society. The fragmentation of the hundred acres originally owned by the Compsons represents the broader trend of the "Old New South" toward the fragmentation of the large plantations of the Old South, just as Jason Compson's eventual sale of the land to residential developers in order to become a cotton speculator himself represents economic trends of the New South (Kirby 1987). Similarly, the absence of Dilsey's children and Luster's parents from the Compson household, Frony's marriage to a Pullman porter from St. Louis, and their eventual migrations to urban centers South and North, that is, Memphis and Saint Louis, reflect the impact of mass black migration from the South between 1915 and 1946, when Faulkner wrote the famous Compson "Appendix" to *The Sound and the Fury.*[3]

The trajectory of change that rages through the 1928 novel

takes the forms of trauma, physical transformation, death, flight, and exile; obsessions and grudges, anachronistic styles, values, and beliefs; and repetitions or substitutions that fall short of the desired or remembered original. In the novel, however, this trajectory of change is organized largely around Caddy and the impact on the household of her sexual awakening, pregnancy, marriage, annulment, fatherless infant, and exile. In other words, Caddy is thematized as the primary cause of change, although other sources, types, and levels of transition are clearly at issue in the novel. My intention in this essay is to deepen our understanding of the various changes for which the complex and overdetermined figure of Caddy stands and, in the process, to bring a contestatory notion of Southern history to bear on the novel.

Critics have traditionally seen the novel's treatment of the upheavals experienced by the Compsons as exemplary of Southern history in general, particularly at the point of transition from the Old South to the New South. However, with greater attention to formerly neglected historical perspectives, our understanding of this transition is changing. Mainstream historiography in the post-Reconstruction South has been construed primarily from a white Southern viewpoint, emphasizing political and economic restructuring and rebuilding. This is the story of the South most people know. This is the story of *Gone with the Wind*. In contrast, the story told by African-American historiography, focusing on the history of black struggle against racial violence and the phenomenon of migration from the South to the North, has not reached such a broad audience. It has not yet made its way into our shared ideas about the Southern past and its broader impact on American history and culture.[4] This story, which has been consigned to relative silence, casts Faulkner's writings in a startling new light.

Before investigating the impact of this context on *The Sound and the Fury*, however, and because it is not a story everyone knows, I offer a brief overview of the black migration that began in 1915. Although most historiographers see World War I and its aftermath as a turning point in Southern history, African-American historians emphasize the importance of black migration.[5] Stimulated by the demands of a rapidly expanding war industry and the labor shortage created by a sharp decline in European immigration, migration offered the black masses in the South their first real opportunity to leave. With the encouragement of black newspapers, particularly the *Chicago Defender*, letters and testimonies from migrants, and rumors and debates about the prospects of a better life up North, the 1916 recruitment of black Southerners by Northern railroads led to the leaderless mass migration from the South that did not reverse itself until the 1960s. Whereas 90 percent of American blacks lived in the rural South at the turn of the twentieth century, 6.5 million had migrated out of the South by the 1960s.[6] In itself, black migration, urbanization, and proletarianization altered socioeconomic conditions throughout the nation, leading to labor shortages in the South, the formation of urban ghettoes in the North, and a flurry of debates over the meaning and likely consequences of black migration. In the context of the broader trajectory of twentieth-century African-American history, this migration represented the early stages of black protest.[7]

As James Grossman points out, most historians have examined the Great Migration "as an aspect of the changing wartime labor market or as an essential element in the development of northern urban ghettos and racial problems" (5). Few historians have adequately studied the perceptions of the migrants themselves as shaped by the experience and phenomenon of migration. As Grossman argues, "the migrants represent a crucial transition in the history of Afro-Americans, American cities, and the American working class. That transition was shaped by a complex interaction between structural forces in the South, the migration experience, structural forces in the North, racial attitudes, and the migrants' perceptions of each of these" (5). A concern with this "total context" enables Grossman to stress the importance of Southern racial ideology and culture on the attitudes, expectations, and experience of black migrants. Conversely, Grossman's argument suggests the need to examine the impact of black migration on Southern racial ideology and culture.

White Southerners were reluctant to acknowledge the message of self-determination and protest they dimly perceived in the mass migration of half a million African Americans between 1915 and 1920 and a million more during the 1920s. The migration demonstrated that African-Americans could participate in the historical process, act in protest against their lot in the South, and change their destiny. From this perspective, white Southern resistance to and attempts to impose restrictions on black migration were informed not only by economic demands but also by Southern racial ideology.[8] White Southerners did not wish to acknowledge the protest against Southern racialism and the evidence of black agency that were implicit in migration.

As a result of this widespread denial by white Southerners of the message of protest implicit in black migration, and as a consequence of the exclusion or marginalization of black migration in hegemonic narratives of American history, Faulkner's career-long meditation on the developing meaning, impact, and significance of black migration on his life and culture has received little critical attention. His own culturally constituted disavowal of black migration as a condemnation of Southern racialism and racialized violence and injustice contributed largely to the indirection with which black migration emerged as a crucial element in his corpus. Even though migration did eventually become an explicit theme in Faulkner's writing, it is habitually treated in the negative, that is, in terms of what is *not* there, of what is absent, missing, or lost. Thus, to disclose Faulkner's response to black migration, we must still turn to the history of black migration and, in relation to this history, demonstrate what is absent from Faulkner's texts.

Black migration had been "charted and graphed, analyzed and evaluated, deplored and defended in the newspapers, on public platforms, and in legislative committees" since 1916, and there is no doubt that Faulkner was aware of it (Spear 129). Moreover, the specifics of Faulkner's personal life during the first peak of black migration, 1915–18, drew him even closer to this phenomenon. To avoid being in Mississippi for the wedding of Estelle Oldham, whom he had hoped to marry himself, Faulkner left by train to visit his friend Phil Stone in New Haven, Connecticut. Having been rejected for military service on the basis of his small stature, he took his first trip out of the South with no specific plans for the future. Still hoping to serve in the military, however, Faulkner did manage to enlist in the Royal Air Force by successfully impersonating a British subject. In July, after a brief stop in Mississippi, he was headed for flight school, taking a train to Toronto.

As Faulkner's first experiences away from the South, these train trips served to draw Faulkner closer to the lived experience of the first stage of the Great Migration. When Faulkner took the train from Mississippi to New Haven in April 1918 and from Mississippi to Toronto the following July, he joined the stream of northbound migration. Venturing from the South by train during the peak of migration, Faulkner, like half a million black Southerners, discovered the geographical limits and hence the cultural specificity of Southern racialism. Crossing the Ohio River, the northern boundary of the Jim Crow South, migrants encountered for the first time a world in which not all aspects of everyday life were organized by racial hierarchy.

Outside the South, where public transportation was not segregated by race, Faulkner, like countless black migrants, encountered a startling breach of Southern racial etiquette. Today, the fact that blacks in the North could sit next to whites in public may seem insignificant, but for Southerners at the time, black and white alike, it raised the promise and the specter of a whole new world. Although Faulkner did not comment on his experience of nonsegregated public transportation in the letters he wrote home from New Haven and Toronto in 1918, he does reflect on it in the Quentin section of *The Sound and the Fury*. Riding streetcars in Massachusetts, the transplanted Southerner Quentin Compson takes note of the presence (or absence) of blacks, their proximity, and the difference between Southern and Northern racial etiquette (86, 89, 94).

The experience of sitting beside the racial Other on these northbound train rides is a longstanding *topos* in the literature of migration. Richard Robert Wright, later the bishop of the African Methodist Episcopal Church, recalled his experience of riding the northbound train ride in terms of the dawning of his awareness of Southern racialism. "Here I was sitting beside a white man, and he said nothing. He did not try to make me get up or in any way embarrass me; where I came from the white man would have said 'Boy, get up from here, and let me sit down,' and I would have had to get up. Finally I gained courage and spoke. 'How far is Chicago?'" (cited in Grossman 1). By observing and verifying the differences between Southern and Northern racial etiquette, Wright was motivated to alter his own behavior, in other words, to remain seated next to a white man and even to venture a question.

In *American Hunger*, the novelist Richard Wright also linked an early experience of racial awareness to the train journey north, specifically to his arrival at the depot in Chicago in 1927:

I looked about to see if there were signs saying: FOR WHITE − FOR COLORED. I saw none. Black people and white people moved about, each seemingly intent upon his private mission. There was no racial fear. Indeed, each person acted as though no one existed but himself. It was strange to pause before a crowded newsstand and buy a newspaper without having to wait until a white man was served. . . . I knew that this machine-city was governed by strange laws and I wondered if I would ever learn them. (Wright 1–2)

Both accounts underline that the journey north produces an awareness of Southern racialism because the particular forms of Southern racialist practices are *absent*. Just as Richard Robert Wright noted that the white man on the train "did not try to make me get up or in any way embarrass me," the novelist Richard Wright focused on the racialist signs *he did not see.*

Explicit commentaries do not accompany Quentin's observations about racialism in *The Sound and the Fury.* In order for a middle-class white Southerner like Faulkner (or his character Quentin) to comment on the racial awareness produced by his journey to the North, he would have had to confront its effects on, and challenges to, his own racialized identity. Whereas Northern racial etiquette promised new freedoms to migrating black Southerners (or perhaps only "strange [new] laws," as the novelist Richard Wright suggested), it threatened to diminish the privileges and liberties of white Southerners. Thus, although Faulkner and Quentin note the absence of Southern racial etiquette, they gloss over the meaning of this absence. To confront it directly would be to recognize the erosion of his culturally constructed "superiority" as a white subject. Faulkner's desire to evade this recognition appears in a letter he wrote his father from New Haven in 1921.

In this letter, Faulkner counteracts the effects of his discomfort with Northern racial etiquette by beating a desperate retreat to Southern racial ideology and etiquette. He attributes racial antagonism in the North to the absence of such racist practices as segregation and prescribed forms of address. "Freedom," he argues, only makes blacks more discontent with their devalued identity as racialized subjects. Therefore, his argument concludes, to diminish their privileges, as is done in the South, is the "only . . . sensible way to treat them" and it actually makes them happier than blacks in the North.

Well, sir, I could live in [the North] a hundred years and never get used to the niggers. The whites and niggers are always antagonistic, hate each other, and yet go to the same shows and smaller restaurants, and call each other by first names. . . . You cant tell me these niggers are as happy and contented as ours are, all this freedom does is to make them miserable because they are not white, so that they hate the white people more than ever, and the whites are afraid of them. There's only one sensible way to treat them, like we treat Brad Farmer and Calvin and Uncle George. (*TH* 149)

This defense of the benighted racist discourse he inherited demonstrates Faulkner's reluctance in 1921, five years after the Great Migration began, to confront the injustice and inhumanity of Southern racialism. In view of the eloquent testimony of the half a million black Southerners who migrated from the South during these five years, Faulkner's argument that blacks were happier in the South seems hollow and defensive. Black migration refuted this argument, and its demonstration that black Southerners were neither content nor unable to act to change their destinies also struck at the heart of Southern racialism.

Faulkner's reluctance to admit the relationship between Southern racialism and black migration contrasts sharply with black voices of the period. Wherever they could speak without fear of reprisal, blacks emphasized the impact of Southern racism on black migration. The *Chicago Defender* emphasized racialized injustice in the caption of a front-page photograph illustrating throngs of blacks beside the railroad tracks in Savannah, Georgia, waiting to catch a northbound train during the Great Northern [Migration] Drive of 1916: "The exodus of labor from the South has caused much alarm among the Southern whites, who have failed to treat them decent. The men, tired of being kicked and cursed, are leaving by the thousands as the above picture shows" (cited in Grossman 83). As the perpetrators of racialized injustice, however, white Southerners were reluctant to speak of it. This reluctance to acknowledge their role in encouraging black migration produced a response to migration and its roots in Southern racialism characterized by silence, indirection, contradiction, and denial.[9]

Faulkner's writings consistently illustrate yet also struggle against this culturally constructed denial, in order to articulate a critique of Southern racialism and the construction of racialized subjects. As Faulkner noted in a 1993 retrospective introduction to *The Sound and the Fury,* "We [Southerners] seem to try in the single furious breathing (or writing) span of the individual, by means of oratory, our heritage, to draw a savage indictment of the contemporary scene or to escape from it into a makebelieve region of swords and magnolias and mockingbirds which perhaps never existed" (Cohen and Fowler 279). In the same "single furious breathing," Faulkner's writings are both "savage indictments" against Southern racialism and attempts to evade or deny it. "Sunset," a brief sketch Faulkner published in the *New Orleans Times-Picayune* in 1925, is the first of his writings to broach the experience of migration. A cautionary tale, it appears to make the typical white Southern argument that rural blacks lacked the preparation to survive let alone succeed in the harsh, anonymous, and exploitative urban environments to which migration was leading them. However, other aspects of the sketch work against this simple argument. First, it is set in New Orleans rather than in the urban North, which turns the argument about the harshness and danger of the North back on the urban South. Second, it arouses sympathy for the migrant by showing that his confusion is a result not simply of ignorance or naiveté but of the contradictions of black life in the South. Third, it criticizes the white community for failing to comprehend or provide for the migrant's needs and for allowing him to pursue a trail of misunderstandings that leads to his death. Thus, "Sunset" seems less a caution to black Southerners against migration than an accusation against the white readers of the *New Orleans Times-Picayune* for exploiting and scapegoating its new urban working class.

Given his own privileged position as a racialized subject and a member of the middle class, how did Faulkner come to sympathize with the black migrant? What made him place himself, by writing in "indirect free style," that is, by using the third-person "he" yet freely entering into the thoughts and feelings of the migrant, both in and out of the migrant's shoes?

What led him to recognize the white community as exploitative, intolerant, and indifferent? These may not be answerable questions, but they suggest that Faulkner began to feel sympathy for the black Southern plight he had simply denied in the 1921 letter to his father already discussed. With "Sunset," Faulkner began to criticize Southern racialism, yet he shielded himself from this critique by denying his own role as a racialized subject and identifying himself with the black migrant.

With *The Sound and the Fury*, Faulkner turned away from such easy identification with his racial Other and began to scrutinize his actual position as a privileged white subject within the politics and culture of Southern racialism. Having achieved an uncharacteristic lucidity with regard to Southern racialism, Faulkner was caught in a dilemma. Like the migrant in "Sunset," he might have wished to leave the South and its predicaments behind, yet he could neither find a hospitable home outside the South nor escape his attachment to it. *The Sound and the Fury* reflects Faulkner's fundamental uncertainty about how to negotiate his role in the South, during a period in which its contradictions were growing increasingly difficult to deny. Like Jason, whose efforts to control his destiny ultimately "ravelled out about him like a wornout sock," Faulkner "could see the opposed forces of his destiny and his will drawing swiftly together now, toward a junction that would be irrevocable" (*SF* 313, 307). Jason's failure to overcome his destiny at this irrevocable historical junction is echoed by the failures of such later characters as Horace Benbow in *Sanctuary* and Gavin Stevens in *Intruder in the Dust*. Their failures suggest that Faulkner was resigned to achieving only limited success in opposing and transforming Southern culture and his privileged position as a racialized subject within it.

Like that of the 2.5 million black southerners who migrated from 1915 to 1930, the experience Faulkner had in the North spurred his development of racial awareness, in other words, of the cultural specificity of Southern racialism. *The Sound and the Fury* reflects on this experience in the Quentin section. Given the climate of white Southern response to migration, it is not surprising that Faulkner approaches black migration indirectly, especially insofar as he perceives its links to Southern racialism. A striking example of this indirection is that although the Quentin section draws on Faulkner's 1918 experiences in the North and articulates a response to black migration, it is set in 1910, before the Great Migration began.[10]

By seeing the Quentin section as a response to black migration, in spite of Faulkner's efforts to separate it from this historical phenomenon, we can better account for the important role Faulkner assigns to it. In the context of the other sections, all of which are set in 1928, the Quentin section bears the role of the historical past. Quentin's despair and suicide, however, do not in themselves seem to bear enough on the present to serve as a historical explanation of it. What is the significance of Faulkner's eliminating Quentin from the historical present? I argue that Quentin's migration and development of racial awareness, which led him to experience the dissolution of his racialized identity, represent a geographical and spiritual path not taken by the white South.

Quentin's racialized identity dissolves as a result of his experience of Northern rituals of racialization, for instance, on the streetcar, with the Deacon, a black migrant, and with Gerald Bland, an unreconstructed white Southern transplant.[11] Riding on a streetcar in Cambridge beside a "prosperous looking" black man who is wearing "a derby and shined shoes" leads Quentin to reflect on the forms and rituals of Southern racial etiquette (86–8). Quentin remembers riding the train from Massachusetts to Mississippi the previous Christmas. The train had stopped somewhere in Virginia (i.e., back in the South) and was blocking a road crossing. He looked out the window, "and there was a nigger on a mule in the middle of the stiff ruts, waiting for the train to move. How long he had been there I didn't know, but he sat straddle of the mule, his head wrapped in a piece of blanket, as if they had been built there with the fence and the road, or with the hill, carved out of the hill itself, like a sign put there saying You are home again" (86–7). As if to reinforce an identity threatened by the racial etiquette he experiences in the North, Quentin engages the black bystander in a Southern form of racialized ritual play.

Although he begins the ritual by taking on the role of his racialized Other, namely, by asking for a "Christmas gift," he reasserts his appropriate role in the ritual by throwing out a quarter and enjoining the other man to "Buy yourself some Santy Claus." "Yes, suh. . . . Thanky, young marster," replies the black man, who knows his lines in the script. Quentin's subversion and reassertion of this ritual reveals his anxious new awareness of its cultural constitution and of the threat black migration poses to it. Soon, black Southerners would refuse to serve as an unmoving and immovable fixture of the Southern landscape, a "sign put there saying You are home again." Instead of remaining the stable sign of labor, social inferiority, and contentedness, black Southerners would trade their mules for a ticket on a northbound train. In 1928, Faulkner knew what Quentin only suspected in 1910, namely, that black Southerners would no longer sit, "shabby motionless and unimpatient," "waiting for the train to move," but would abandon the South en masse.

Given his insights into this racial dialectic, Quentin cannot any longer trust the racialized identity he derived from his intimate relations with blacks, for example, with "Roskus and Dilsey and them" (86). Now he realizes that these intimate relationships might signify little more than culturally enforced racial rituals. For middle-class white Southerners like the Falkners and the Compsons, raised in plantation-style extended households with mammies at their center, this threat to the sincerity and stability of their relations with blacks was not insignificant. Black migration reinforced the suggestion that these household retainers were not absolutely devoted to their "white folks" but – like their white folks – were playing roles that were culturally constructed and enforced.

As more and more household retainers migrated, their constitutive role in the material life and racialized identity of white Southerners, more apparent in the breach than in the observance, was increasingly felt if not acknowledged or articulated. In the absence of faithful black servants, white masters and mistresses could not perform the rituals of identity that reinforced their "benevolence" (Katzman 1978). The ironic reversals that result from Quentin's performance of benevolence and concern vis-à-vis the "black and secret and friendly" little girl he meets in the bakery, for example, demonstrate the impasse such culturally constructed benevolence had reached (*SF* 135). An outgrowth of change, this impasse gave rise among white Southern males to what Raymond Williams defines as a new "structure of feelings," that is, to inarticulate feelings of anxiety, dissatisfaction, and frustration.

As opposed to Quentin, who participates in and demonstrates one possible structure of feeling produced by the emergence of black migration, the unreconstructed Southerner Gerald Bland, "the unchallenged peripatetic john of the late Confederacy," participates in and demonstrates another, stubbornly sustaining himself as the privileged subject produced by outmoded rituals of racialization (106). To this end, Gerald and his mother ritually reenact the vanishing racial dialects that produced Gerald as a white Southern male subject, by telling such stories (in Quentin's whimsical and bitter rewording) as "how Gerald throws his nigger downstairs and how the nigger plead to be allowed to matriculate in the divinity school to be near marster marse gerald" (107). Caroline Compson attempts to participate in similar rituals with her son Jason, "the only one . . . that isn't a reproach" to her (181), yet Jason is all too aware that she cannot make good any of the promises of these rituals. Quentin, however, feels as if he never "had a mother" to whom he "could say Mother, Mother" (117, 213), and with whom he could reenact and sustain his identity as the subject produced by a vanishing racial dialectic with "Roskus and Dilsey and them."

The relation of the mother to the dialectics of identity and especially to Southern racial dialectics is central in this novel of transition, and it comes together in the figure and the body of Dilsey, the black mammy.[12] This explains Dilsey's importance in the novel as the site of a vanishing dialectic of racial identity and the culture it produced and sustained.[13] The black mammy, who was both a surrogate mother and an object of illicit sexual desire, was at the center of an inarticulate structure of feeling among white Southerners who experienced black migration as loss and abandonment (Tucker). Although abandonment and loss are fundamental preoccupations of *The Sound and the Fury*, Faulkner treats the loss object not in terms of the old and hobbling Dilsey but as the young and sexually desirable Caddy. It is clear, however, that Caddy stands in the place of the black mammy. Both a nurturant mother and an object of sexual desire, Caddy lives her sexuality, as Quentin protests, "like nigger women do" (92). This sexual independence stands for, and was often confused with, the broader-scale initiative and independence required of black women who managed to migrate from the South (Jones 1985). Just as Faulkner's journey north was linked to his loss of Estelle Oldham, Quentin's development of racial awareness in the North is connected to the loss of Caddy and the themes of separation and changing social relations.

Despite the taboo against incest, Faulkner could more readily explore the feelings of abandonment provoked by black migration as an imaginary loss of a sister, a beloved yet forbidden object of desire, than as a loss that might ultimately point to the black mammy. These links between migration and maternal love, sexual desire, and abandonment help explain why Caddy bears more than her share of meaning, or is overdetermined, as a figure of loss. She bears multiple, contradictory, and even illegitimate meanings that go beyond our expectations of her importance as Quentin's sister (e.g., sexual promiscuity, abandonment, migration, blackness, among others). Beyond serving as a figure for displaced feelings provoked by black migration, as already suggested, Caddy serves as a figure for feelings provoked by the changing role of women. When she ceases to play the Southern belle, she effectively disrupts the Southern dialectic of gendered relations, just as black migration disturbed a dialectic of racialized relations. Like black migrants in relation to the Southern dialectic of race, Caddy "ran right out of the mirror" of a Southern dialectic, producing disturbing effects in the gendered Other (77, 81).

Aware of these dissolving dialectics and unable or unwilling to reconstruct himself in the context of a newly reconfigured racialized and gendered dialectic, Quentin himself dissolves, leaving the future to . . . well, to what? Reflecting on the novel in 1933, Faulkner tried to explain the reactions of each of the three Compson brothers to the overwhelming impact of change:

I knew that someday the peaceful glinting of that branch was to become the harsh cold flood of life itself and that it would sweep [Caddy] further than she could return to comfort [Benjy]. And that he must never grow beyond this moment. *He must never grow up to where grief could be leavened by comprehension and hence rage [and hence alleviation] as in the case of Jason, and the alleviation of oblivion as in the case of Quentin.* (Cohen and Fowler 281, my emphasis)

Their sister, Caddy, did not produce and cannot account for all the changes and losses that transform "the peaceful glinting branch" of their childhoods into "the harsh cold flood of life itself." In contrast to Benjy, who "must never grow beyond this moment" of loss and grief, Quentin and Jason represent different modes of leavening their grief.

Whereas Quentin's journey to the North exposed him to black migration, to the limits and effects of Southern racial ideology, and to the dissolution of his identity as a racial subject, Jason's entrenchment in the South leads him to deny the phenomenon of black migration, its relation to and impact on the Southern dialectic of race, and his own inextricability from this dialectic. This denial takes the form of a general refusal to acknowledge the dynamics of dependency. According to him, he cannot depend on anyone yet everyone depends on him. He claims not to "need any man's help to get along. I can stand on my own feet like I always have" (*SF* 206, 211). Far from providing him with any opportunities, his family has saddled him with unwanted responsibilities.

I reckon the reason all the Compson gave out before it got to me like Mother says, is that [Father] drank it up. At least I never heard of him offering to sell anything to send me to Harvard. (197)

Well, Jason likes work. I says no I never had university advantages. . . . Then when [Caddy] sent Quentin home for me to feed too I says I guess that's right too, instead of me having to go way up north for a job they sent the job down here to me. (196)

Governing relations not just within the white Southern family but also within the black and white household and culture at large, the racialism of this dynamic of dependency is precisely what black migration began to overturn. Jason refuses "to slave [his] life away" for others or to believe that anyone is slaving their life away for him (118). According to Jason, blacks work too little and eat too much (180, 185–7):

What this country needs is white labor. Let these dam trifling niggers starve for a couple of years, then they'd see what a soft thing they have. (190–1)

Like I say the only place for them is in the field, where they'd have to work from sunup to sundown. They cant stand prosperity or an easy job. Let one stay around white people for a while and he's not worth killing. (250)

Embedded in Jason's casual allusion to racist terrorism is the belief that the racialist institutions of the New South, such as economic exploitation, racial discrimination, and segregation, could prevent the transformation of Southern racialism.

Jason's identity as a racialized white Southern male is centrally constructed on the effort to deny, resist, and prevent this
transformation by any means necessary; and black migration,
as *The Sound and the Fury* seems to have foreseen, represented the ultimate triumph over efforts such as his.

When Caddy's illegitimate daughter, Quentin, escapes with
Jason's illegitimately acquired assets and, in spite of Jason's
vigilant efforts to confine her, flees the South like a black
migrant, Jason's identity is undone. With the realization of his
worst fears, Jason's "invisible life ravelled out about him like a
wornout sock" (313). At this point, "something – the absence
of disaster, threat, in any constant evil – permitted him to
forget Jefferson as any place which he had ever seen before, [or
as the place] where his life must resume itself " (314). Assuming that black migration would continue and recognizing it as
the realization of the worst fears of the white South, *The
Sound and the Fury* glimpsed, in 1928, that this migration
would eventually force white Southerners to yield their positions as racialized subjects if not institutionalized racialism.
As Luster admonished Benjy, Faulkner's text indirectly urged
the white South to accept the transformation of its familiar
landscape: "'they aint coming back here no more. . . . Looking
for them aint going to do no good. They're gone'" (4, 73). Yet
when he wrote this novel, Faulkner could not have known
that, between 1928 and 1942, black migration and the projected dissolution of Southern racialism would be hindered by
the Great Depression. Unfortunately, the invisible life of a
white South attached to an unjustly racialized social order and
resistant to its transformation would take several more decades to unravel.

Faulkner's exploration of his Southern context, its fundamental racialism, and the resistance of white Southerners to
its transformation thus began earlier than many of his critics
believe, and involved not simply a historical investigation of
this context but, more crucially, a desire to oppose and transform it. As Richard King has demonstrated, Faulkner's writ-

ings were engaged in the process of "working through" the Southern past (King 1980). Dominick La Capra argues that fundamental psychoanalytic concepts such as "working through," "denial," "acting out," and "transference" are crucial to the process of historical understanding because they allow us to grasp the human complexity of coming to terms with shameful and traumatic aspects of the past. As La Capra argues, the process of working through "requires the recognition that we are involved in transferential relations to the past in ways that vary according to the subject positions we find ourselves in, rework, and invent" (125). Unless we enter into such active and situated exchanges with the past, we will simply deny its shameful and traumatic aspects and "reprocess" the past to satisfy and "act out our own desires for self-confirming or identity-forming meaning" (125).

But to be critical and self-critical, this undertaking must be sensitive to the problem of the possibilities and limits of meaning, including the threat of finding oneself at the point of irrecoverable loss and empty silence. The quest for a "positive" identity or for normalization through denial provides only illusory meaning and does not further the emergence of an acceptable future. A reckoning with the past in keeping with democratic values requires the ability – or at least the attempt – to read scars and to affirm only what deserves affirmation as one turns the lamp of critical reflection on oneself and one's own. (126)

We should not be so bold as to think that the American South alone has a past that requires working through or that we are as able and willing as Faulkner was to turn the lamp on ourselves and our own.

NOTES

I wish to thank Jim Carothers, Alan Feuer, Melanie Johnson, David Katzman, Mark Luce, Jennifer Roth, Barry Shank, Theresa Towner, Bill Tuttle, Philip Weinstein, Norm Yetman, and especially Philip and Julia Barnard, without whose encouragement, friendship, and generosity I could not have written this essay. Special acknowledgment is also due the University of

Kansas's General Research Fund for supporting my research during the summer of 1993.

1 On the family as an "ideological state apparatus" and on ideology as a mode of reproducing the social order, see Louis Althusser's classic essay "Ideology and Ideological State Apparatuses." See also Stuart Hall's critique of Althusser, which seeks to provide a better explanation of oppositional culture and the relationship between ideology and identity formation.

2 For discussions of the ideological construction of Yoknapatawpha County or, more broadly, of Faulkner himself, see, for example, Duvall, Lester, Matthews (1987), and Schwartz.

3 For a historical and critical discussion of the "Appendix," see Lester.

4 From a white Southern point of view, the New South emerges in 1913, the year when the Southern-born Woodrow Wilson became president and reintegrated Southern whites into the political and economic process of the nation. George Brown Tindall's classic study, *The Emergence of the New South: 1913–1945*, for example, begins with the statement that "half a century of Southern political isolation ended with the inauguration of President Woodrow Wilson on March 4, 1913" (1). Yet, as C. Vann Woodward's *Origins of the New South, 1877–1913* explains, 1913 was widely celebrated by African-Americans as the Year of the Jubilee, the fiftieth anniversary of emancipation, which ironically marked the fact that, apart from a small black elite, blacks had made little material progress up to this time.

5 For a variety of contemporary perspectives on the Great Migration, see Harrison as well as Trotter.

6 For demographic figures on black migration, see Johnson and Campbell.

7 For a broad sketch of African-American migration, see Katzman (1991).

8 Justifying their response in terms of economics, Southern states resorted to restrictive legislation and extralegal force to staunch the flow of migration (Scott and Grossman). Not believing that blacks were deciding to leave the South on their own initiative, the South tried to stop migration by prohibiting anything designed to entice migration. They prohibited or obstructed the activities of labor agents and banned advertisements, letters, and newspapers promoting migration. When these sanctions failed, Southerners attempted to render northbound trains inaccessible to blacks; would-be migrants were refused tickets, restrained from boarding, and physically removed from trains; trains themselves were kept from stopping wherever migrants might readily board them. Determined to leave the South, blacks evaded these restrictive measures, just as they proved deaf to the deliberately circulated rumors concerning the misfortunes suffered by migrants in the North. All else failing, some Southern

communities made conciliatory gestures toward blacks, hoping to dissuade them from leaving.

9 On the role of silence and denial in historiography, see La Capra. Kirby describes the same phenomenon with regard to the settlement of accounts between landowners and tenants. Whereas black tenants and sharecroppers were extremely clear about how a system that cheated them worked, white landlords were typically silent, indirect, or contradictory about the subject (142 5).

10 In 1910, the native son of Massachusetts W. E. B. DuBois moved back to the North to join the NAACP, and Leroy Percy, the last Delta planter to occupy a major political office in Mississippi, was involved in the bitter senatorial campaign he lost to James K. Vardaman in 1911. Angered by hecklers during a speech he gave on July 4, 1910, Percy called Vardaman's followers "cattle" and "rednecks"; thereafter, Vardaman's supporters wore red ties, as does the carnival pitchman that Caddy's daughter, Quentin, runs off with in *The Sound and the Fury*. Despite their class differences, the Falkners supported Vardaman (cf. Blotner, Kirwan 191–231, Railey).

11 On the dialectic of racial identity as played out between Quentin and the Deacon, see Bryant.

12 On the figure of the mother in *The Sound and the Fury*, especially in relation to Kristeva's semiotic, and an overview of other discussions of the topic, see Weinstein, 29–41.

13 Faulkner himself gradually realized the importance of his mammy, Caroline Barr. It was not until after her death in 1940 and after he had written *Go Down, Moses* (which is dedicated to her memory), in which a mammy plays a central role, that Faulkner could even suggest, as he does in the 1946 "Appendix," that Dilsey would leave "her white folks" and migrate.

7   Race in *Light in August:* Wordsymbols and Obverse Reflections

In *The Sound and the Fury,* Quentin, reminding himself that while in the East he must "remember to think of [blacks] as colored people not niggers," goes on to assert that a black person is "a form of behavior, a sort of obverse reflection of the white people he lives among" (86). Although Quentin's reflections have obviously been conditioned by his Southern background and are hardly intended to serve as any sort of universally applicable commentary, both his concern with the language of racial designation and his judgment that race is a conceptual and behavioral issue as much as (or rather more than) a biological one are salient. Moreover, they thematically anticipate Faulkner's most profound meditation on the topic, *Light in August.* It is striking – and may seem paradoxical – that the Faulkner novel most centrally concerned with an issue that suffused so much of his corpus contains not a single significant character who is identifiably African-American, but that absence only emphasizes the text's predominant concern with race as a linguistic and social construct rather than a biological given, its focus more on the concept of race than on actual race relations. In the course of the novel, Faulkner not only provides a provocative consideration of the issues surrounding racial notions in the American South in the early part of the twentieth century – indeed, in Western culture generally, if one takes into account the novel's connection with important theoretical and historical writings about race

146

– but, while investigating the operations of the concept of blackness, he also manages to explore the role of language in the construction of subjectivity.

Late in *Light in August*, Gavin Stevens offers a biological explanation for Joe Christmas's unfortunate behavior, the tragic course that had led him down a thousand lonely and savage streets to a violent end. Stevens suggests that Christmas's "blood would not be quiet," that his "white blood" compelled him in one direction, his "black blood" in another, with the latter leading him to his ultimate doom, "beyond the aid of any man" (*LA* 449). Although Stevens's credentials – Phi Beta Kappa, a Harvard degree – suggest that his interpretation might be considered plausible, the complexities of the preceding action and the depiction of Joe Christmas clearly reveal it to be simplistic, inadequate to the nature of events and character as represented. As Faulkner himself said, it is simply "an assumption, a rationalization which Stevens made" (*FU* 72). Even the notion of "black" or "white" blood seems, either in or out of context, not only ludicrous but sinister. Moreover, although Joe himself is depicted as tragically conflicted by the possibility of a mixed heritage, with only brief moments of wry awareness that "if I'm not [partially black], damned if I haven't wasted a lot of time" in self-destructive behavior (254), there are no solid grounds for assuming that he is in fact racially mixed. Joe's appearance is fully "white," he has been raised entirely by whites, and the sole source of information about his "blackness" is his demented grandfather, Doc Hines. This "fact" originates in Hines's intuition about the "real" lineage of Joe's seemingly "Mexican" father and is backed up only by the equally questionable testimony of the circus owner who employed him; it is conveyed to Joe in an ambiguous way, to other characters in the novel by gossip, and to the reader in a deferred and convoluted fashion, during a conversation among Bunch, Hightower, and the Hineses that occurs late in the text. In every instance, the validity of this information is profoundly open to question and entirely unverifiable by empirical means, yet so potent is the idea itself that few recipients entertain serious doubts.

Both the notion of Joe's "blackness" and the multiple responses to it might in many respects seem almost laughable were it not for the compellingly tragic resonance of the novel, emphasized even now by the disturbing awareness that such ideas retain their potency many decades later: the power of racial thinking has been recently reaffirmed by the varying reactions to the Rodney King case and the Los Angeles uprisings, as Cornel West and Robert Gooding-Williams have noted. In addition, *Light in August,* as numerous Faulkner critics and historians have pointed out, has a distinct and exemplary relationship to prevailing concepts as well as events of the period in which it was written. Thadious Davis, for example, notes that the Southern Renaissance of 1925–39, in which Faulkner was so central a figure, was also an era in which racial segregation and white supremacy were ingrained patterns in Southern thought, having become increasingly codified after World War I (23). Eric Sundquist locates the appearance of *Light in August* at the "crest of a forty-year wave" of Jim Crow laws that grew out of the "separate but equal" doctrine of *Plessy v. Ferguson* (1896), a case involving a "Negro" who was "seven-eighths white" and could pass as white; these laws flourished during the period after World War I when blacks made increasing demands for racial equality (1983, 68–9). Sundquist also notes that the novel draws on the "mass of theorizing" about Jim Crow, black regression, and the concept of the "white nigger" that pervaded race theory of the 1930s (1987, 12). Others, from W. J. Cash, writing in the 1940s, to Joel Williamson in the 1980s have explored the psychological etiology of the myth of the "black beast rapist" and the violent propensities of the "mind of the South" that made lynching and other vigilante action possible; they frequently invoke Faulkner's 1932 novel as a dramatic embodiment of the impact of such thinking on both an individual and a community.

Light in August and Faulkner's masterpiece of four years later, *Absalom, Absalom!*, may now be the best-known and most highly regarded novels of their era that are centrally, if not exclusively, concerned with race, but they were certainly neither the first nor the only ones of significance. *Light in August* has a particularly intriguing intertextual relationship with two works that immediately preceded it, *Quicksand* (1928) and *Passing* (1929), the only novels by the long neglected African-American writer Nella Larsen. Considered either individually or in tandem, the Larsen texts have many of the same thematic concerns and structuring devices as Faulkner's 1932 novel. The protagonist of *Quicksand*, Helga Crane, comes, like Larsen, from a racially mixed background, undertaking to reconcile the psychic division that seems to be a consequence of her genetic legacy by moving from one geographical location and social milieu to another in a futile quest, while *Passing* depicts the agony of racial masquerade and its potential for both psychological and literal violence. Like *Light in August*, *Passing* also conflates racial confusion with sexual uncertainty, incorporating a homoerotic subtext. Moreover, its central character, Clare Kendry Bellew, undergoes a series of experiences with similarities to those of Joe Christmas. The product of a difficult childhood, Clare moves from a natural family ruled by a formidable and violent father to an adoptive white family whose religiosity is equaled only by its repressiveness and its obsession with industriousness. Capable, with her light coloring, of "passing," Clare self-destructively marries a white racist who repeatedly denounces "black scrimy devils" and prides himself on having "no niggers in [his] family" (171–2), but her unrelieved "hankering" after her own people leads her ultimately to exposure and a violent death. The tragic trajectory of Clare's life, like the carefully structured format of the tale and the narrator's brooding about the "burden of race" and the cursed quality of "Ham's dark children" (225), in many ways anticipates Faulkner's later novel, although the gender issues in Larsen's work give it a somewhat different thrust, as does the protagonist's persistent yearning to reconnect with her African-American past, which distinguishes her from Faulkner's profoundly ambivalent Joe Christmas.

Although the preoccupation with racially based thinking and codes of behavior links *Light in August* with significant other fiction of its era, even as it connects the novel closely with its specific sociopolitical Southern context, it also resonates with concepts that had perfused Western culture generally for a century or more. As Lucius Outlaw notes in his recent essay on the history of the concept of race, that concept originated in the human need for classificatory ordering in the social world. Its ultimate precursors include Plato's theory of forms, and it was given impetus by the typological thinking that accompanied the emerging scientific praxis of the eighteenth century in the West. During the nineteenth century, "race" came to signify biologically distinguished groups, its use having been generated by the association of the color black with evil, death, and Christian sin, by mounting tensions among groups of peoples in Europe, by the urge to account for human diversity, and by the growth of the slave trade. Outlaw notes that as of 1990, the nature and usage of "race" was continuing to evolve, in part because of the rise of the "global village" and the increasing unlikelihood of genetic homogeneity; any "race classification" is to some degree a product of chance and can become obsolete in a relatively short time.

Not only does the word "race" have a slippery connection to the idea, the idea itself is always changing; similarly, "black" and "white" have a problematic linkage to the concepts they putatively represent. Still, such words have profound impact on individuals, being part of the encompassing construction, language, that belongs to and indeed largely constitutes the Symbolic order, the cultural law that dictates and constructs the development of the speaking subject. It is, says psychoanalytic theorist Jacques Lacan, "the world of words that creates the world of things"; the individual is, a priori and infallibly, "the slave of language." Thus it is "inconceivable," asserts Lacan, that the elementary structures of culture and its ordering of exchanges, indeed what we think of as "experience" itself, could exist "outside the permutations authorized by language." Culture, he says, "could well be reduced to language" (148); the "letter . . . produces all the effects of truth in man" (158).

Although Lacan's discussions of the construction of subjectivity in and via language do little or nothing to explore the consequence of elements such as race or class, focusing instead on sexual difference, his well-known drawing of identical bathroom doors marked "Ladies" and "Gentlemen," and his wry mention of the way in which one's public life "is subjected to the laws of urinary segregation," seem quite relevant to the issue of "blackness" and "whiteness" as it pervades *Light in August*. Because the only disparity between the doors is the word above, it is solely the signifier that serves to articulate the difference between them. Yet, says Lacan, for those who see them, "LADIES and GENTLEMEN will be henceforth two countries . . . between which a truce will be . . . impossible" (149). Not only does this passage invoke the actual Southern practice of racially segregating bathrooms and other public facilities, it indirectly addresses the issue of racial categories themselves. In the consideration of fictional characters like Faulkner's Joe Christmas and Larsen's Clare Kendry, the simple substitution of "blackness" or "whiteness" for the words over the Lacanian bathroom doors does much to elucidate their plight; the signifiers of racial classification, however arbitrarily they may be assigned to individuals, can prove psychologically deterministic.

In *Killers of the Dream*, Lillian Smith's autobiographical memoir, after meditating on "the edgy blackness and whiteness of things" that dominated her Southern childhood and the way in which blackness and whiteness had become "breathing symbols" (12), Smith goes on to tell an anecdote with provocative connections to Faulkner's 1932 novel and Lacan's illustrative example of bathroom doors. When Lillian was a child, a "little white girl" in her town was discovered to be living with a black family. A group of local clubwomen that included Smith's mother had the child removed by a town marshal and brought to the Smiths' house to live. Over time, Lillian developed an emotional bond with the other girl, but this was abruptly severed one day when a telephone call resulted in the return of the white child to "Colored Town." Distressed, Lillian protested, "But she's white!" The answer came: "We were mistaken. She is colored." Lillian insisted, "But she looks—" yet the response was "She is colored. Please don't argue!" Lillian's pleas, grounded in the evidence available to her eyes as well as in emotional connection, went unheeded and the girl was taken away. Smith refers to this wrenching event — clearly parallel to some of Joe Christmas's early experiences although viewed from a different vantage point — as emblematic of "the drama of the South" (34–6). Even invisible "blackness" becomes the determinant of individual fate.

Smith notes in her subsequent reflections on the "distorted frame" put around every black child from birth that the same "frame" also surrounds whites. "Each is on a different side of the frame," she says, "but each is pinioned there" (39). Despite the invisibility of his imputed blackness, Faulkner's Joe Christmas is also pinioned by this distorted racial frame. Verbally, the constrictive framing of Christmas — racial and otherwise — is established within the narrative by a complex series of textual moves, some quite obvious, others more subtle. Christmas has, of course, been "framed" by a number of critics over the years, some describing him as a type, a memorable example of the "tragic mulatto," others treating the novel as a work about racial masquerade, about "passing." Critics of the 1940s, such as Maxwell Geismar and Joseph Warren Beach, typically referred to Christmas as "a mulatto" and accepted the "fact" of his "black blood," undoubtedly because, as Irving Howe said, the mulatto, "trapped between the demarcated races" is "an unavoidable candidate for the role of a victim" (128). Nevertheless, Faulkner asserted in 1957 that Joe "didn't know what he was, and there was no way possible in life for him to find out" (*FU* 72), and Regina Fadiman's 1975 study of Faulkner's revision of the *Light in August* manuscript shows that Faulkner deliberately sought to mystify the racial identity of Joe Christmas.

Recent critics, emphasizing the complexities of Faulkner's intention and the subtleties of his method, have explored the manner in which the figure of Joe Christmas eludes definition, racial or otherwise. Although James Snead refers to Christmas as both black and white, a tragic mulatto, he goes on to reflect on the different ways in which this pivotal Faulknerian figure remains "the quintessence of indeterminable essence" and so "resists signification" (87–8, 81). Martin Kreiswirth has analyzed the complex method of the novel, noting that every time a narrative begins to emerge that will clarify some of the ambiguities, new and disruptive materials break in. Christmas's contradictory being cannot be rendered as narrative, says Kreiswirth, and the "fundamental indeterminacy" of his identity becomes duplicated in the reading experience itself (74–5). But essentially indeterminate as Christmas may be, both the operations of the Symbolic order into which he is inscribed at an early age and a series of textual strategies serve to define and to "frame" him. It might even be said that while the novel clearly exposes – in order to indict – the pernicious (though virtually inevitable) effects of the prevailing codes, its structure and other aspects of the narrative method to some degree subtly participate in the process of "framing."

Certain passages in *Light in August* provide suggestive, if sometimes oblique, commentary on the problematic process of signification and on the coercive effects of language, despite its ambiguous relation to the reality it purports to define. In one such instance, Byron Bunch, confronting the birth of Lena's baby and his consequent realization that "she is not a virgin," goes on to wonder whether all the individuals playing parts in the human drama that has been unfolding "were just a lot of words that never even stood for anything, were not even us." What Byron finds most difficult to accept is the identity of the father, saying, "It aint until now that I ever believed that he is Lucas Burch. That there ever was a Lucas Burch" (401–2). While Byron is simply reflecting on his own dawning awareness of some truths about the human situation in which he has become emotionally enmeshed, his comments point to the highly tenuous connection between signifier and signified. Also indirect, though provocative, is the earlier scene in which Joe Christmas is being punished by his adoptive father, MacEachern, for refusing to learn the Presbyterian catechism. MacEachern's voice is described as "cold, implacable, like written or printed words" (149), a comparison that subtly invokes the paradox that by refusing to undertake the verbal mastery of and by the catechistic text with its repressive codifications, Christmas brings upon himself another sort of violence. Whether he resists or capitulates to the Symbolic effects of the Protestant code, Christmas will be punished, either directly or indirectly.

In both of these passages, male ideas and language are foregrounded and linked with the Father – God, the Church, the adoptive father, the biological father, or the would-be surrogate father. Indeed, throughout the novel, masculine figures and their precepts are the explicit representatives of the Symbolic order. Many of these characterizations are sufficiently extreme that they would appear entirely comical if they were not vicious and violent: the sheriff who is both leader and agent of community opinion and cries out, "get me a nigger," beating the one found at hand in an attempt to elicit information about Joanna Burden's murder (291–2); Percy Grimm, the white supremacist vigilante in military guise who claims to be dedicated to "the protection of America" and kills and castrates Joe Christmas so that he will "let white women alone, even in hell" (454, 464); and Doc Hines, who sees himself as God's instrument, charged with the eradication of abomination and bitchery and thus feels justified in murdering his daughter's lover as well as letting the daughter herself die unattended in childbirth. In these three male figures, one cannot help but notice the metonymic movement from repressive rhetoric to physical violence. As in the scene between Christmas and MacEachern, the connection between classificatory verbiage and literal brutality is suggestive.

Doc Hines is a grandfather, one of several in the novel whose ideas have a resounding impact on their progeny; these figures tend to be profoundly racist as well as fanatically religious and sexist. Hines is the most obviously pernicious of these, responsible not only for murder and death by neglect but also for the abandonment of his only grandchild to the deprivations of orphanage life and the vilifications of those like the dietitian who call the boy "little nigger bastard" – all because Hines believes that Joe is "tainted" by a racially mixed heritage. The concepts of the innocent child's grandfather set in motion the tragic course of his life, while Joe's subsequent internalization of those ideas results in extremely self-destructive behavior.

Joanna Burden, later Joe's lover as well as his counterpart in a number of ways ranging from social marginality to confused sexual identity, is also in some sense a victim of grandfatherly behavior, as well as of paternal rhetoric. Joanna is brought up to believe that her grandfather, killed in Mississippi for his actual advocacy of blacks, was murdered "by the curse which God put on a whole race." Blacks, she hears, are "cursed to be forever and ever a part of the white race's doom and curse for its sins." This message, delivered to the four-year-old Joanna, who has been forced to accompany her father to the cedar grove where her grandfather is buried, is appallingly dehumanizing and frightening in its invocation of biblical "authority," and its impact on the child is heightened by the surroundings in which it is heard. Conceptually and emotionally distorted as a result, Joanna comes to see blacks "not as people, but as a thing, a shadow in which I lived, we lived [a] black shadow in the shape of a cross" which she must work to "raise" (252–3).

That Joanna subsequently dedicates her life and her inheritance to "raising" the stature of black people hardly offsets the fact that she is also capable of treating individuals such as Joe, who she believes is partly black, as "a thing": her initial behavior toward Joe causes him to feel she has "niggerized" him, for the meal she leaves him appears in his sensitive eyes to be "set out for the nigger" and ironically includes "Ham," which he furiously hurls against the wall (238). Even after they become sexually involved, she apparently sees Joe as irretrievably racially Other: she calls out "Negro! Negro! Negro!" when they make love and then tells him she is pregnant with their "bastard Negro child" (266). She also pressures him to become more "officially" black by attending a Negro school. Indeed, Joanna turns out to be the figure in Joe's life who uses racial designations the most, the one who makes the most extensive effort to "place" him. Admittedly her "racism" is more benign than that of others with whom Joe makes contact, but the couple's intimacy makes it more problematic. Joe's ultimate attempt to decapitate Joanna – to remove the source of such categorizing intellection from the body with which he has shared pleasures – could perhaps be seen as emblematic of the larger struggle that has engaged so many of his energies: the attempt to resist the coercion of language and its attendant classifications.

Given the power and phallocentricity of the language and codes that govern the society represented in and by the town of Jefferson, it is hardly surprising that so few figures show the capability of challenging them in any way. Although Lacan himself asserted the potential for the speaking subject to achieve *la parole pleine* and for language to renew itself perpetually – and indeed the extraordinary multivalence of Faulkner's fiction bears eloquent testimony to the suppleness and the radical possibilities inherent in at least one Western language – almost none of the characters in *Light in August* does other than submit to its more constrictive operations, to the rule of the murderous wordsymbols.

This applies even to a figure such as Lena Grove, seen by many critics as an almost mythic figure, an earth goddess, and at the very least a female whose extramarital pregnancy and obvious vulnerability challenge the assumptions and responses of all the intradiagetic figures who come in contact with her, making her part of one of those "alternative communities" about which John Duvall has written. When one examines Lena in terms of language – both that which she uses and that employed to describe her – she is seen to be utterly constricted. Indeed, Lena's depiction, however "subversive" it may by in some ways, seems calculated to disclose the emptiness of routinized language, its inadequacy in the face of the reality that it seeks to convert into words. Lena's statement which opens the novel – "I have come from Alabama: a fur piece" (3) – is obviously comic, serving hardly at all to render the physical arduousness and emotional difficulty of pursuing, without funds or maps or adequate facts, and in a state of advanced pregnancy, the lover who has abandoned her. Further along, the first time Lena speaks more than the brief and superficial expressions of gratitude that mark her interchanges with the Armstids, she tells the tale of Lucas's departure in such a way that reveals she has totally internalized his way of thinking about the situation. This is evident in the monologue that begins "he had done got the word about how he might have to leave a time before that [night she told him about the baby]. He just never told me sooner because he didn't want to worry me with it" (18–19). Lena's rhetoric in this passage reveals her linguistically to be entirely the captive of anOther. At the same time, however, it eventually becomes clear that Lena's dogged adherence, in her speech, to male-dominated ideas and bland banalities serves as a linguistic shield, preventing her from acknowledging the potentially horrific circumstances to which her condition may condemn her. Her severely limited use of language ironically operates as a form of protection.

For a figure such as Christmas, on the other hand, the encounter with language and its implications, particularly in terms of his preoccupation with received notions about race, about blackness and whiteness, is a traumatic and ultimately destructive one. In this regard, it is notable that Joe devotes no reflective time to his biological parents or any other of his relatives; conceptually, his struggles with his supposed racial background and, during one period, with the ideas of his powerful adopted father dominate his existence. Joe's earliest direct exposure to racial epithets, and to the thinking they so intensely convey, occurs at the orphanage, where he has been left by the grandfather who regards him as "a sign and a damnation for bitchery" (127). They are inflicted upon him primarily by the angry dietitian who keeps calling him "you little nigger bastard" without any real evidence and despite the awareness that in a group of black children he would look "just like a pea in a pan full of coffee beans" (125, 130); the racial imputations echo what she has heard from others and may constitute the projection of her own guilt about sexual transgression, with Joe as the innocent recipient. By the time Joe is an adolescent, he, too, projects his confused feelings outward, in one notable instance regarding the young black girl in the shed awaiting his sexual assault as "a black well," a "womanshenegro" to whom he responds with a series of brutal kicks (156).

Subsequently Joe believes his putative blackness to be a powerful weapon in the white world; he imagines shocking his adoptive father with the news that "he has nursed a nigger beneath his own roof" (168) and takes pleasure in upsetting women with whom he has lain by telling them that he is partially black. As confused about his sexual identity as about his racial identity, he conflates the two during intimate moments with Joanna Burden, seeing himself as "drowning" in "a black thick pool" (260). The multiple pulls and psychic confusions are most explicit in the scene in which Joe enters Freedman Town, feeling himself surrounded by the smell and voices "of invisible negroes." The entry takes the form of a descent into "a thick black pit" where he is threatened by a sense of having returned "to the lightless hot wet primogenitive Female" and rapidly flees, ascending with relief to "the cold hard air of white people" (114–15). During this same period, he is drawn for refuge to Negro cabins, but sees himself as "hunted by white men at last into the black abyss which had been waiting, trying, for thirty years to drown him" (331), and thinks of the borrowed Negro shoes as a "black tide creeping up his legs, moving from his feet upward as death moves" (339). The divergent impulses of flight and return, like his conceptual oscillations between blackness and whiteness, signify how powerfully Christmas is torn apart by the linguistic oppositions that rule his psychic life.

Whereas the passages in question portray Joe directly grappling with the issues raised by his early designation from without as "nigger bastard," which proves more a prophecy than a statement of fact, still others, from which Joe is absent, further disclose the manner in which his racial status is constructed by language rather than by visible, verifiable data. In one of these, a white male (perhaps it should be "apparently white" because the story's very interrogation of Christmas's heritage should obviate the tendency to impose categorical racial designations), Byron Bunch, tells another, Hightower, about a discussion between still other white males that followed Joanna's death. Dismayed to be found in suspicious circumstances, Brown/Burch reportedly says to the sheriff, "Accuse the white and let the nigger run" (97), evoking the responses "You better be careful what you are saying, if it is a white man you are talking about. . . . I dont care if he is a murderer or not. . . . A nigger . . . I always thought there was something funny about that fellow" (98–9). In almost parodic fashion, race proves more important than murder and hearsay is quickly accepted as fact. At another point, the townspeople discussing Christmas, disoriented because "He dont look any more like a nigger than I do," nevertheless accept his "blackness" as explanatory of his behavior, of his violence toward a white woman and his subsequent failure to elude capture – "it must have been the nigger blood in him" (349).

Although such hyperbolic passages by their very nature serve as critiques of racial definition and explanation, their recurrence may nonetheless persuade first-time readers of the novel that they too should accept the notion of Joe's partial (and invisible) "blackness." Such passages are, moreover, reinforced in subtle ways by other elements in the text, including the repeated use of the word "shadow" when Joe is introduced as a small child – appropriate for his size and reticence, perhaps, but still capable of resonating intratextually with the passage in which Joanna describes the black people as a "shadow" that must be raised. Less directly, the moment in which the child Joe kneels to eat with his hands "like a savage, like a dog" (155) resonates with that in which Burch looks at the black youth who will take his message to town as "a beast" (435), just as the use of the adjective "inscrutable" for some of the few actual blacks in the novel seems somehow linked with "the veil, the screen" that renders Christmas incomprehensible to some observers. Descriptions of the adult Joe as watching his naked "body grow white out of the darkness like a kodak print emerging from the liquid" (108) or lying in bed with his ebony woman attempting to breathe in "the dark and inscrutable thinking and being of negroes, with each suspiration trying to expel from him the white blood and the white thinking and being" (225–6), while expressive of his psychic condition, the spiritual torment he undergoes in attempting to locate himself racially, also keep before the reader the black–white oscillation associated with Joe and thus, implicitly, the notion of mixed blood. Although this notion is subsequently revealed as absurd during Gavin Stevens's elucidation, it remains a potent force for much of the narrative.

It also seems relevant that descriptions of nearly all of the characters who live at the social margins, whether these descriptions are provided by viewers or by the narrative voice itself, tend to contain the word "dark." Not necessarily racist, the term is nevertheless suggestive. Joanna's house and her person have an aura of "something dark and outlandish and threatful" (47), and "dark" or "darkness" occur no less than seven times in two paragraphs about Hightower (76). Moreover, in at least one instance a black figure is described by the ambiguously located narratorial voice in what can only be called a racist way – the Negro woman seen outside Hightower's house spelling aloud the letters on his sign "with that vacuous idiocy of her idle and illiterate kind" (59). The demeaning racial otherness of this woman, so fleetingly depicted, is echoed more subtly in the presence of other black female characters who prove to be doubly mediated, their subjectivity totally inaccessible to the reader. These include the girl Christmas encounters in his abortive early sexual experience, seen only through the distorted lens of his own confusion, "prone, abject," smelly and terrifying, a "black well" that threatens to engulf him (156); Old Cinthy, the slave who belonged to Hightower's grandfather, a virtual caricature of the loyal family retainer and present only in the aging Hightower's tortuous memories; and the "high brown" cook employed by Hightower, represented only in the racist gossip of the communal voice, which reflects that "if a nigger woman considered [Hightower's sexual request] against God and nature, it must be pretty bad" (72). Because all these black females are assigned marginal roles as well as being subjectively unavailable, their otherness seems reduplicated.

Various textual strategies have something of the same effect on additional figures who are marginalized by gender and class as well as race, and thus quietly reenact the procedure as it occurs in the larger society. A few of these are evident at the outset of the novel, establishing the way in which individuals are objectified, inserted into preexisting structures. In the first several pages, Lena Grove provides an intriguing example. She is initially depicted from an interior vantage point, reflecting on the surprising extent of her travels from Alabama; additional information about her early deprivations and childhood experiences begins to turn her into what Forster would call a "round character" and thus to engage the reader's sympathy. The passage is followed by further memories of her trip and the anticipation of a reunion with Lucas ("And then he will see me and he will be excited. And so there will be two within his seeing before his remembering" [91]). By the end of this scene, the reader's amused awareness of Lena's naiveté is balanced with a concern for her plight and knowledge of her conditioning by early experiences. Yet suddenly there is a turn to an external and far harsher point of view, that of the male watchers Armstid and Winterbottom, whose focus is entirely on her pregnant body. Their first comment is "I wonder where she got that belly" (9) and is followed by speculation about who she is and where she has come from. The narratorial voice subsequently offers comment that further "places" Lena, first turning her into a quasi-mythic emblem of fecundity and then, by quietly mocking her rural speech patterns, emphasizing her class status. It describes her as moving "swollen, slow, deliberate, unhurried and tireless as augmenting afternoon itself" and notes, after she buys a box of sardines, that "she calls them *sour-deens*" (10, 27).

Something similar occurs with the males during these scenes, whose social placement, their otherness to the implied (urban, sophisticated) reader, is also established. The narrator notes that the male clerk who waits on Lena "also calls them *sour-deens*," and, commenting on Armstid's negotiations with Winterbottom for a cultivator, describes him as proceeding "with the timeless unhaste and indirection of his kind" (27, 10). However, in the case of Armstid, it is notable that the classification of "his kind" is followed by a movement to his point of view, which includes bits of interior monologue; this has the effect of recuperating his subjectivity and thus allowing him a more complex identity. The process constitutes a reversal of what happens narratively to Lena, whether this is fortuitously or intentionally gender-based. Though her location – mythic/poor white – is ambiguous, it is a position of otherness.

At the same time as such subtle textual moves seem to reinforce the process by which individuals are racially classified, "framed," and located at the fringes of society, the novel as a whole quite explicitly assails both the human tendency to categorize and the validity of the categories themselves. The linguistic and cultural codes that construct subjectivity are revealed as perhaps inevitable but absolutely inadequate for capturing the fullness of individual experience and, moreover, capable of deforming it. It may be that the "spirit" cannot exist without the "letter," but it is equally obvious that the letter is constrictive, capable of violence at many levels.

In several of its facets, from individual characterizations to particular scenes to the overall structure, *Light in August* discloses the imperative to classify even as it deconstructs actual classifications. Obviously, race – or, more properly, the oppositional blackness–whiteness binary – is the most central and problematic of these, as the depiction of Joe Christmas makes all too clear. The tragic effects of racial categories – indeed of the concept of race itself – however far they may be removed from verifiable biological "fact," are everywhere evident in the novel. The text amplifies these effects, placing them in an even larger context by examining the function of linguistic-cultural structures generally, and the setting of a closed and xenophobic small Southern town of the early twentieth century is particularly effective in this regard. As critics have pointed out, André Bleikasten and John Duvall among them, the town's ideology is rigidly codified and thus harshly judgmental of any person or concept that challenges it, yet it is regularly assaulted, though rarely with real success. For the individuals depicted within the novel, flight, death, or perpetual apartness are the outcome of such assaults on the system.

What makes *Light in August* particularly effective as a

piece of narrative fiction, even beyond its memorable portraits of several doomed individuals struggling to locate themselves within sociolinguistic structures whose constrictions they attempt to resist, is the way in which the very architectonics of the work duplicate the oscillating imposition and subversion of such structures. Although this sort of oscillation is visible even within a single scene – the introduction of Lena Grove already mentioned, with its subjective–objective variations, is one example – it is also possible to see it occurring in the narrative as a whole. While analysis of the overall structure of *Light in August* has chiefly focused on the interweaving of the stories of the three principal characters – Joe, Joanna, and Hightower – and on the containment of Joe's tragic tale by Lena's more hopeful one, it is helpful to a discussion of the procrustean operation of language to recognize the novel's contrapuntal movement between the imposition and subversion of categorical thinking, between objectifying phraseology and subjective counterassertion.

The novel, considered as a whole, has a certain triadic quality, for it contains extensive opening and closing segments, chapters 1–4 and 13–21, which expose the coercive process by which linguistic classification is imposed, and a middle portion, focused almost entirely on the story of Christmas, which reveals both the destructiveness of that process and its fundamental inadequacy. "Habit," reflects Byron Bunch, is "a right good distance away from truth and fact" (74); broadly construed, the opening and closing of the novel are about "habit," while the middle portion is concerned with "truth and fact." At the same time, the recurrent small-scale oscillations evident within this larger movement serve to amplify and underscore it.

The first chapter, as I have already said, subtly discloses the process of categorically "framing" an individual such as Lena or Armstid, and the second, whose opening treats the arrival of Christmas at the sawmill, explores it more explicitly. Although Irene Gammel has asserted that Christmas's identity is initially fixed by the gazes of the onlooking workers, perception is always linguistically mediated, as Gooding-Williams has pointed out. Moreover, it is only in the moment when the workers hear the name of the new mill hand that the question of race arises and motivates the effort to locate him fully. "Did you ever hear of a white man named Christmas?" asks the foreman, and Byron Bunch sees the name as an augury of "what he will do," an "inescapable warning" carried with him like "a rattlesnake its rattle" (33). Because Christmas holds a "negro's job" at the mill, he is classified as inescapably marginal. Brown's name, too, raises questions for Byron, its commonness suggesting that he has adopted it as a disguise, and he is also consigned to the fringes as Christmas's "disciple," the two men being seen as "like to like" (43, 45) (the latter phrase is subsequently applied to a different pair of marginal figures, Christmas and Hightower). In this same chapter, Byron "fixes" the two main women characters linguistically — Lena is "a young woman betrayed and deserted . . . whose name is not yet Burch" and Joanna "is a Yankee" who is "mixed up with niggers," one believed to claim "that niggers are the same as white folks" (52–3) — and the narrational voice defines Hightower as an "outcast" (49). Chapters 3 and 4, dominated by the voices of the townspeople and the telling of Brown's story by Byron, contain several instances of the same sort of compulsion to impale individuals verbally, often pursued to the point of self-parody: Hightower's "wife went bad on him"; "the town believed that good women dont forget things easily . . . bad women can be fooled by badness"; the "revelation" that Joe is part black confirms the judgment that there is "something funny about that fellow" (59, 66, 99). Obviously the ironic tone of these passages subverts and counterbalances the rigidity of their assertions, but the frequency of such judgments discloses the force of "habit"-based thinking.

The middle portion of the novel focuses on Christmas's story, told mostly from his point of view, and it also contains the voices of figures who do the same sort of categorizing. The most important of these proves ironically to be Joanna, who, though presumably the character the most sympathetic to blacks, is noteworthy for her destructive, and ultimately self-destructive, attempt to impose on Joe the classification of "negro," less viciously racist than that of "nigger" as used by others but still reductive and tormenting. More broadly cari-catured are MacEachern, with his designation of Bobbie Allen as "Jezebel" and "harlot," and the restaurant owner, who calls Christmas everything from "Romeo" to "Beale Street play-boy." The overriding focus in this portion, however, is on Christmas's struggle with and against these categories as well as the inevitability of their imposition. At some early stages, Joe's ignorance of such things leaves him unable to find terms for his own experience, as when he overhears the sexual en-counter between the dietitian and the intern and does not comprehend what happened. Although in this case a lack of "wordsymbols" to impose on the raw experience leaves him vulnerable to the dietitian's verbal assaults, a later lack, his failure to recognize that Bobbie Allen should be classified as a prostitute, allows him to court and care for her. Subsequently attempting to cope with the black–white and male–female division within and without – these categories proving inade-quate to contain or define his own needs and experience – turns out to be a fatal undertaking for Christmas.

This center segment of the novel manages, through the complicated portraiture of Joe Christmas, both to depict the ineluctable operations of the prevailing sociolinguistic code and to call them profoundly into question. It is followed by the chapter focused on the town's reaction to Joanna's death, which reveals the comforts of easy classification, however in-adequate it may be to the nature of individuals and events. Those gathered around her burning house see it as a "crime committed not by a negro but by Negro" and are filled with outrage. None had ever been in her house and some had previ-ously shouted "nigger lover" when Joanna passed on the street, but they are ready to spring into action against the "negro" who "murder[ed] a white woman the black son of a" (288–92). For the duration of the novel, various figures attempt to explain Joe's actions, past and present, by his "nigger blood," in a process that culminates in Gavin Stevens's lengthy "explanation" of the mixed blood pulling him in opposing directions. Some individuals may be disturbed by the disjunction between the visible and the verbally imposed, including the man who calls Christmas a "nigger murderer," then says "he dont look no more like a nigger than I do" (346), but the linguistic designation eventually prevails, allowing Percy Grimm to feel justified in carrying out his atrocious vigilante action.

As *Light in August* reveals, the letter indeed killeth, the murderous wordsymbols having provided the classification that Joe disastrously struggles with and that serves as the rationale for his inhuman treatment by others. Virtually all the figures in the narrative are affected by the agency of the letter, either procrusteanly using or being used by the language that necessarily structures their existence; too few of them discover its suppleness and subversive potential. The tremendous achievement of Faulkner's novel is that it not only makes absolutely central the tragic paradox of racial designation, it also examines in profound and subtle ways the means by which such concepts construct individual subjectivity and determine the functioning of an entire culture.

8 *Absalom, Absalom!:* (Un)Making the Father

> Wind ye down there, ye prouder, sadder souls! question
> that proud, sad king! A family likeness! aye, he did beget
> ye, ye young exiled royalties; and from your grim sire only
> will the old State-secret come. – Melville, *Moby-Dick*

Since the 1970s, feminist literary critics have both expanded
the American canon and called into question the masculinist
values on which it is based. Expansion has led to the incorporation of many previously neglected female writers, from
Stowe and Jacobs in the nineteenth century to Cather and
Hurston in the twentieth. Meanwhile, the work of Sandra
Gilbert, Susan Gubar, and Jane Tompkins, among others, has
served to reveal the (sometimes obsessive) misogyny at work
in canonical male texts, as well as the masculinist bias of the
canon makers themselves. Yet it has more recently become
clear that a feminist criticism limited to rescuing important
female writers and demystifying important male ones – what
Elaine Showalter long ago called gynocriticism and feminist
critique, respectively – cannot adequately address the questions raised by the work of certain already canonical American writers such as Hawthorne, Melville, and Faulkner. Their
work presents an engagement with gender that is far too complex to be treated as merely symptomatic of the American
canon's masculinist bias. Just as Stein and Dickinson, arguably the only female writers with full canonical status in the

168

United States before the feminist revision, have received rein-
vigorated critical attention from feminist critics who regard
gender itself as a cultural construction, one that is – in the
words of Frann Michel – "socially and historically variable,"
as well as "internally contradictory" (5), a similar understanding of gender makes the work of even a Hawthorne, that infamous protester against a "damned mob of scribbling women,"
the site of renewed feminist analysis for critics such as Joel
Pfister and Lauren Berlant. As the recent issue of *The Faulkner Journal* devoted to "Faulkner and Feminisms" indicates,
Faulkner has already provoked a good deal of such critical
attention, as well he should, since there are few American
novelists of his magnitude more engaged with gender – not
only as the cultural institutionalization of sexual difference
but, further, as a historical predicate for both social power and
cultural dysfunction.

The thematic nexus of gender in Faulkner's major novels
from *The Sound and the Fury* through *Go Down, Moses* is the
family, the original locus of individual psychic struggles as
well as the central social structure that both provokes and
contains them. It is little wonder, then, that critics concerned
with gender have so far drawn heavily on psychoanalysis,
since it affords the best available theoretical tools and models
for understanding the modern, Anglo-European family as a
major site and vehicle for the construction of gender identity.
Feminist psychoanalytic criticism has proven particularly effective in pursuing the questions raised by Faulkner's complex treatment of motherhood, especially in *The Sound and
the Fury* and *As I Lay Dying*, where by any accounting the
mother – whether dead or alive, woefully absent or dolefully
present – figures centrally in the family economy of loss and
desire. But as Faulkner's social canvas broadens with *Light in
August*, and as his historical focus deepens with *Absalom
Absalom!*, the critical pressure of his attention to the family
gradually, and then decisively, shifts to the father. Recall, for
example, that the Quentin Compson of *The Sound and the*

Fury who laments, "If I could say Mother Mother" (*SF* 95), returns in *Absalom* to meditate, often obsessively, on fathers: "Yes, we are both Father, or maybe Father and I are both Shreve, maybe it took Father and me both to make Shreve or Shreve and me both to make Father or maybe Thomas Sutpen to make all of us" (*AA* 210).

I do not mean to suggest that fathers displace mothers, as if Faulkner had decided to give their roles equal time. Rather, I mean that the question of the status and function of fatherhood that *The Sound and the Fury* poses and that *Light in August* begins to address more fully, with its elaborated array of fathers and grandfathers, leads finally in *Absalom* to a concerned interrogation of fatherhood as the enigmatic source and vehicle of social identity and political sovereignty – the "grim sire," as Melville says in *Moby-Dick*, who harbors "the old State-secret" (155). Once it is recognized that this "state-secret" belongs not to any father, living or dead, but to the patriarchal social system on which Anglo-American fatherhood itself depends, it seems no accident that Faulkner should focus more insistently on the father as he broadens his social perspective from the "nuclear" families of *The Sound and the Fury* and *As I Lay Dying* to the genealogical histories unfolded in *Absalom* and *Go Down, Moses*.

As I have argued in "Symbolic Fathers," if Faulkner's most ambitious exploration of motherhood, *As I Lay Dying*, produces in Addie Bundren a deep analysis of maternal subjectivity, it also delivers an excoriating critique of fathers and the language of patriarchy. *As I Lay Dying* thus opens the way for the multiple registers in which fatherhood is explored in *Light in August*. From Old Doc Hines and Calvin Burden through MacEachern, fatherhood is repeatedly inflected as the site of a punitive social discipline fueled by religious fanaticism and racial hatred. But in *Absalom, Absalom!*, Faulkner addresses the authority of patriarchy itself, that authority on which Anse Bundren no less than Doc Hines rely. Further, the narrative excavation here conducted to unearth the story of

Thomas Sutpen, a "grim sire" indeed, exposes the structure of patriarchy itself to a corrosive critical scrutiny that is far more ambitious than anything Faulkner had attempted before. Consider that in *Light in August* as in *The Sound and the Fury*, it still makes sense to talk about "bad" fathers and "good" ones. Mr. Compson, as John Irwin has demonstrated, is a bad father, and Byron Bunch, we may safely infer, will be a good one to Lena's child. But much as Addie Bundren's monologue distinguishes her from Mrs. Compson – whether Addie Bundren is a bad mother becomes less important than the question "What is a Mother?" – Thomas Sutpen's story definitively raises the stakes on the father. That is, whether Sutpen is a good or a bad father is virtually irrelevant to the question implicit in Quentin's effort to hypothesize a patrilineal line – the question of what makes a father. It is to this question that Sutpen's story provides an answer, one that a feminist analysis of Faulkner needs to take into account.

While a writer in residence at the University of Virginia in 1957, Faulkner was asked whether he thought of the title or the story first when he wrote *Absalom, Absalom!* "They were simultaneous," he replied. "As soon as I thought of the idea of a man who wanted sons and the sons destroyed him, then I thought of the title" (*FU* 76). Although we know that Faulkner's memory did not always serve him correctly, obviously enough it always served him well. In this case, the record provides some confirmation. Writing to his editor, Harrison (Hal) Smith, in February 1934, Faulkner announced a novel he had begun, to be called "Dark House." "Roughly," he concluded, "the theme is a man who outraged the land, and the land then turned and destroyed the man's family" (*SL* 78–9). By August, Faulkner had decided to put the project aside, but meanwhile he had decided on a new title: "*Absalom, Absalom:* the story ... of a man who wanted a son through pride, and got too many of them and they destroyed him" (*SL*

83–4). Whether or not there was a punctual moment at which title and character sprang forth, it is clear that between February and August 1934, Faulkner's conception of Sutpen had come into sharper focus. Sutpen had become for him not only a man who "outraged the land," not only, that is, a man *with* a family upon whom that land turned in revenge, but more specifically a "man who wanted a son through pride." Indeed, throughout the Virginia sessions, Faulkner repeatedly described Sutpen as a man who "wanted a son," wanted to "establish a dynasty," to "make himself a king and raise a line of princes" (*FU* 98).

Clearly, Faulkner was underscoring a view of Sutpen not merely as a father but as a dynastic father, and the difference this makes begins to emerge in the answer he gave to yet another question posed by a student at Virginia. Asked whether Sutpen ever acknowledged Clytie as his daughter, Faulkner patiently explained that "it would not have mattered" whether he did so, since she was "female," and Sutpen would "have to have a male descendant" if he was "going to create a dukedom" (*FU* 272). What "makes" a dynastic father, Faulkner here indicates, is a son, and as *Absalom* amply illustrates, that son must bear the father's name. That is, he must be a recognized heir, legally capable of passing on that name to *his* son, and so on, thus generating "a line of princes." A dynastic father, then, would seem to be a particular kind of father, one who belongs to that tiny subset of all fathers in which we find the "founders" of great families, among whom – a tinier subset still – are also to be found hereditary monarchs. But if their historical numbers are small, such dynastic fathers instantiate the model of patriarchy on which Sutpen's design is built.

What sets Sutpen's dynastic purpose in relief, making it seem not so much particular as deviant, is also what most clearly distinguishes Sutpen from Faulkner's other legendary father figures such as Colonel Sartoris and L. Q. C. McCaslin: Sutpen is, to put it colloquially, a redneck. As such, his career in pursuit of wealth and status not only sets him apart from the other ancestral father figures in Faulkner's work, it also situates him in another mythic context – the one popularly known as the American Dream. It thus locates him among a company of literary protagonists – Melville's Ahab, Fitzgerald's Gatsby, Dreiser's Clyde Griffiths, or even James's Christopher Newman whose ambitions may be understood as demonic, romantic, or tragic, but can hardly be called dynastic. Sutpen looks even more deviant among them than he does among the Sartoris and Compson clans; indeed, the wedding of the upwardly mobile American hero's dream of success to the Southern planter-aristocrat's paternalism has frequently puzzled Faulkner's readers. But if we look briefly at the novel's prehistory, we can at least see how Faulkner may have found his way toward this union and discovered its manifold opportunities.

As Elizabeth Muhlenfeld's splendid account of the novel's genesis indicates, Faulkner drew on three earlier stories as he began to conceptualize the plot and narrative form of *Absalom:* "The Big Shot" (written earlier than 1930), "Evangeline" (written in 1931), and "Wash" (1933) (Muhlenfeld xi–xxxix). Notably, in all three stories, despite their radical differences in both focus and quality, the central conflict turns on a daughter's fate, not a son's. In "The Big Shot," Dal Martin's efforts to buy respectability center on his daughter's social status, and in "Evangeline," it is Judith's engagement to a (white and unrelated) Charles Bon that provokes the central conflict. Only in the last written, "Wash," does the specter of a son even arise, and thus the specter of a Sutpen who wants one. Yet even here, as the title indicates, it is primarily Wash's story, one that develops as a result of his granddaughter's bearing another daughter. Neither "The Big Shot," Dal Martin, who has risen to the position of a "millionaire," nor the Wash of the short story has a son, nor apparently any desire for one. When we recall that Flem Snopes – whose story Faulkner was also working on in this period – is yet another man with only a daughter (and that not even his own, biologically speaking), it appears that rednecks have daughters whereas aristocrats have sons.

Unlike the "Big Shot," Wash, of course, has not risen anywhere above the fishing camp that Sutpen has allowed him to inhabit for many years, but like Dal Martin, Wash has invested whatever pride he possesses in the social recognition due his female descendant, here a granddaughter. Wash himself has fathered only daughters and granddaughters, and he is surprised that Sutpen has "gotten" only a daughter on Milly, a fact that suggests to Wash that Sutpen has gotten old and impotent. " 'Gittin a gal,' " Wash says to himself in "astonishment," "thinking for the first time in his life that perhaps Sutpen was an old man like himself" (CS 543). In "The Big Shot," it is "the boss" himself who turns the young Martin away, not the black butler, and in that traumatic moment, "he – the man [the boss] – had got an 'implacable purpose' upon that female part of every child where ambition lies fecund and waiting" (US 510). Here, the potency of "the man" is allied with his dominant class status, whereas the redneck child's ambition lies waiting like an egg in his "female part" to be inseminated. Indeed, it seems as if not only do poor whites father only girls, but their very ambition is female as well. In Absalom, by contrast both the planter boss and the young boy rejected from the front door are distinctly and, as we shall see, crucially male figures.

Between "Wash" and Absalom, Faulkner transformed Sutpen by giving him a humble origin and then substituting a son for a daughter as the vehicle for his pride. We can only speculate as to what came first, the recognition that a desire for a son would rechannel the poor white's frustration into a dynastic purpose, or the realization that the aging Thomas Sutpen of the two earlier stories lacked a biographical past and could thus be reconfigured as an antebellum "big shot." Perhaps, as Faulkner was later to insist, it all happened at once, "out of quiet thunderclap." Perhaps the opportunity opening from the twin recognitions – of Sutpen's missing son and his missing personal history – struck Faulkner at the same time. But that Sutpen was reshaped, and vastly enlarged, as a result is clear enough. The Thomas Sutpen who first appears in "Evangeline" is an aging caricature of the old Southern planter. Even in "Wash," as Elizabeth Muhlenfeld points out, although no longer the "undeveloped" figure of the "florid, portly man" he was in "Evangeline," Sutpen is still not yet the Sutpen of *Absalom, Absalom!*. While Sutpen's character grows larger, darker, and more "imposing" in "Wash," it remains the case that "for the second character, the plantation owner, Faulkner simply used a convenient character he had recently noticed, one ready to hand in his 'lumber room'" (Muhlenfeld xviii). But once Sutpen is recast as a peasant, and once the son replaces the daughter as a symbolic vehicle of the father's pride, the Sutpen of *Absalom* emerges.

This Sutpen "who wanted a son" also enabled the reconfiguration of race in relation to both class and gender. For once it is recognized that there must be a son if there is to be a father – the fundamental premise of dynastic fatherhood – the potential lying "fecund and waiting," as it were, in "Evangeline" is quickened into life. This ghost story, centering on the triangle of Charles, Henry, and Judith, afforded Faulkner his narrative matrix. By rewriting Charles Bon not merely as Judith's suitor and eventual husband, rejected and finally killed by her brother Henry because of an octoroon wife, but as himself part black and Sutpen's oldest son, Faulkner in effect located Sutpen's missing son. It is noteworthy that here again, a gender shift is at work. In "Evangeline," the so-called black blood both originates and surfaces in the female, Bon's New Orleans wife, whose racial identity threatens no patrilineal bloodline but only Henry's provincial code of honor, he refuses to countenance Judith's marriage to a man who has slept with and even married and fathered a child by a mulatto woman. But in *Absalom*, although the origin of the supposed "black blood" remains the female Eulalia Bon, its "issue" is

the male Charles Bon. The career of Charles Bon, when compared with that of that earlier "tragic mulatto" Joe Christmas,
redirects the black man's revenge at the denial of his masculine identity from the "womanshenegro" (*LA* 157) Joe hates
(as well as the "bitchery" his grandfather blames) to the white
father whose paternal recognition he seeks, so that the course
of revenge and violence runs not in Joe Christmas's fated circle
but straight back into the father's house.

By linking the redneck with the master in the figure of a
dynastic father, Faulkner's design also opened the opportunity
to reinscribe the racial hatred of the white underclass within
the planter class that historically both fostered and depended
on that hatred. Dal Martin is sent away from the boss's front
door by the boss himself, whereas Wash is sent away from the
back door by a black servant, but both exemplify a "mystical
justification of the need to feel superior to someone somewhere," which finds expression in an "antipathy" toward "negroes" (*US* 508). Wash's identification with Sutpen is fueled
by the "mocking echoes of black laughter" (*CS* 538), which
the Sutpen of Absalom will also hear and react to with compa-
rably filiocidal consequences. If Wash ends by killing his own
granddaughter and infant great-granddaughter, Sutpen ends by
propelling his sons into a fratricidal conflict. (Note how the
alignment of the subordinate gender with the subordinate
class is reiterated with what Faulkner might call a "fateful
fidelity" [*Sartoris* 299].) But once again, it is because the
mockery of black laughter threatens to sound forth from within the "dark house," because, that is, the black butler's face
has returned as the exiled black son's, that the class hatred
long displaced and deflected through racial-hatred now returns to bring down a house that is at once the father's and the
master's. In *Absalom*, the poor white's abject racial hatred is
transfigured by its incorporation into Sutpen's design, where
it dooms *not* his rise to wealth and status, but his dynastic
dream.

According to David Paul Ragan, the story "Wash" "may

have been the turning point that suggested the means of combining the disparate elements of the three stories into a unified whole" (6), a point that gains force if we consider, again,
how Faulkner first described Sutpen to Hal Smith: "a man
who wanted a son through pride, and got too many of them
and they destroyed him." The Sutpen of "Wash" has lost his
only son in the Civil War and wants another to replace him.
By returning to "Evangeline" and rewriting the lost son, Henry, as himself the replacement for firstborn son, Bon, Faulkner
in effect gave Sutpen the kind of son he needed to become the
kind of father Faulkner's design required – one whose dynastic dream of kingship, like David's, founders not because there
is no son, but because there are too many.

If what makes a father is a son, according to the dynastic
formula, then what makes a son a father? An absurd question,
we might respond. What makes a son a father is, after all, the
sexual act of "begetting" a child who turns out to be a boy, an
act that requires a woman who becomes a mother by the same
token. But the natural, physical domain in which conception
and childbirth occur has little to do with the "making" of
fathers in the dynastic register of Sutpen's story. Here, if what
makes a dynastic father is a legitimate son, one who can both
bear the name of the father and pass it on to yet another son,
generating what Sutpen envisions as "the fine grandsons and
great grandsons springing as far as the eye could reach," what
makes a son into a father only "incidentally" – as Sutpen puts
it – entails "a wife" (*AA* 218, 212). In the dynastic register of
Sutpen's "design," in order for there to be a father, there must
be a son; but in order for there to be a son, there must *already*
be a father. No wonder Quentin struggles backward and forward, imagining on the one hand that the sons make the father (it took "Shreve and me both to make Father"), and on the
other, that the father makes the sons ("or maybe Thomas
Sutpen to make all of us") (210). In this putatively pure male
domain, ironically enough, there is apparently a chicken–egg
dilemma: Which comes first, the father or the son? "In the

beginning was the Word, and the Word was with God, and the Word was God," says the Book of John; the New Testament – unlike the Old, which is unequivocal – tries to fudge the question and for good reason. There must – somewhere, somehow – be an already existing Father in order for there to be any fathers, and the patriarchal system on which this dynastic regime depends supplies one; in the Lacanian vocabulary of today, he is the "Symbolic Father," but in the biblical vocabulary on which Faulkner drew, he is God the Father. The Sutpen to whom Quentin and Shreve attribute the vision of an infinitude of male progeny is thereby being located in this Symbolic father's position, "still there, still watching," "even after he would become dead" (218). From what Quentin and Shreve imagine as the vantage point of the illegitimate son, Charles Bon, "no man had a father," that is, "no one personal" father. Rather, "all boy flesh that walked and breathed stems from that one ambiguous eluded dark fatherhead" (239–40). Like the "young exiled royalties" whom Melville's Ishmael enjoins to seek out their "grim sire," Quentin and Shreve are launched on a quest to discover that "ambiguous eluded dark fatherhead" represented by Thomas Sutpen, a man who appears to Quentin at the novel's very outset as God, enunciator of the "*Be Sutpen's Hundred* like the oldentime *Be Light*" (4). Although I think it could be demonstrated that the dead Sutpen functions as the symbolic father on whom depends the very symbolic order of language through which the novel's various narrators represent him, what I want to pursue here is the living Sutpen and, even more narrowly, the explosive moment at which the boy Sutpen becomes the man-who-would-be-father.

It should not be surprising that those critics who have attended most fruitfully to Faulkner's representation of father figures have relied on Freud and Lacan, since this theoretical tradition is centrally, indeed one might argue obsessively, concerned with the father as the figure of power, authority, and law, and with the son as his tortured victim and emulator. Although John Irwin in his justly influential psychoanalytic treatment of Quentin Compson in *Doubling and Incest, Repetition and Revenge* is generally more concerned with sons and brothers and their narcissistic doubling than with the father, he does offer a useful starting point for understanding Sutpen's initiation into patriarchy.[1]

After his traumatic affront at the planter's front door, the young Sutpen, Irwin argues, "rejects his [own] father as a model and adopts the plantation owner as his surrogate father" (Irwin 98), whereupon his course is set along some readily recognizable Freudian lines. That is, Sutpen chooses not to kill the father but instead to become him. Clearly enough, Sutpen's anguished meditation following his rebuke at the planter's front door can be read as fitting the pattern described. "*But I can kill him. – No. That wouldn't do no good,*" Sutpen tells himself repeatedly before deciding to emulate the man who owns the "land and niggers and a fine house" (*AA* 191–2). Although this is not his point, Irwin's analysis forces us to recognize what has too often gone unacknowledged – that Sutpen's dynastic purpose cannot be accounted for by reference to the image he tries to replicate. For it is not that the white planter – himself invisible to the boy at the door who faces and is faced down by the black butler – is represented as a father: he is not. Rather, the image of the planter has long since imprinted itself on the imagination of the young Sutpen, who "would creep up among the tangled shrubbery of the lawn and lie hidden and watch the man" who "spent most of the afternoon . . . in a barrel stave hammock between two trees" being served by a black servant (184). This "man who owned all the land and the niggers and apparently the white men who superintended the work" presents himself in the boy's eye as a master, an owner, as someone who enjoys an astonishing leisure (184). But there is nothing in this image that is specifically paternal. What Irwin's analysis makes clear is that Sutpen's desire to become a father and found a dynasty stems instead from structural forces set in operation by his traumatic encounter, that Faulkner binds the dream of equality to the regime of patriarchy by means of the psychological process unleashed in the "boy" who finds suddenly that "he would have to think it out straight as a man would" (191).

Irwin describes this process with admirable cogency. The young Sutpen "incorporates into himself the patriarchal ideal from which that affront sprang in much the same way that a son comes to terms with the image of his father as a figure of mastery and power by impersonalizing and internalizing that image as the superego, accepting the justice of the father's mastery even though that mastery has been exercised against the son" (98–9). Irwin's analogy between Sutpen's incorporation of the "patriarchal ideal" and the case of any Freudian son who negotiates the Oedipal crisis enables him to generalize this as the "mechanism by which the son tries to overcome the mastery of the personal father while maintaining the mastery of fatherhood – a mechanism in which the personal father dies without the son's having to kill him" (99). If this highly abstract description of Sutpen's ordeal seems remarkably apt, it is partly because that ordeal is itself already abstracted in Faulkner's (quite literal) representation of it. That is, Sutpen's crisis is not merely readable as an instance of the dilemma confronting the Freudian son who must try to become the father rather than kill him. Rather, it is constructed as the very *model* of that dilemma itself. In other words, it is not only that Sutpen "incorporates into himself the patriarchal ideal . . . in much the same way" that the generalized Freudian "mechanism" demands of all sons who would be fathers, but that this mechanism is precisely what is set in relief as the operating rule of patriarchal authority when the boy Sutpen is portrayed as literally incorporating "the patriarchal ideal."

Irwin thus opens a path he leaves unexplored. For even though at times he seems to recognize that patriarchy is a system, not a fact of nature, he ends up ontologizing the "patriarchal principle" by arguing that "fathers are inherently superior to sons" (103). Their authority "is not accidental to fatherhood, it inheres in its very nature," he insists, because "the essence of the authority, the mastery, that a father has over a son is simply priority in time" (103). But Faulkner's portrayal of Sutpen's crisis, far from essentializing the father's authority as a function of "the very nature of time," traces its social formation as a function of patriarchy's own rule. If patriarchy provides Faulkner with the most ambitious formatting device, as it were, for encompassing a historical field that reaches back to both Locke and Lear, and beyond, it is not because it is essentially eternal and given, but because it has perpetuated itself again and again – a reiteration to which the novel testifies amply in its own reiterative structure.

When I say that Faulkner literally represents an already abstracted model of the Freudian son's ordeal, I mean that the account given of Sutpen's boyhood trauma systematically foregrounds the very distinction between the "personal father" and the "mastery of fatherhood" on which that model depends if the "mechanism" is to achieve its ends. What needs to be recognized here is that two ends are served by this mechanism – one personal, one impersonal. When "the son tries to overcome the mastery of the personal father while maintaining the mastery of fatherhood," his personal stake in the enterprise is to become the man his father is, or at least appears to be. But quite obviously, if this personal goal is to be accomplished, the "figure of mastery" inscribed in the father's position must itself be preserved. Otherwise, the son's whole endeavor to become the father would lack both meaning and purpose. (Indeed, under such circumstances, when confronted by the father's power and the threat it poses, the son might just as well kill him.) By demanding that the son "internalize" as his "superego" an impersonal image, the patriarchal model thus ensures that the "mastery of fatherhood" itself will remain secure. Needless to add, the individual father, who has presumably already negotiated this excruciating impasse, also has a large stake in the perpetuation of this impersonalized "figure of mastery." But the whole mechanism can also be viewed as serving to perpetuate that very "figure of mastery," in which case what is at stake is by no means merely personal, whether we are speaking of the son or the father. What is at stake is the self-perpetuation of the patriarchal mechanism itself.

In the depiction of Thomas Sutpen's traumatic boyhood encounter we witness not only the "internalization" but the very emergence of the "figure of mastery," what Lacan designates as the "Law" of the "Father" (Lacan 321). Despite the degree to which Lacan's version of Freud also ontologizes patriarchy, it is nonetheless useful in understanding Sutpen, since Lacan's theory hypostatizes this figure of mastery as "the Absolute Master," a "symbolic" father (305). By detaching "the paternal function" from its mere operation in the domain of images, what Lacan calls the "Imaginary," and according it a transcendentalized status in the symbolic domain, the "locus" of what he calls the "Other," Lacan enables us to see how the mechanism of patriarchy operates in order to perpetuate itself (310, 305). Of particular relevance here is Lacan's emphasis on speech as the register in which the Other is made evident. Always already a "he who knows," the Other is known, first and last, as an "it which speaks." Indeed, "it is from the Other that the subject receives even the message that he emits," once he is fully a subject, that is, one "split" by his insertion into language (305). While the Other stands beyond and authorizes the "figure of mastery" represented within the social domain by the "name of the father," or what Lacan calls "the paternal metaphor," the Other is not itself an image but the necessary, always already given of a discourse. For Lacan, indeed, this discourse is language itself, and its "privileged signifier" is the phallus, an "image of the penis" raised to symbolic status by its function as the signifier of a lack it serves to mask (319).

With Lacan's terms in view, we can see how Faulkner's

treatment of Sutpen's crisis brings the patriarchal mechanism into focus. Not only does the figure of mastery emerge in the course of Sutpen's crisis, to be embodied in the phallic "monument" in which his "innocence" is finally imaged, but also the process itself unfolds as a dialogue, out of which an "it which speaks" emerges to be installed as a "he who knows," a fully credited Other, as it were.

When he leaves the big white house, the boy Sutpen retreats into a "cave" where he begins to deliberate with himself regarding what "would have to be done about it" (*AA* 188–9). In a process already initiated in the novel's opening pages, two voices now emerge, the "two of them inside that one body" and these "debaters" argue back and forth, one repeatedly insisting, "But I can shoot him," and the other saying, "No. That wouldn't do no good" (190). Each time, the first voice then asks, "What shall we do then?" and the other replies, "I don't know" (190) When we recall that both have already "agreed that if there were only someone else, some older and smarter person to ask," the question might be answered, it becomes clear that a longing for some authoritative voice has already installed itself in the conversation, subordinating the one who asks the questions to the other who answers them (189). Split into two voices, that is, Sutpen the boy projects an other to address, an other who is already invested with the authority to say "No" effectively to the proposal of "shooting him." Yet this other speaker's "I don't know" is equally resonant because it reveals that although he knows that killing the man "wouldn't do no good," he still does not know why it wouldn't, much less what would.

By the time that knowledge does emerge, of course, a great deal has happened that could readily repay psychoanalytic scrutiny. Indeed, the tableau itself is already all too replete with Oedipal resonance. The young Sutpen who has been turned away from the door of that "smooth white house" (189) could readily be seen as the son denied access to the mother's body. But in keeping with Faulkner's shift in title, from "Dark House" to *Absalom, Absalom!*, it is the father–son crisis itself, the power struggle rather than its ostensible object, which Faulkner foregrounds here as throughout the novel, with its reiterated emphasis on doors and thresholds. Needless to say, the repressed returns, as mothers, sisters, and spinster aunts collectively work, wittingly or not, to undermine Sutpen's dynastic project. Even in this episode, the maternal element could be read as displaced onto the "cave" into which Sutpen first retreats to meditate, but let us pursue Sutpen's psychological acceleration from boyhood to manhood along the purely masculine lines it predominantly, indeed insistently, follows. If Sutpen's traumatic transformation from boy to man is registered, like so much else in the novel, by the shifting relations between two voices caught up in a dialogue, this dialogue punctuates what it also foregrounds – the stages through which the boy passes as he is thrust into manhood.

In the first stage, as we have seen, the issue confronting Sutpen is relatively straightforward: he has been hurt by an explicable insult, so deeply hurt, indeed, that he wants to murder the man who has hurt him. But the other he has projected as a voice of authority to consult blocks this desire to kill the master, invoking as its reason "that wouldn't do no good." As the dialogue then moves on in the effort to discover what *would* do any good, it has in fact already begun to reveal – by virtue of the very necessity to which this other voice's emergence testifies – why mere murder would not: because there would be no grounds on which even to define what "doing any good" or "doing any harm" could mean, and this because there would be no law, no legitimate authority, to make the distinction between good and harm. Just as in Hobbes's version of the state of nature there can be no concept of justice until a sovereign authority is instituted outside and above men, for Sutpen there can be no revenge that would "do any good" because there is no sovereign rule of law yet in place that can dictate to him a measure by which to judge his

injury against the compensation it demands. The other voice
that has already emerged, then, will finally swell to encompass and silence all others in order to dictate that measure,
"instructing him as calm as the others had ever spoken" (192).
Between this voice's initial emergence and its final installa-
tion as the voice of the Other, however, Sutpen's "thinking"
proceeds along lines worth tracking.

When Sutpen goes home, "the thought" strikes "him for
the first time as to what he would tell his father when the old
man asked him if he had delivered the message" (191). Finding
himself again within the domain of his own father, and one
whose command the boy has failed to carry out, Sutpen's attention shifts from his injury to his failure. Like Joe Christmas in the orphanage, the boy Sutpen expects retribution, but
rather than passively awaiting his punishment as Joe does,
Sutpen considers ways of avoiding it – specifically, by lying.
But he decides that "if he did lie he would be found out maybe
at once, since probably the man had already sent a nigger
down to see why whatever it was his father had failed to do
and had sent the excuse for was not done" (191). It is here, at
the moment when Sutpen recasts the undelivered message as
an "excuse" sent by his own father to the master for work
"not done," that the substitution of the latter as what Irwin
calls his "surrogate father" begins. By coding the undelivered
message as his father's "excuse," Sutpen in effect displaces his
own failure onto his own father, while displacing the authority capable of punishing them both onto the master. (Clearly
enough, it is the latter whose actions the boy imagines will
have *already* led to the boy's being "found out," and not those
of his personal father.) So while Sutpen still awaits punishment, the authority capable of inflicting it has already been
displaced from the personal father to the impersonal master,
himself imagined as already having acted. But meanwhile,
this retrospective assignment of punitive authority to the
master is generated not by the boy's pain but by his fear, a fear
that allies him with a father who has failed. Indeed, as if in

imitation of his own father's fecklessness, the boy now fails to do his own work, "not refusing, not objecting" when his sister tells him to fetch the wood, but "just not hearing her."

When his father finally does arrive, he makes "him fetch the wood," to be sure, but there is "still nothing said about the errand" (191). And it is this silence that will ultimately engender "the terrible part of it," the realization that "it cant even matter, not even to Pap" – not, be it noted, to *either* "Pap" (191, 192). For once it becomes apparent to the boy that the master has sent no one "down" to expose any lie the boy might try to tell in order to avoid his punishment, the man on whom he has already shifted the burden of retribution lets him down too. This silence triggers the return of the boy's outrage at the insult he has suffered, an outrage still festering as he awaits the moment of retribution. But because now he realizes that this moment may never come, the fear of punishment gives way to a renewal of his own desire to punish. Accordingly, just as, before, he had displaced the function of punisher from his own father to the master, now he displaces his rage along the same track. Imagining that the man "will get paid back that much" because at least "he wont know it aint done until too late," Sutpen fantasizes a different content for the message, one that recodes excuse as warning and thus retroactively imposes punishment on the master: "if it only was to tell him that the stable, the house, was on fire" (192).

Note how the scene at the door has changed as a result of this fantasy. If the message is a warning of disaster rather than an excuse for failure, the boy's own failure to deliver it is going to matter, and primarily to the master. Thus the master will "get paid back . . . for what he set that nigger to do" (192) in the coin made familiar by Ab Snopes in "Barn Burning." This fantasy recodes the affront itself as a scene in which the master's *verboten*, his denial of Sutpen's entry into the house, will have already brought that house down (prophetically enough) in a flaming holocaust. But this fantasy yields its satisfactions at the cost of its raison d'être. For it doesn't merely express a wish to punish the master rather than being punished by him, it turns the one into the other and leaves no one either to punish or be punished. Because the wish is expressed as what Rosa would call a "might have been," as a wish, that is, to have already punished the master in the very moment of having been punished by him, the retroactively fantasized revenge cancels out the very source of the injury that provoked it. It recasts the master as already destroyed by his own will – blind and inexplicable as that remains – and it recasts the boy as a figure whose rage no longer has a legitimate target.

In fact, the only target remaining is the black servant, whose role as blocking agent resurfaces here with the repeated thought "the nigger never give me a chance to tell him" (191). Since the "warning" fantasy recodes the boy as himself an agent of the master, it is not surprising that it drives the black butler into view again: the boy's effort to deliver the warning has been thwarted, after all, by another agent of the same master. But the butler has already long since been dismissed as a target for Sutpen's revenge. If killing the master "wouldn't do no good," neither can the solution inscribed as a "might have been" in this fantasy, but the fantasy helps to reveal why: in both cases, the act of revenge would erase not only the target of the boy's rage but also the very authority on which that act depends if it is to be effective. That authority must be secured somewhere, somehow, before any action he takes can "do any good."

To grasp how Sutpen finally resolves the crisis, we need to focus on the master's silence and its definitive impact. What his own father's failure to ask about the errand signals to the boy is that he has suffered his injury for no purpose, that "it cant even matter, not even to Pap." Whether the undelivered message be an excuse or a warning – and in a sense it has retroactively become a sign both of failure and of its punishment – the entire event is finally understood as a sign of Sutpen's impotence, an impotence he protests with mounting despair as he repeats, "he never even give me a chance to say it. Not even to tell it, say it" (192). But if the boy has not been allowed to speak, to emit his message, the Master has himself remained silent. However, the Master's silence cannot itself be read, as can the undelivered message sent by Pap, as a sign of impotence. If the master emits no message, that is, it is not because he lacks the power to do so but because he is indifferent: "he can't even know that Pap sent him any message and so whether he got it or not cant even matter," Sutpen thinks (192). Just as the master has shoes he does not even need to wear, he has "a nigger" he has not even bothered to send down to find out why his father has failed to do his work. But the indifference expressed in and by the master's silence signals a more fundamental feature of his position – he *need* not speak at all. He has subordinates to do that for him. Even had he sent "a nigger" down, his servant would still be speaking for him, speaking in his name, just as it was his servant who spoke for him at the front door of his mansion. The master occupies a position made familiar to us in the political register of the West by the king and in the theological register by the god of Christianity.

The king's symbolic power is traditionally expressed through the distance he maintains above his subjects by means of the mediation afforded by his servants. Indeed, strategically speaking, the king actually depends on that mediation to sustain his power. The more, that is, he is spoken for, the more decrees are issued in his name while he remains invisible and aloof, the more absolute his power both seems and becomes. In this sense, it is not only that the king *need* not speak, but that he *cannot* himself speak directly to his subjects, since this would threaten to bring him "down" into their contingent domain. Kings, being nevertheless and to their great embarrassment always human and contingent after all, have resorted to a host of stratagems in the effort to shore up and perpetuate their symbolic power. In this endeavor, they were much aided by Christian theology, whose model of absolute power they struggled repeatedly to reiterate. Most famously, they relied on the legal principle of the "king's two bodies," which ensured that the figure of mastery remained immortal and absolute. The king, according to this doctrine, never dies, he merely suffers a "demise," a separation of his mortal from his immortal part (see Kanterowicz 371). The king is, then, only the agent of his crown, itself symbolic of a power both eternal and absolute. It is little wonder kingship was both theorized and practiced in accord with the theological model Filmer tried to make its origin as well.[2] For that model presented a remarkable blueprint for success.

The God of the Old Testament has to speak repeatedly to his chosen people in order to keep them in line, and although he disguises and hides himself in a variety of ways in the process, he must keep on issuing his warnings again and again. Not even handing down his laws succeeds in definitively installing in them his absolute mastery over them. But once he sends his son to deliver his message once and for all, God the Father can safely recede into his omnipotent and invisible silence. With the institution of his Church, moreover, an infinite mediation machine is permanently established, so that he need not bother ever again to speak to His flock. His message has always been emitted, and now stands as an external law and covenant. Men not only may but must speak in His name, if they are to be members of the body of Christendom.[3]

No doubt, one major reason for God's success in establishing himself as absolute master is his choice of his own son to deliver his message. Whom else can he trust? After all, if we are to judge from the Old Testament, experience has shown him that his appointed servants often fail him, sometimes with disastrous results to his design. (A servant might, for example, send away someone bringing a warning.) A son, therefore, must be created if the message is to get through, and creating that son makes God the Father. That son, of course, must die, must be sacrificed so that the father's mastery is sealed once and for all, but at least this will have made a difference. In any case, being God the Father now, he can take that son back in to his bosom, restore him to his original heavenly mansion, just as Sutpen will dream of doing, at least according to General Compson's account.

When Sutpen finally overcomes the desire to kill the father with a desire to become him, then, he aspires to the position of an absolute master explicitly patterned on God's. What propels him into that position is that the specific master who has insulted him has remained silent, leaving a vacuum where there should be a voice. Into this vacuum, then, rushes "something shouting": "I went up to that door for that nigger to tell me never to come to the front door again and I not only wasn't doing any good to him by telling it or any harm to him by not telling it, there aint any good or harm either in the living world that I can do to him" (AA 192). An outcry of impotent rage, these are the last words of protest spoken by the voice of the boy Thomas Sutpen; the next voice to be heard belongs to that "innocence instructing him as calm as the others had ever spoken," and Sutpen the man accepts that instruction (192). In between the boy's final outcry and the man's obedient submission to his master's voice, comes the "explosion," a "bright glare that vanished and left nothing, no ashes or refuse, just a limitless flat plain with the severe shape of his intact innocence rising from it like a monument" (192). What Sutpen at once faces and violently repudiates here is his own impotence, an impotence whose discovery immediately produces the phallic monument in which it is at once enshrined and disavowed.

It is crucial to note that this Other's voice is not that of the master himself; indeed, we never hear that voice any more than Sutpen does. Instead, the voice of Sutpen's innocence arises to fill the vacuum opened up by the master's very silence. In Lacan's words, the "phantom of the Omnipotence . . . of the Other" entails "the need for it to be checked by the Law" (311). The "innocence" that Sutpen had begun by realizing "he would have to compete with" has assumed the position of the Other, and the message it now emits dictates the terms of a revenge he believes can "matter," can "do some good." The boy's innocence, in other words, his lack – of experience, of knowledge and power – has been displaced upward, as it were, to speak with the voice of God, to assume the paternal function. By according the "it which speaks," the "he who knows," the mind of a boy, Faulkner sets in stark relief the patriarchal mechanism, which demands that – in Lacan's terms – there *be* an Other with no Other, that is, that there be an absolute Law. As Lacan puts it, "when the legislator (he who claims to lay down the Law) presents himself to fill the gap, he does so as an imposter." And yet, he continues, "there is nothing false about the Law itself, or about him who assumes its authority" (311). The voice of Sutpen's "innocence," which emerges to fill the gap left by the master's silence, is an imposter, but there is nothing "false" about the structure thereby secured, the order of authority thereby assumed. Once installed in the symbolic position of the Other, this voice speaks in the name of the father, enforcing the authority of his Law.

That authority remains in itself absolute, as is evident from the conversation Sutpen has many years later with General Compson. Reporting on this conversation, Quentin says that his grandfather believed that Sutpen named Charles Bon, since his "conscience" – as the voice of innocence is now designated – "would not permit the child, since it was a boy, to bear either his name or that of its maternal grandfather, yet which would also forbid him to do the customary and provide a quick husband for the discarded woman and so give his son an authentic name" (*AA* 214). Like so much of Sutpen's design, Charles Bon's lack of a paternal name ironically mirrors the social structure that has generated it, in this instance, the black slave child's lack of a patronymic. Sutpen not only refuses to give his son the name of his own father, but denies him the name of *any* father, as the antebellum slave code dictated for all black sons, who thus remained legally "boys." That this denial is enacted in the "Name of the Father" – that is, on the instructions of a conscience speaking from the position of the Other – only serves to reveal the perverse irony with which a strict obedience to the Law of the Father repeatedly undermines Sutpen's dynastic design. He is left forever baffled, searching, for the "mistake" he has somehow made. But Sutpen has made no mistake, at least not in pursuit of his dynastic project. He has simply made literal the impersonal "Law of the Father," and in the process of telling his story, Faulkner reveals, after all, what makes a father.

"What is the Father?" asked Freud. "It is the dead father," according to Lacan (310). André Bleikasten invokes Freud and Lacan in his extended analysis of "Fathers in Faulkner," where he concludes that Sutpen is only the latest in that series of failed fathers in Faulkner's work that begins with *Sartoris.* Like his earlier "analogues," that is, Sutpen is "dead, but not dead enough" to "act the role of the dead father" (1981, 143) who guarantees the law.[4] On this reading, it is Sutpen's failure as father that matters most; fatherhood itself remains intact, even as its social authority declines. What such failure reveals is a world in which "the dead father no longer functions as a symbol of cultural order" (1981, 125), as Bleikasten says of *Sartoris,* a novel which thereby repeats the familiar modernist myth of patriarchy's decline, "nostalgically reinstating the lost transcendence of myth (of the Father, of God, of the Chief)," as Mikkel Borch-Jacobsen describes it (73). Bleikasten is certainly right about *Sartoris,* as he is about so much else in his brilliant analysis. But I would argue that in *Absalom,* Faulkner has moved well beyond repeating the myth of patriarchy's decline. I suggest instead that Sutpen's story reveals the colossal destruction wreaked not by a father who fails to represent the law, but by one who succeeds, precisely, at identifying with it. In other words, unlike his precursor, Colonel Sartoris, Thomas Sutpen does not fail to function as a "symbol of cultural order" but, rather, reveals the symbolic function on which that order depends.

On this view, the story of Sutpen's failure to found the dynasty he intends affords Faulkner the opportunity to "unmake" the father, as it were, in the effort to expose what makes him. Clearly enough, that opportunity emerges as a consequence not merely of Sutpen's having "too many" sons, but of the firstborn being putatively black. What enables Faulkner to excavate the "grim sire," in other words, is the racial discourse of "blood" that a black son introduces into the dynastic line. If what makes the father is a son, what "unmakes" Sutpen as the Father he would be is a son whose legal inability to bear and pass on the Name of the Father generates a serial catastrophe that not only dooms Sutpen's design but meanwhile fractures and thus lays bare patriarchy's social structure. Obviously enough, this demonstration would require many more pages, but let me close by offering an example of where it would take us.

Sutpen's infamous "proposal" to Rosa Coldfield in effect blurts out what the woman's function under patriarchy really is, "to become a womb to bring forth men children," as Deborah Clarke puts it (64). As feminist theory from Gayle Rubin to Luce Irigaray has made clear, patriarchal society is founded on the exchange of women by men, and the only social positions its structure accords women are those of wife and mother, virgin, or prostitute. In rejecting Sutpen's proposition, Rosa chooses to remain a virgin, and insofar as her anger flows from her consequent exclusion from any legitimate domain for enacting her sexual desires – an exclusion she shares, so far as we know, with every woman in the novel save Bon's octoroon mistress – her protest is waged on behalf of her body, "long embattled in virginity" (AA 4). Rosa's refusal to accept the terms of patriarchy's proposition leads her to become, as she puts it in the course of her lascivious tribute to the sensual in the novel's fifth chapter, "all polymath love's androgynous advocate" (117). Just as Rosa's exclusion from the role of wife enables her to enunciate the sexual body on behalf of all those denied its pleasures by a patriarchal regime, her exclusion from the role of mother enables her to wage a campaign of revenge that both speaks for, and acts on behalf of, Ellen Coldfield and Eulalia Bon as well as Milly Jones – the mothers whose failure to meet Sutpen's genealogical demands document the truth his proposal blurts out.

But what brings Sutpen to the point of blatantly instrumentalizing patriarchy's genealogical demand, of course, is that he still lacks a son, since Charles Bon has forced Henry to murder him, and Henry has disappeared. Bon's strategy for forcing the question of paternal recognition, furthermore, reflects the demands made on men entailed by the same exchange system whose structure Sutpen's proposition to Rosa reveals. That is, by threatening to marry Judith, Bon insists on his rights, as a man under patriarchy, to participate equally with other men in the exchange of women. That such a marriage would violate the incest taboo – among other things – serves to underscore the proposal's status as threat. But what has provoked that threat, at least as Quentin and Shreve imagine it, is Sutpen's denial of paternal recognition in the first place, a denial "justified" by Sutpen's belief that Charles is black. And it is the same "black blood" that Sutpen uses to justify sending forth his son Henry as his agent to block Charles's marriage to Judith. Denied the Name of the Father, the son Charles Bon wreaks his revenge by threatening to become his son-in-law. Finally, by forcing Sutpen to force Henry to kill him, Charles wrecks Sutpen's dynasty, in effect "unmaking" the father who has refused him entry into the father's house. It is left to Wash Jones, the poor white, to kill Sutpen, but in forcing Sutpen to make a murderer of Henry, Bon not only kills himself but, by the same token, destroys Sutpen as father. Without a father, no son, but without a son, no father.

The rich contributions of Cheryl Lester and Judith Wittenberg on the racial issues already impinging on *The Sound and the Fury* and centrally informing *Light in August* invite me to add a final speculative comment. If in *Absalom, Absalom!* the "black blood" assigned to the eldest son in a dynastic line proves a faultline in the geological structure of patriarchy, in *Go Down, Moses*, Faulkner may be seen trying to recuperate the Father in assigning "black blood" to the fathers – both Sam Fathers and Lucas Beauchamp. This is not to say that fatherhood is more important than the issues of racial identity and white supremacy in this novel; rather, they are deeply linked. That Faulkner by no means meant to give up on fatherhood is indicated readily enough in the description Edmonds offers of Lucas: "He is both heir and prototype simultaneously of all the geography and climate and biology which sired old Carothers and all the rest of us and our kind, myriad, countless, faceless, even nameless now except himself who fathered himself, intact and complete, contemptuous, as old Carothers must have been, of all blood black white yellow or red, including his own" (*GDM* 118). Here, one might argue, Faulkner works hard to resuscitate the patriarchal ideal inscribed in the figure of mastery, using the discourse of blood to redefine the father in terms that work to exorcise racial difference. In this novel, the dynastic formula no longer holds; certainly neither Lucas nor Sam is made a father by having a son. But it might be worth exploring the possibility that the premise of the black father enabled, even as it entailed, the recuperation of a patriarchal ideal.

NOTES

1 On the question of brothers, see in addition to Irwin, Rene Girard and Juliet Flower MacConnell. By bracketing the issue of brothers, I do not wish to imply that the fraternal rivalry so abundantly on display in the novel is irrelevant to the concerns addressed here. On the contrary, as Sutpen's story unfolds, the fratricidal conflict Sutpen's dynastic fatherhood has generated unravels even as it dooms his patriarchal design. A full treatment of the novel's address to patriarchy – which this is not – would necessarily pursue the issue of the son as brother.

2 Filmer, in effect, considerably undermined the monarchic power he wished to defend when he tried to unite the symbolic and the contingent

by genealogizing the king as Adam's heir. For useful commentary on Filmer's position, see Schochett and Pateman.

3 See John 1:12–13: "But as many as received him, to them gave he power to become the sons of God, even to them that believe on his name: Which were born, not of blood, nor of the will of the flesh, nor of the will of man, but of God." Needless to say, it is the God of Western, Christian tradition whose definition as Father is operable here. Other religious traditions by no means necessarily define either deity or paternity in the same way.

4 For a fuller discussion of Bleikasten's argument, see my "Symbolic Fathers and Dead Mothers."

Conclusion:
The Stakes of Reading Faulkner
– Discerning Reading

As I write, we approach the hundredth anniversary of William Faulkner's birth, and the turn of a century and a millennium. Considering the advances and promise of this past century, we may look forward to beginning a new era. Seeking lessons from this century's failures, we may meditate on a period that has been, despite all its real advances, murderous on a scale beyond precedent and perhaps beyond comprehension. This century has witnessed, and continues to witness, the violent destruction of unnumbered millions of people and a ravaging of the earth we're only now beginning to reckon. At this point in a hundred years of awesome accomplishment and promise coupled with sickening destruction, it seems appropriate to ask some questions here about reading a famous literary record of this time.

What's at stake in *reading* Faulkner? To whom does it matter? Why does it matter?

Or, why ask why? These questions may seem to be unnecessary or to answer themselves. On the one hand, it is well known that Faulkner matters, and has mattered, to many readers. The preceding essays in this volume testify to, even as they critically examine, Faulkner's importance for an international reading public. To ask what is at stake in reading a writer who obviously has had such an impact may seem superfluous at this point. The reading public has spoken.

On the other hand, since the italics direct attention to the

197

activity of *reading* Faulkner, reading is such a private act that it seems the only thing at stake goes without saying: the satisfaction of the solitary reader. Alone with a Faulkner novel or story, the reader is moved or left cold, enlightened or puzzled, delighted or provoked, or all these by turns. From this standpoint, it doesn't really matter whether Faulkner has a major reputation with the reading public. His writing either suits each particular reader's taste, becomes an acquired taste, or doesn't. The reader's subjective state is what is at stake, and Faulkner has to matter to *you* or *me*. Why he matters is simply your business or my business. The reader has spoken.

End of discussion?

The beginning, rather. Although the two common objections I have raised to my questions have some validity, they need to be revised and reunderstood. Doing so should clarify something of what is at stake in reading Faulkner in our time. For as Faulkner's writings may enable us to see, such typical statements contain the rudiments of a tragic divisive tendency. The tendency amounts to a cultural mistake this century's devastation should have taught us we cannot afford. Faulkner's writings struggle intimately with this divisiveness as a tragic error within Faulkner's own cultural roots in Southern, American, and Western cultures.

The objections are common because they stem from these roots or similar ones. Thus, this resistance to discussing the consequences of reading Faulkner, itself points to a major stake: whether reading Faulkner will reinforce this harmful tendency or combat it.

What is this mistake at stake? The problem with the common objections I mentioned is that they harbor the unexamined assumption that there is an absolute division between the public and the private. The objections imagine that Faulkner as read by a large public is on one side of an impenetrable wall, and on the other side is Faulkner as read by a particular reader, you or me, as you or I relate to Faulkner in private. *Either* "the reading public has spoken" to establish what mat-

ters about Faulkner, *or* "the reader has spoken." This amounts
to saying that nothing on one side of the wall really matters to
anything on the other side; there is no influence, no feedback
between them. This assumption rests on a false either/or, as
does the cliché "the individual versus society." Both pose a
false choice, an exaggerated split between the single subjectivity (in this case, the solitary reader's) and the plural subjectivity (here, that of the readers who collectively make up a
reading public). Both imagine phantom abstractions.

A basic working assumption of Faulkner's writing tells us
why such abstractions are phantoms: simply put, everything
is connected – yet distinct. This principle is deceptively
simple and easy to state. It is hard, however, to put into practice in thought, feeling, and action. It says that in the final
analysis there are no impenetrable walls. Everything mutually
penetrates with everything else as it participates in temporal
change and continuity, in history not as merely the story or
the events of the past but as the ongoing process Faulkner
called motion. Because of this intermingling, to attempt to
erect such eternal walls in act, thought, or feeling is to invite
disaster. Faulkner's understanding of this fluctuates in intensity and clarity; he didn't always like what he understood and
(like everyone) didn't always follow his best understanding.
Explaining the source of his writing, Faulkner said he listened
to his voices and wrote down what they said; sometimes he
didn't like what they said, but he put it down anyway (Cowley
114). Sometimes, I think, he didn't put it all down; sometimes
the voices that are too dominant suppress his best understanding.

It is not surprising that Faulkner's writings themselves are
embroiled in false dichotomies pervasively produced by the
United States and other cultures; it would be amazing if they
were not. Yet Faulkner's work is a key instance of how multiple possibilities in culture(s) can also produce a healthy opposition to destructive cultural mindsets and habits. His writing
career drew on these alternative potentials, these other inter-

nalized cultural voices, to struggle against a whole family of dichotomies. In critiquing these tragic elements in its own cultural roots, his fiction offers its readers a stake in the effort not to conceive of others in this divisive fashion.

The struggle is twofold: (1) to resist the strong pull of this false either/or in one's culture(s), without (2) falling into the mirror-image oversimplification that there are *no* significant differences to be discerned between the single, private person or subject and the collective subjectivity of a public. In this sense, the challenge to us is to be *discerning, or acknowledging, readers* of difference and connection. It is to acknowledge that there are indeed important distinctions to be made between others and oneself – or the Other and ourselves – while simultaneously acknowledging the influential, formative bonds and interdependencies that link us as participants in life's motion. (A particularly enlightening television series, *Connections*, starring David Attenborough, explores in entertaining historical detail the usually indirect, thus usually invisible, connections that in time bind different people's lives in the most astounding ways, through the ripple effects of events. Faulkner's much discussed ripple image in *Absalom, Absalom!* [210] epitomizes his similar point.)

It is this crucial discerning recognition of difference within relatedness and relatedness within difference that Faulkner's people often need and fail to receive. Prominent in his fiction are children denied acknowledgment from their parents, like all the younger Compsons from their mother and father in *The Sound and the Fury*, and Charles Bon, Judith, Henry, and Clytemnestra from their father, Thomas Sutpen, in *Absalom, Absalom!* Or lovers failing to give acknowledgment to each other – like Joe Christmas and Joanna Burden in *Light in August*. Or black people deprived of it by white people – like Rider, Eunice, Thomasina, and Terrel (Turl) in *Go Down, Moses*, and Joe Christmas and Charles Bon insofar as they are perceived as black.

As all these names may remind us, at issue more generally

is the ability at all levels to discern differences without making these differences into false, oppressive divisions. These are not only differences between oneself and others, but also, for example, between each man or woman and the society or subgroup each belongs to, or between genders, "races"/ethnic groups, classes, regions, religions, sexual orientations, and other affiliations and conditions of life. These examples go a long way toward indicating the discernments or acknowledgments often tragically lacking in Faulkner's represented world. This world is not only "the South"; among other influences informing Faulkner's representations is an awakening public revulsion against the disastrous master-race ideologies in Nazi Germany, militarist Japan, and elsewhere in the 1930s, when Faulkner did his most acclaimed work. As I write, in the 1990s, headlines continue to trace our century's violent history of similar racist, ethnic, religious, and political hatreds around the world.

The social fracturing of blacks from whites in Faulkner's South is important not only in itself but as the most obvious indicator in his fiction of people disastrously riven from one another because recognition is lacking. Faulkner's writing focuses the suffering that is spread by this separation as well as the poignant acknowledgments that occur in the privileged moments of his writing. His work thus implicitly recommends to his readers a powerful criticism of the divisive attitude of simplistic binary opposition, at whatever level.

This criticism clearly can be directed at his own texts as well. The positive features of Faulkner's cultural criticism help us grasp its own limits. As in this volume of essays, even contemporary admirers increasingly condemn the occasions when Faulkner's writing wittingly or unwittingly collaborates with his culture's failures to acknowledge difference within connection, connection within difference. But, to recall the earlier point, Faulkner's is not just any "piece of culture." Faulkner's exemplary capacity for self-criticism and revision throughout much of his career has rightly been praised

in recent commentary (see especially Moreland and Morris).
Further, as a particular, distinctive artifact of culture, his
work, like his culture(s), contains many possibilities for readers to draw from, and it cannot dictate how, or if, it will be
read. Readers too have their differences because they are particular, distinctive members of many-sided culture(s) making
up, in total, an international reading public.

To repeat, at issue is whether it will be the most ethically
enabling, nonpolarizing potentials of Faulkner's writing that
his readers come away with, or the divisive elements it both
contests and re-produces. (Faulkner does not, as is carelessly
said, *force* his readers to see the need for discerning reading or
to see anything else – how could he, or any single writer?
Such a statement, I think, comes short of discerning reading.
But he can persuade us, if we're persuadable; influence us, to
the degree we're influenceable by him.)

The attempt to avoid false polarization, it must be said, is
not a pretense that oppositions and conflict are to be avoided
at all costs. Far from it, as we shall see shortly in the example
of *Go Down, Moses*. After all, to avoid the simplistic either/or
habit is to struggle against this outlook both internally and
externally. Rather, the goal is to oppose the false dichotomy
without falling into it. This means that when I oppose the
Other I can guard against the tendency to think of the Other
as if it/they were some utterly alien demon but instead can be
alert to the larger, ongoing historical forces concretely linking
us even in conflict. For the same reason it means there is no
simple escape or refuge from the Other – no excluding *sanctuary*, to borrow one of Faulkner's titles, from an often dismay-
ing world. It means to understand that the fates of all the
parties in a conflict are ultimately bound together in the mortal interindebtedness, as Herman Melville called it, of life's
ongoing motion. This understanding, if it is firm enough, can
make a difference in how we handle the differences we encounter every day and the kinds of opposition and cooperation
we enact.

Pursuing all these ramifications of our topic is, of course, impossible in this essay. (For related criticism on reading Faulkner, see, for example, Morris, Wadlington, and Weinstein; for more on black–white divisiveness, see Snead and Sundquist; for more on acknowledgment/discernment and Faulkner, see Wadlington and Weinstein, and for related theoretical discussions, Cavell and Paul Smith.)

Our focus on reading here, then, examines one symptom of a potentially dangerous practice. A vital lesson of this century is that the powerful technologies of our time make this widely prevalent habit simply suicidal. With these larger implications in mind, in the rest of this essay we'll explore more specific stakes involved in the general issue of discerning, acknowledging reading.

I return to my starting point, then, to trace the ties between the private, subjective state of reading (which looks a lot more separate than it is) and the status of Faulkner as a major literary figure, a literary institution of our time. To consider private state and public status together is to relate two apparently wholly different spaces. In line with the goal of discerning difference, I want to recognize what is distinctive in them while acknowledging what ties them inseparably.

One space is the special refuge all lovers of reading know, which we call settling down with a good book. As I settle down with, say, a novel, I settle down with myself. I create a solitude momentarily free of the stresses of our usual dealings with people and practical matters, with nothing to do but turn my own mind to communing with the book. By contrast to television or a movie, a novel allows me to set it in motion by myself, to play director and also to act out the characters and "voice-over" narrator, to stage action and language in my own consciousness entirely, as it pleases me to do. This precious independence and solitude are the more precious because they are populated by the fictional beings my imaginative performance as a reader helps bring to life. I give them a lifelike effect by cooperating with the novelistic intelligence and voice(s) of the writer that I set in motion as well. If Faulkner suits me, then ensconced in this wonderfully populated privacy I might seem entitled to say, with Satan in *Paradise Lost*, that the mind is its own place.

The other place is a public literary institution. As we come to it after the coziness of private reading, it may seem as if we were walking into a skyscraper brightly decked with the giant name *William Faulkner*. This is an institution constructed and constantly repaired by quite practical dealings among many people dedicated to what Faulkner represents for them. At least part of what he represents is that, as a (some even say *the*) major U.S. writer, Faulkner has the power to make people money and confer prestige on them. Because of this power, many have a stake in Faulkner; he exists in all but name as Faulkner Incorporated, an institution that maintains its existence within institutions that directly or indirectly promote the reading of Faulkner.

Publishing firms (which are increasingly becoming subsidiaries of large corporations with a careful eye to profit and loss) commit large resources to keep Faulkner's writings in print or to publish literary criticism (like this collection of essays) that study them. A writer's career may be made if she or he is compared favorably to Faulkner in the pages of that venerable institution of what we call high culture, the *New York Times Book Review*. Success becomes even more likely if the writer is awarded one of the most prestigious U.S. literary prizes, the PEN–Faulkner Award, an accolade from the distinguished international writers' group PEN, which chose Faulkner's name as a yardstick of excellence. Academic literary critics can similarly make their careers by teaching and writing about Faulkner in their institutions of learning. To support their research and writing, these critics seek financial assistance, which comes from either charitable or profit-seeking corporations or public, tax-supported agencies like the National Endowment for the Humanities. Most of the books published on Faulkner have had such support.

If Faulkner were a movie actor, Hollywood producers would say that he is a name you can take to the bank, a bankable name at least in the "high culture" industry (though popularizing adaptations of Faulkner in television and movies have also been successful). A huge network of public institutions thus fosters the reading of Faulkner. When we pick a Faulkner book from the shelf and retire to what seems the purely independent, nonpublic act of reading, this step can be seen as the last link in a long chain of cultural activities – economic-political-academic-literary – that attach us to invisible public connections by putting the book in our hands. The very fact that we are reading Faulkner rather than someone else is part of a largely concealed, ongoing process of selection, beginning in Faulkner's lifetime and extending into ours, in which publishers, reviewers, critics, and the reading public at large interact with one another, with Faulkner's work, and with their historical circumstances. (For a denigrating but informative discussion of the politics of constructing Faulkner's reputation, see Schwartz.) From this process emerges his reputation, which is to say his availability on the shelves of libraries and bookstores, and his prominence on the school reading lists that send the most numerous target audience, students, to those shelves.

As we shall see, a similar selective process within culture shapes the way we read the text once we are "alone" with it at desk or armchair. But even at this point, perhaps it begins to be clearer why, despite all the dissimilarities, I suggest that the private act of settling down with book and the public activity of participating in the institution of Faulkner need to be thought together. They indicate the two faces of reading. Reading in private is reading in public. Or rather, although key distinctions exist between the two faces, they are really inseparable. To understand that is to understand better some of the less obvious stakes in reading Faulkner.

It is easier, I know, to make such a claim than to make it stick, because of how different the private space and the public market of reading can feel. The first space is as warmly personal as a favorite chair in which we sit with our book, the second – however much it echoes with genuine enthusiasm for Faulkner – is so much more cool and distant. Swirling with corporate budgets, publishers' advertisements, editorial-board meetings, award committees, lectures, exams, applications, tax paying, and deadlines – all saturated with official and unofficial politics and politicking – this second space is made of exactly the sort of public busy-ness that the leisured privacy of reading wants to shun (unless, of course, the literary text has converted such public activity into interest and pleasure, in a gripping story, say). But from this public space it is easier to grasp that such private leisure is much more available for some people than for others, and that why this is so has a great deal to do with general social conditions stretching throughout and beyond the market economics of reading.

We should admit at once that at its best the private reading experience is the pleasure all lovers of fiction know, the entrance into a well-imagined world. So many different satisfactions may be found there that they are probably innumerable, innumerable by me at any rate. But to appreciate such private satisfactions in their subterranean connections to public space, we could do worse than to draw on one of Faulkner's best-known descriptions of the stakes of writing and reading.

Although he admitted the impossibility of achieving the goal completely, Faulkner said that writers try to capture the motion of life and to still it in such a way that when we read, it moves again (*LG* 253).

What would an approximation of achieving this vast ambition for writing and reading mean? Unlike those too frequent moments in life that come and go too quickly, that are upon us before we are ready, then scatter and vanish, here in the book everything would be gathered, connected, concentrated. Life lost becomes life regained – not embalmed and sealed in a museum case but coiled in the artful words, ready to be released by us. This stilled motion we set moving again as we read; it moves, and it moves us as we share in life's inexhaust-

ible drive, energies, and fluidity, without the losses that usually accompany this changefulness.

The writing/reading ideal Faulkner describes would seem
to fill the needs of his characters, if only they could read his
books as well as inhabit them. Experiences often come to
Faulkner's people too early or too late, leaving wounds or nostalgia; they are over too quickly to be appreciated, leaving
regrets; they are too slippery or ambiguous to be grasped, leaving confusion. Or they are intense but inherently transitory,
leaving aversion or the increasing desire of insatiable emotional addiction. Faulkner's prominent characters typically
suffer acute loss. His most "romantic" ones seek ways, usually inadequate, to have intense experience without losing
more than they gain from it. But as we readers witness the
characters' losses and their often futile efforts to contain
them, even at our most empathetic or participatory we are
still spectators and not literally inhabitants of the characters'
fictional world. As a result we can find even the characters'
losses and failures to contain loss preserved there on the
printed page – collected, patterned, and distilled for *us*,
though not for the fictional people we help to give the effect of
life. In its resourceful arrangements of style and form, Faulkner's language works to track the characters' experience of loss
and attempted recovery and to render visible the invisible
weavings of differences and connections.

If, however, reading a Faulkner text does not "work" for us,
it may be because we find our reading experience too simply
like the life experiences of the characters. Perhaps these experiences are insufficiently mediated for us by those words on
the page, which themselves can become too confusing. Some
readers of Faulkner find that the words are overwhelming in
their complexly ambiguous arrangements; along with the
characters, these readers suffer loss with no recompense of
adequate gain.

For other Faulkner readers, however, his remarkable language contributes much to creating the literary effect of

spending vitality without loss, or comparable effects of balancing loss and gain. At Faulkner's best, for these readers, his narrative prose gives the impression that it opens new channels of eloquence revitalizing the force of words to stir us without losing their power to sharpen our critical eye and ear. This audience finds in Faulkner's prose some balancing mixture, perhaps a mix of empathy and critical insight, that makes the writing satisfy instead of overwhelm.

His innovative fireworks of style and form spend tremendous energies, as his characters often do, yet again we readers have what they do not: Faulkner's language on the page, ready for us to spend again as we stage it in our mind's eye and mind's ear. For those contemporary readers for whom language is a touchstone, a further refinement is possible. (See especially Matthews 1982.) In this reading, the major interest is not the once and for all containment of loss but the endless interplay between the formation of meaning and its vanishing. Here reading participates in an open-ended linguistic process of assembling worded experience into significance yet necessarily dissolving and dispersing it. The text is read as itself the unending, because simultaneous, regaining and re-losing of meaning. An important satisfaction of this kind of reading is the conclusion that in our lives language similarly both constructs and deconstructs meaning because words always say both less and more than we mean.

Although we're far from having considered all the varieties and combinations of reading practices, this survey lets us specify more exactly some important consequences of reading. To restate the paradox, at issue in reading Faulkner is spending profusely yet somehow still possessing what one has spent. It is what we can call a private, subjective *economics* in which readers are offered the opportunity to gain from the book's spendthrift energy some means, if only temporary and imperfect, of dealing with the losses endemic to life's unending motion. Because we would have the tonic energies of life's motion without its losses, time's changes would become wholly positive (at least temporarily). In economic terms, we would have free-spending prosperity without the following hangover of depression.

But having seen this much, readers familiar with Faulkner's texts can recognize more. Faulkner places his people firmly within far-reaching historical processes. Everyone and every thing, as he said more than once, is part of motion (e.g., *FU* 65, *LG* 253). The motion of life that exhilarates yet threatens loss to the psyche blends with the temporal changes of history in which Faulkner's people have their being. These are the processes of loss and agonizing recovery in post–Civil War Southern history, including the long-continuing impact of regional, national, and international economic depressions of the 1920s and 1930s. This means that the economics of private, psychological gain and loss are bound tightly to the economics of profit and loss in public, social life. The interworkings of these public and private economics supply Faulkner's narratives with motive and conflict.

Faulkner's immense hopes for writing/reading coincide with his characters' common impulsion to expend desire freely yet paradoxically still save it all. The obverse desire is to borrow money and incur other obligations freely but still be unindebted – to balance one's books with others in order to be free of all obligation even as one enjoys the benefits one has gained from others. Anse and Addie Bundren in *As I Lay Dying*, the reporter in *Pylon*, and Lucas Beauchamp in *Intruder in the Dust*, asking for his receipt as the novel ends, are striking or subtle instances of one or both sides of the coin of desire. But private desire constantly interweaves with the economies of the material world. So the stakes of private desire are raised by the stakes of public existence. So, potentially, is even our most private reading of Faulkner open to its public dimensions.

Much of Faulkner is in this two-sided desire: spending all yet still having all, or being wholly in debt yet unindebted. It carried him to ingenious inventions of people, prose, and literary form that follow out the many manifestations of the paradox. One of its sexual versions is the image of a promiscuous or fecund yet paradoxically virginal female his narrative voice and male characters evoke and envision. Eula Varner, especially as seen by Labove in *The Hamlet*, is the most direct living representation of this sexuality, like "the goddesses in [Labove's] Homer and Thucydides: . . . at once corrupt and immaculate, at once virgins and the mothers of warriors and of grown men" and herself but the result of "one blind seed of the spendthrift Olympian ejaculation" of life (113, 147). The male version of this image is fabulously epitomized in the inexhaustible dog Lion in *Go Down, Moses*, as Weinstein describes him: "Lion embodies . . . the male lust for virginity," profoundly untouchable, self-contained power whose desire can yet be wholly slaked in the hunt (Weinstein 145). Similarly, each in his own way, Thomas Sutpen and Flem Snopes depend on dense networks of mutual indebtedness yet strive to keep themselves untouched, unindebted, nonrelated to their relations.

The lures of escape from human interindebtedness and from the losses of time take shape as untappable reservoirs or inexhaustible floods of potency, or paradoxically both at once. They are fascinations, problems, provocations for Faulkner's people, and offered as such for his readers.

The examples of Ike McCaslin in *Go Down, Moses* and Harry Wilbourne and Charlotte Rittenmeyer in *The Wild Palms* are instructive. In their attempts at inexhaustible life they try to divide private from public desires and so unintentionally demonstrate their inseparability. Ike desires the great woods in which he hunts, desires to have them in a way that keeps his desire unadulterated. These woods for him represent his desired fecund and promiscuous yet unchanging female – he thinks of them as a combined mistress-wife-mother. In other words, he wants to take part wholly in the great woods' inexhaustible cycle in which death's loss is always instantly recoverable by the production of more life: "the deathless and immemorial phases of the mother who had shaped him. . . . He would marry . . . but still the woods would be his mistress and his wife . . . that place where dissolution itself was a seething turmoil of ejaculation tumescence conception and birth, and death did not even exist" (GDM 311–12). To have this unspendable profligate life Ike gives away everything else. Having the woods, then, entails the paradox of not holding legal title to them, or indeed any other property, especially the McCaslin land and other wealth to which Ike is the rightful heir. In giving away his inheritance, Ike attempts to divide the economy of private desire neatly from public economics. He is convinced that to maintain this desire he must separate it wholly from the monetary realm of ownership, profit, and loss.

This conviction is based partly in Ike's rejection of the legacy of slave ownership at the heart of his family's wealth. And the legacy, in turn, is summed up in a violation of acknowledgment by the founder of the family's prosperity. Old Carothers McCaslin, Ike discovers, has committed incest with his black daughter Thomasina (resulting in the mother's suicide) and established a small monetary legacy to the son of the union, Terrel, because it was "cheaper than saying My son" to a slave offspring and so perhaps feeling obligated to free him and lose his value as human property (258).

Faulkner's commentators have pointed out that Ike condemns himself to futility with his well-meaning decision to wall his desire off from such a flawed public, social world by giving away his inheritance. One indirect consequence of his repudiation is that the woods he has idealized in his mind as the immortal sanctuary of desire are destroyed by logging companies, since he lacks the economic power to stop them — for example, by buying the woods himself or in cooperation with others. For our purposes what needs to be stressed even more is that both his decision to give up legal private ownership and his desire for the "unspendable" woods are far from being free from public economics, despite his desire to make them so.

Both Ike's desire and his relinquishment are based on an alternative economic wish, a visionary communal ownership. The seeds of this alternative cultural attitude and practice are planted in Ike's mind by his hunting mentor, Sam Fathers (a man of mixed African and Native American descent, sold by his Indian father to be raised as a slave by Euro-Americans). His mentor's powerful tales of "the old people," the dispossessed and departed Indians, make young Ike feel that communally, as a people, they remain the true owners of the land. He is but a guest there whose private legal possession would be "trivial and without reality" (165). From this vision of ownership by a whole people in "communal anonymity" springs his interpretation that the Bible commands people to hold the earth or any portion of it only in these terms of brotherly sharing, not as private property to be handed down within one's family (246).

Thus, even attempting to split private desire entirely from the public marketplace of his white forefathers, as Ike tries to do, means shaping desire around another economy that serves as the basis of the attempted split. Ike shapes his desire around the fragile traces of an economy of communal ownership in his multiculture, speaking to him in the voice of his alternative Fathers, Sam, who is "the mouthpiece of the host" of the old people (165).

Harry Wilbourne and Charlotte Rittenmeyer play out a variant on this ubiquity of economy. They try to live wholly wrapped up in the privacy of their romantic passion, without losing any of this intensity to workaday outside commitments such as job or family. Not only are they, like Ike, constantly frustrated by the unshakable practicalities of their economic circumstances. More subtly but powerfully than this outside force, a certain kind of marketplace thinking forms the very interior of their love-refuge from the outside world, as in Charlotte's statement that "love and suffering are the same thing and . . . the value of love is the sum of what you have to pay for it" (*WP* 48).

With Ike, Harry, and Charlotte, private desire is imprinted by the public means of producing, distributing, and exchanging desired goods and services that we call an economic system. Other cultural elements such as religious habits and the circumstances of one's historical moment are emphatically part of the web of mutual influences. We can see the marks of a grim Southern Calvinism, multiplied by the novel's Great Depression–era setting, in Charlotte's subjective economy, where love must be bought by suffering. On these terms of emotional trade, after Charlotte's death Harry at the end of the novel vows to preserve their love in his painful memories of it.

If in Faulkner the public shapes the private, the private always marks the public too (the second part of this sentence contemporary criticism tends to underplay). No one encounters some monolithic phantom abstraction like the Public, the Economic System, or the Culture. Like Ike, everyone absorbs these large realities through the agency of particular people, thoroughly filtered and marked by their different particular subjectivities and private projects. And everyone adds his or her own distinctive twist as well, usually not by conscious effort but by the pervasiveness of differences within and among people. So Ike doesn't simply encounter "Communal Ownership by Indians." What he encounters is Sam Fathers, in a specific, individual set of circumstances that is nonetheless representative.

As Faulkner stresses, Sam Fathers persuasively tells Ike of "the old people" without having any firsthand experience of the life they led (165). Sold to whites in infancy, he could not have participated directly in the old Indian economy, and even his Native American father in selling him as a marketable black child evidences the economic changes piercing the older culture. Nevertheless, his stories do have a material basis.

From his own socioeconomic history as a master hunter forced to be a mastered slave, and from who knows what secondhand accounts he heard of how the old people possessed the land, he constructs stories to embody his desire for an alternative to the loss and lostness (165) he has experienced.

It is Sam's vision of an entire people owning a land, a vision passed through a minority culture voice at once subjectively and historically based, that subtly marks Ike's psyche with a desire to abandon private ownership. But, also inseparably, Ike must cooperate with this marking by his own interpretive performance of these stories on his own mental stage: "Gradually to the boy those old times would cease to be old times and would become a part of the boy's present, not only as if they had happened yesterday but as if they were still happening, the men who walked through them actually walking in breath and air and casting an actual shadow on the earth they had not quitted" (165).

Similarly, it isn't a disembodied Slave Economic System whose profits Ike refuses to inherit but the particular, private family version of it he learns, a history spotlighting economic power and the abusive desire it can create. The way he learns is especially instructive for us, because it vividly illustrates not just the interweaving of public and private desire but specifically the public–private faces of reading. After Ike has been influenced as the audience of Sam Fathers's hunting stories, he is also marked by reading privately the old family ledgers of financial transactions where, again, the people involved "took substance and even a sort of shadowy life with their passions and complexities as page followed page and year year; all there, not only the general and condoned injustice and its slow amortization but the specific tragedy which had not been condoned and could never be amortized" (254). As he actively reconstructs a picture of slave-owner economics between the lines of the ledgers, he receives a family story combining failures to acknowledge difference with glimmers of

hope of discernment. Ike learns of both his grandfather's secret abusive sexual desire for two slaves and the compara-
tively benign actions toward slaves by Ike's father and uncle,
who allow their slaves to buy their freedom.

By serving as reader or audience of these private versions of
public history available in the ledgers and in Sam Fathers's
stories, Ike's subjectivity takes from them a quite distinctive
combination of attractive and repulsive examples of desire's
mixed economies. Private and public circumstances are inseparably blended in the discourses Ike reads and hears as well as
in his active interpretation and mental staging of events.
Within this context of the double face of reading, Ike makes
his economic choice of refusal designed to let him have his
woods and hunt them too. In doing this, he discerns difference
to a degree, but in what he acknowledges we can locate the
cultural limits of his insight.

Note the tremendous incongruity. Ike is someone whose
life remarkably records the intimate blending of public and
private economies of desire. Yet he attempts to live wholly
within private desire, simply sealed off from the dominant
public economies of his time and place. We can, of course,
empathetically understand why he does this in the sense that
we are privy to the moving experiences that leads to his decision. Yet the incongruity of his plan of action can be grasped
as the product of a culture (Ike's, Faulkner's, "ours," depending on what culture[s] the reader belongs to). It is a whole way
of life that does so much to drive a wedge between public and
private desires and actions, that it induces in Ike an exaggerated sense of the importance of a single person's unilateral
actions and blocks the appraisal of other courses. Acting by
himself, he can only be something of an escapist Don Qui-
xote, out to combat the world's evils single-handedly, and thus
admirable, tragic, and absurd all at once, a version of "the
individual versus society."

What is all but entirely missing from Ike's cultural conceptions, then, is the alternative to his fatalistic lone-man ap-

proach: the option of planned cooperation. As some critics have noted, joining in concerted action with others is clearly the most fitting means to deal with a disturbing problem in society Ike has uncovered, the limitations of the economics of private property (cf. King, 1982, and Morris 17–18). The addressing of such a social and political problem could only be a form of social effort since it lies beyond the bounds of a single person to handle. Yet Ike finesses the realization that this is so in order to retire to the sidelines with his private desires supposedly untainted by the corruptions of public economic desires.

In its own heavily self-conflicted way, the novel points to this crucial vacancy in the range of options Ike can conceive. As Ike ruminates with his cousin over why Ike is rejecting his inheritance in favor of the cousin, the novel implicitly invites us to see unified action as the one, most logical option Ike needs at least to consider seriously but unwittingly avoids. At the same time, the novel in its conflicted manner also works to cover up this glaring gap in Ike's seemingly all-encompassing discussion of the relevant matters with his skeptical cousin. This cover-up may well leave readers stranded in a false either/or – either "Ike should accept his inheritance" or "Ike should reject it." Here many readers seem to have gotten bogged.

My point, of course, is that whether Ike *unilaterally* does either is not the decisive issue. If Ike were to consider the option of cooperation with others who share, or might be persuaded to share, his concern, then how his inheritance might be used or not used for this purpose would take on a different meaning. He might at least avoid his noble-but-foredoomed gesture at "purifying" desire by trying to live only within nature's processes and not concretely in history's motion as well.

One subtle pointer the novel directs at the gap in Ike's conception of his options is the striking contradiction between the communal vision that drives Ike's decision – that anonymous community of brotherly shared ownership – and the lack of any communal, cooperative dimension to his action. Ike's conception of history's motion depends on a similar gap. He sees history as a divinely directed lesson in loss, where God is invisibly at work to teach people the evils of their possession of hereditary private property by having them suf fer the consequences, through the destruction of wilderness and similar losses. But nowhere in his fatalistic version of history is there any interest in how this process would or does actually come about, the concrete organizations or joint ef forts that produce this school of disaster. The single partial exception is revealing: war, specifically the Civil War and its attendant suffering.

A similar gap is displayed in the story "Delta Autumn" when, many years later, the hunters discuss the contemporary (c. 1940) political scene. In discussing the dangers of dictators such as Hitler at home or abroad, they discourse, even though vaguely, on collective effort to stop the Hitlers by war. Yet they are noticeably silent about cooperation to deal with the economic-political problems of the Depression that are also mentioned: "Half the people without jobs and half the facto ries closed by strikes. . . . Too much cotton and corn and hogs, and not enough for people to eat and wear" (323). Outside of war, it seems that the only forms of cooperative action the characters can conceive are hunting – a blend of each hunter's skill and group effort in ritual violence – and the weak, tem porary semblance of collective effort Gavin Stevens organizes for the funeral ritual in the title story, "Go Down, Moses."

The shared habits and energies of cooperative action are siphoned off into periodic wars, sports, and mourning rituals within Ike's (Faulkner's, "our") culture. Their crucial absence in Ike's decision is also only hinted at in the novel's own representations of that culture. Thus, at both levels this form of public, economic life maintains only a minimal, ghostly existence that creates the (dimly) visible absence in Ike's cul tural menu of choices. The gap and the novel's partial cover-up are the more remarkable because collective action was prominently debated in the contemporary Depression public discussions to which the novel cautiously opens itself.

Yet it is significant that Faulkner continues to struggle with the false binaries between private and public, individual and collective. After *Go Down, Moses* he immediately began to write *A Fable*, the story of two immense, though finally defeated, collective actions in the revealing form of soldiers' strikes *against* war. In Faulkner's attempt to make such dangerous cooperations credible (to himself and to his public, inseparably), he follows a major unfolding direction of his work, a struggle with trying to say – and mean – "we" as well as "I" (*FAB* 321).

Dividing "I" from "we," "us" from "them" is a tragic cultural mistake in Faulkner. Learning to say "I" as well as "we," "we" as well as "I" is a major part of what is at stake in reading him. On Faulkner's showing, what is at stake in his reading, then, is going against the grain of much that his/"our" culture teaches in the informal and formal learning and relearning that make up our lives as subjects of culture. In numberless ways, that culture makes it easy to think an exaggerated difference between ourselves as private persons/readers and faceless others who are the public, part of an alien economic and political "outside world." A whole family of destructive, isolating partitions supports and is supported by that division.

Yet no more than Ike McCaslin's does our reading take place in a vacuum of privacy. And there are more people thronging that privacy than the imagined fictive ones I mentioned earlier. Like Ike, and like Quentin Compson in *Absalom, Absalom!*, our privacy is populated as we are populated, by a "commonwealth" (*AA* 7) of the other persons and practices that have left their shaping influences within us.

As with the stories that predispose Ike's young mind to read as he does in the ledgers, these shapings precede and supplement the formal learning of reading at home or at school. As we advance in literacy, we learn selectively according to our own specific development and the kinds of reading practices available on our school's menu of choices – but not only, or even primarily, on the menu of school learning. In our time, clearly of major importance in the United States are the skills we develop as audiences for electronic media, the products of an immense economic enterprise soliciting certain kinds of attention, desire, and satisfaction from us and leaving others undeveloped.

As a result, when I retire to privacy with my book, what I call *my* reading is really the personal twist I put on a public inheritance of culturally learned reading skills that influence every level of my subjectivity, beginning with my selection of privacy for reading and extending to every aspect of what I have learned to pay attention to and what to skim over or not notice at all. Inseparably, too, the culturally marked inheritances of my generation, nationality, class, "race," gender, region, and so on either broaden or narrow the range of literacy I have had the opportunity or desire to develop.

One example of the generational changes in reading will have to stand for all the variability in reading opportunities and practices. In Faulkner's lifetime an accelerated shift took place in the United States from the more public forms of reading aloud at home, at school, and elsewhere to the more private "silent" reading that dominates today on the post–elementary school menu. Both kinds of reading have their strengths and limits. But this shift took place in tandem with economic, political, and other accelerating privatizations of life, the total of which can easily create an illusory sense of absolutely private space and an "I" sealed off there apart from the "we" or "they" outside.

For all these reasons and more, when we test Faulkner's writing according to our personal judgment and taste, we are doing in miniature what the seemingly distant and alien public institution of Faulkner Incorporated does. This is so even if we have only the most indirect contact with, or even awareness of, William Faulkner as major writer, as public institution.

The point is, both we and the institution of Faulkner exist within the same overall network of connections and differences, forming one another in an endless motion. The economies of desire our reading activates in Faulkner's writing are our own particular versions of the economies of Faulkner Incorporated and the larger economies with which all of these commingle, whether in conscious or unconscious cooperation or opposition. The private and the public faces of reading are both distinctive and inseparable, constantly shaping each other.

To understand this is to move toward saying "we" as well as "I." But as Faulkner came to see, the saying, hard as it may be, is not enough. Inherent in the pattern we have traced in his writing is the difficult corresponding movement to action, a cooperative way of doing that matches this saying. In Faulkner's life, this movement is visible in his emergence after *A Fable* as a public figure urging cooperation to address social problems without at the same time aggrandizing the power of the state over the individual (e.g., *ESPL* 203–33, esp. 230–1; cf. *FU* 100–1).

I think that "we" may be what speechless Benjy in *The Sound and the Fury* was in effect "trying to say" to the girls by attempting to join them and leave the enforced isolation of his all too perfect private subjectivity. It is noteworthy that Benjy is castrated for his attempt. Metaphorically speaking, there is a large cultural investment in seeing that Benjy remains a maimed child all his life, feeling loss yet hardly aware of what he has lost.

Faulkner's writing offers the possibility of weighing such costs. Committed to recouping loss, it registers the power of history's living motion in the tragic turbulence surrounding islands of private subjectivity. Discerning reading in that Faulknerian turbulence is a good way to mark a centennial and a millennium.

WORKS CITED

Adams, Richard P. "Faulkner: The European Roots." In *Faulkner: Fifty Years after "The Marble Faun,"* edited by George H. Wolfe, 21–41. Tuscaloosa: University of Alabama Press, 1976.

Adorno, Theodor. *Aesthetic Theory,* translated by C. Lenhardt, edited by Gretel Adorno and Rolf Tiedemann. London: Routledge & Kegan Paul, 1984.

Negative Dialectics. New York: Continuum, 1973.

Agee, James, and Walker Evans. *Let Us Now Praise Famous Men: Three Tenant Families.* Boston: Houghton Mifflin, 1960.

Althusser, Louis. "Ideology and Ideological State Apparatuses: (Notes Toward an Investigation)." In *Lenin and Philosophy.* New York: Monthly Review Press, 1971.

Austin, J. L. *How to Do Things with Words.* London: Clarendon Press, 1962.

Bakhtin, Mikhail. *Speech Genres and Other Late Essays,* translated by Vern W. McGee, edited by Caryl Emerson and Michael Holquist. Austin: University of Texas Press, 1986.

Benjamin, Walter. "Der Erzähler: Betrachtungen zum Werk Nicolai Lesskows." In *Illuminationen,* 413. Frankfurt: Suhrkamp Verlag, 1955.

"The Work of Art in the Age of Mechanical Reproduction." In *Illuminations,* translated by Harry Zohn, edited by Hannah Arendt, 217–51. New York: Schocken, 1969.

Berlant, Lauren. *The Anatomy of National Fantasy: Hawthorne, Utopia, and Everyday Life.* Chicago: University of Chicago Press, 1991.

Bleikasten, André. "Fathers in Faulkner." In *The Fictional Father,* edited by Robert Con Davis, 115–46. Amherst: University of Massachusetts Press, 1981.

The Ink of Melancholy: Faulkner's Novels, from The Sound and the Fury *to* Light in August, 149–62. Bloomington: Indiana University Press, 1990.

221

"*Light in August:* The Closed Society and Its Subjects." In *New Essays on Light in August*, edited by Michael Millgate. Cambridge: Cambridge University Press, 1987.

Blotner, Joseph L. *Faulkner: A Biography.* 1 vol. New York: Random House, 1984.

——— *Faulkner: A Biography.* 2 vols. New York: Random House, 1974.

Borch-Jacobsen, Mikkel. "The Freudian Subject, From Politics to Ethics." In *Who Comes after the Subject?*, edited by Eduardo Cadava, Peter Connor, and Jean-Luc Nancy, 61–78. New York: Routledge, 1991.

Broch, Hermann. Briefe. In *Gesammelte Werke, VIII*, edited by Robert Pick, 273. Zurich: Rhein-Verlag, 1957.

Bryant, Cedric. "Mirroring the Racial 'Other': The Deacon and Quentin Compson in William Faulkner's *The Sound and the Fury.*" *Southern Review* (Winter 1993): 30–40.

Calvino, Italo. *Leçons américaines.* Paris: Gallimard, 1989.

Cash, W. J. *The Mind of the South.* New York: Alfred A. Knopf, 1941.

Cavell, Stanley. *The Claim of Reason: Wittgenstein, Skepticism, Morality, and Tragedy.* New York: Oxford University Press, 1979.

——— *Must We Mean What We Say?* New York: Scribner, 1969.

Clarke, Deborah L. "Familiar and Fantastic: Women in *Absalom, Absalom!*" *The Faulkner Journal*, 2.1 (1986): 62–72.

Coen, Joel, director. *Barton Fink.* Produced by Ethan Coen, released by Twentieth Century-Fox. Circle Films, 1991.

Cohen, Philip, and Doreen Fowler. "Faulkner's Introduction to *The Sound and the Fury.*" *American Literature*, 62.2 (1990): 262–83.

Cowley, Malcolm. *Faulkner–Cowley File: Letters and Memories, 1944–1963.* New York: Viking Press, 1966.

Davis, Thadious M. *Faulkner's "Negro": Art and the Southern Context.* Baton Rouge: Louisiana State University Press, 1983.

de Lauretis, Teresa. *Alice Doesn't: Feminism, Semiotics, Cinema.* Bloomington: Indiana University Press, 1984.

Dhareshwar, Vivek. "Toward a Narrative Epistemology of the Postcolonial Predicament." *Inscriptions: Group for the Study of Colonial Discourse*, No. 5 (1989): 135–57.

Díaz-Diocaretz, Myriam. "Faulkner's Spanish Voice(s)." In *Faulkner: International Perspectives, Faulkner and Yoknapatawpha, 1982*, edited by Doreen Fowler and Ann J. Abadie, 30–59. Jackson: University Press of Mississippi, 1984.

Donaldson, Susan. "Dismantling the Saturday Evening Post Reader: *The Unvanquished* and Changing 'Horizons of Expectations.'" In *Faulkner and Popular Culture*, edited by Doreen Fowler and Ann J. Abadie, 179–95. Jackson: University Press of Mississippi, 1990.

Duvall, John N. *Faulkner's Marginal Couple: Invisible, Outlaw, and Un-speakable Communities.* Austin: University of Texas Press, 1990.

Edwards, Jorge. "Yoknapatawpha in Santiago de Chile." In *Faulkner: International Perspectives, Faulkner and Yoknapatawpha, 1982,* edited by Doreen Fowler and Ann J. Abadie, 60–73. Jackson: University Press of Mississippi, 1984.

Ellison, Ralph. "Twentieth-Century Fiction and the Black Mask of Humanity." In *Shadow and Act,* 24–44. 1964. New York: Random House, Vintage Books, 1972.

Fadiman, Regina. *Faulkner's "Light in August": A Description and Interpretation of the Revisions.* Charlottesville: University Press of Virginia, 1975.

Faulkner, William. *Absalom, Absalom!: The Corrected Text.* 1936. New York: Vintage International, 1990.

As I Lay Dying: The Corrected Text. 1930. New York: Vintage International, 1990.

Collected Stories. New York: Random House, 1950.

Essays, Speeches and Public Letters, edited by James B. Meriwether. New York: Random House, 1966.

A Fable. New York: Random House, 1954.

Faulkner in the University, edited by Frederick L. Gwynn and Joseph L. Blotner. New York: Random House, 1959.

Faulkner's MGM Screenplays, edited by Bruce F. Kawin. Knoxville: University of Tennessee Press, 1982.

Go Down, Moses. 1942. New York: Vintage International, 1990.

The Hamlet: The Corrected Text. 1940. New York: Vintage International, 1991.

Light in August: The Corrected Text. 1932. New York: Vintage International, 1990.

Lion in the Garden: Interviews with William Faulkner, 1926–1962, edited by James B. Meriwether and Michael Millgate. New York: Random House, 1968.

New Orleans Sketches, edited by Carvel Collins. New York: Random House, 1968.

Sartoris. New York: New American Library, 1929.

Selected Letters of William Faulkner, edited by Joseph L. Blotner. New York: Random House, 1977.

The Sound and the Fury: The Corrected Text. 1929. New York: Vintage International, 1990.

Thinking of Home: William Faulkner's Letters to His Mother and Father, 1918–1925, edited by James G. Watson. New York: Norton, 1992.

Uncollected Stories of William Faulkner, edited by Joseph L. Blotner. New York: Random House, 1979.

The Wild Palms. New York: Random House, Vintage Books, 1966.

Federal Writer's Project. *Mississippi: A Guide to the Magnolia State.* Compiled and written by the Federal Writers' Project of the Works Progress Administration. 1938. New York: Viking Press, 1943.

Fiedler, Leslie. "Pop Goes the Faulkner: In Quest of *Sanctuary.*" In *Faulkner and Popular Culture,* edited by Doreen Fowler and Ann J. Abadie, 75–92. Jackson: University Press of Mississippi, 1990.

Filmer, Robert. *Patriarcha or, the Natural Powers of the Kings of England Asserted and Other Political works,* edited by Peter Laslett. Oxford: Basil Blackwell, 1949.

Fowler, Doreen, and Ann J. Abadie, eds. *Faulkner and Popular Culture: Faulkner and Yoknapatawpha, 1988.* Jackson: University Press of Mississippi, 1990.

Frisch, Mark F. "Self-Definition and Redefinition in New World Literature: William Faulkner and the Hispanic American Novel." *Critica Hispànica,* 12.1–2 (1990): 115–31.

Fussell, Paul. *The Great War and Modern Memory.* New York: Oxford University Press, 1975.

Gammel, Irene. "'Because He is Watching Me': Spectatorship and Power in Faulkner's *Light in August.*" *The Faulkner Journal,* 5:1 (1989): 111–23.

García Márquez, Gabriel. "Le Maître Hemingway." *Le matin des livres.* August 14, 1981.

Gilbert, Sandra M., and Susan Gubar. *No Man's Land: The Place of the Woman Writer in the Twentieth Century.* 2 vols. New Haven: Yale University Press, 1988–9.

Girard, René. *Violence and the Sacred,* translated by Patrick Gregory. Baltimore: John Hopkins University Press, 1977.

Godden, Richard, and Pamela Rhodes. "*The Wild Palms:* Degraded Culture, Devalued Texts." In *Intertextuality in Faulkner,* edited by Michel Gresset and Noel Polk. Jackson: University Press of Mississippi, 1985.

Gooding-Williams, Robert. "Look, a Negro!" In *Reading Rodney King, Reading Urban Uprising,* edited by Robert Gooding-Williams. New York: Routledge, 1993.

Gramsci, Antonio. *Selections from the Prison Notebooks,* edited and translated by Quintin Hoare and Geoffrey Nowell Smith. New York: International Publishers, 1971.

Grimwood, Michael. *Heart in Conflict: Faulkner's Struggles with Vocation.* Athens: University of Georgia Press, 1987.

Grossman, James R. *Land of Hope: Chicago, Black Southerners, and the Great Migration.* Chicago: University of Chicago Press, 1989.

Hair, William Ivy. *Carnival of Fury: Robert Charles and the New Orleans Race Riot of 1900*. Baton Rouge: Louisiana State University Press, 1976.

Hall, Stuart. "Signification, Representation, Ideology: Althusser and the Poststructuralist Debates." In *Critical Studies in Mass Communications*, 2.2 (1985): 87–114.

Harris, Charles F., and Louis R. Sadler. "The Plan of San Diego and the Mexican–U.S. Crisis of 1916: A Reexamination." *Hispanic American Historical Review*, 58 (1978): 381–408.

Harrison, Afterdteen, ed. *Black Exodus: The Great Migration from the American South*. Jackson: University Press of Mississippi, 1991.

Horkheimer, Max, and Theodor W. Adorno. *Dialectic of Enlightenment*, translated by John Cumming. New York: Continuum, 1987.

Howe, Irving. "Faulkner and the Negroes." *William Faulkner*. Rev. ed. New York: Random House, Vintage Books, 1962.

Huyssen, Andreas. *After the Great Divide: Modernism, Mass Culture, Postmodernism*. Bloomington: Indiana University Press, 1986.

Irigaray, Luce. *This Sex Which Is Not One*, translated by Catherine Porter and Carolyn Burke. Ithaca: Cornell University Press, 1985.

Irwin, John T. *Doubling and Incest, Repetition and Revenge: A Speculative Reading of Faulkner*. Baltimore: John Hopkins University Press, 1975.

James, C. L. R. *The Black Jacobins: Toussaint L'Ouverture and the San Domingo Revolution*. 2nd ed., rev. New York: Random House, Vintage Books, 1963.

"Dialectical Materialism and the Fate of Humanity." In *The C. L. R. James Reader*, edited by Anna Crimshaw. Cambridge, Mass.: Blackwell, 1992.

Jameson, Fredric. "On Negt and Kluge." *October*, 46 (1988): 159–72.

Jay, Gregory S. "The End of 'American' Literature: Toward a Multicultural Practice." *College English*, 53 (March 1991): 264–81.

Jehlen, Myra. *Class and Character in Faulkner's South*. New York: Columbia University Press, 1976.

Johnson, Daniel M., and Rex R. Campbell. *Black Migration in America: A Social Demographic History*. Durham, N.C.: Duke University Press, 1981.

Jones, Ann Goodwyn. "'The Kotex Age': Women, Popular Culture, and *The Wild Palms*." In *Faulkner and Popular Culture*, edited by Doreen Fowler and Ann J. Abadie, 142–62. Jackson: University Press of Mississippi, 1990.

Jones, Jacqueline. *The Dispossessed: America's Underclass from the Civil War to the Present*. New York: Basic Books, 1992.

Labor of Love, Labor of Sorrow: Black Women, Work, and the Family from Slavery to the Present. New York: Basic Books, 1985.

Kafka, Franz. *Die Tagebücher 1910–1923*. Frankfurt: S. Fischer, 1967.

Kanterowicz, Ernst H. *The King's Two Bodies*. Princeton: Princeton University Press, 1957.

Katzman, David. "Black Migration." In *The Reader's Companion to American History*, edited by Eric Foner and John A. Garraty. Boston: Houghton Mifflin, 1991.

Seven Days A Week: Women and Domestic Service in Industrializing America. New York: Oxford University Press, 1978.

Kawin, Bruce F. *Faulkner and Film*. New York: Ungar, 1977.

"Faulkner's Film Career: The Years with Hawks." In *Faulkner, Modernism, and Film: Faulkner and Yoknapatawpha, 1978*, edited by Evans Harrington and Ann J. Abadie, 163–81. Jackson: University Press of Mississippi, 1979.

"The Montage Element in Faulkner's Fiction." In *Faulkner, Modernism, and Film: Faulkner and Yoknapatawpha, 1978*, edited by Evans Harrington and Ann J. Abadie, 103–26. Jackson: University Press of Mississippi, 1979.

Kenner, Hugh. "Faulkner and the Avant-Garde." In *Faulkner, Modernism, and Film: Faulkner and Yoknapatawpha, 1978*, edited by Evans Harrington and Ann J. Abadie, 182–96. Jackson: University Press of Mississippi, 1979.

King, Richard H. "Memory and Tradition." In *Faulkner and the Southern Renaissance*, edited by Doreen Fowler and Ann J. Abadie. Jackson: University Press of Mississippi, 1982.

A Southern Renaissance: The Cultural Awakening of the American South. New York: Oxford University Press, 1980.

Kirby, Jack Temple. *Rural Worlds Lost: The American South, 1920–1960*. Baton Rouge: Louisiana State University Press, 1987.

"The Southern Exodus: A Primer for Historians." *Journal of Southern History*, 49.4 (1983): 585–600.

Kirwan, Albert D. *Revolt of the Rednecks: Mississippi Politics. 1876–1925*. Lexington: University of Kentucky Press, 1951.

Kreiswirth, Martin. "Plots and Counterplots: The Structure of *Light in August*." In *New Essays on Light in August*, edited by Michael Millgate. Cambridge: Cambridge University Press, 1987.

La Capra, Dominick. "Representing the Holocaust: Reflections on the Historian's Debate." In *Probing the Limits of Representation: Nazism and the "Final Solution,"* edited by Saul Friedlander, 108–27. Cambridge: Harvard University Press, 1992.

Lacan, Jacques. *Ecrits: A Selection*, translated by Alan Sheridan. New York: Norton, 1977.

Larsen, Nella. *Quicksand* and *Passing*, edited by Deborah McDowell. New Brunswick: Rutgers University Press, 1986.

Lester, Cheryl. "To Market, to Market: *The Portable Faulkner.*" *Criticism: A Quarterly for Literature and the Arts*, 29 (1987): 371–89.

MacConnell, Juliet Flower. *The Regime of the Brother.* New York: Routledge, 1991.

Macherey, Pierre. *Literature, Society, and the Sociology of Literature.* Colchester, U.K.: University of Essex, 1977.

McMillen, Neil R. *Dark Journey: Black Mississippians in the Age of Jim Crow.* Urbana: University of Illinois Press, 1989.

Martin, Gerald. *Journeys through the Labyrinth: Latin American Fiction in the Twentieth Century.* London: Verso, 1989.

Matthews, John T. "*As I Lay Dying* in the Machine Age." *Boundary 2*, 19.1 (1992): 69–94.

"The Elliptical Nature of *Sanctuary.*" *Novel: A Forum on Fiction*, 17.3 (1984): 246–65.

The Play of Faulkner's Language. Ithaca, N.Y.: Cornell University Press, 1982.

"The Rhetoric of Containment in Faulkner." In *Faulkner's Discourse: An International Symposium*, edited by Lothar Hönnighausen. Tübingen: Max Niemeyer, 1987.

"Shortened Stories: Faulkner and the Market." In *Faulkner and the Short Story*, edited by Evans Harrington and Ann J. Abadie, 3–37. Jackson: University Press of Mississippi, 1992.

Mayoux, Jean-Jacques. "The Creation of the Real in Faulkner." In *William Faulkner: Three Decades of Criticism*, edited by Frederick J. Hoffman and Olga W. Vickery, 172. East Lansing: Michigan State University Press, 1960.

Melville, Herman. *Moby-Dick.* 1851. Boston: Houghton Mifflin, 1956.

Memmi, Albert. *The Colonizer and the Colonized.* 1967. Boston: Beacon, 1991.

Merleau-Ponty, Maurice. *Phenomenology of Perception*, translated by Colin Smith. London: Routledge & Kegan Paul, 1962.

Michel, Frann. "William Faulkner as a Lesbian Author." *The Faulkner Journal*, 4.1–2 (1988–9): 5–20.

Millgate, Michael. "Faulkner's Masters." *Tulane Studies in English*, 23 (1978): 143–55.

Minter, David. *William Faulkner: His Life and Work.* Baltimore: Johns Hopkins University Press, 1980.

Montejano, David. *Anglos and Mexicans in the Making of Texas: 1835–1985.* Austin: University of Texas Press, 1989.

Moreland, Richard C. *Faulkner and Modernism: Rereading and Rewriting.* Madison: University of Wisconsin Press, 1990.

Morris, Wesley, with Barbara Alverson Morris. *Reading Faulkner.* Madison: University of Wisconsin Press, 1989.

Muhlenfield, Elizabeth, ed. *William Faulkner's Absalom, Absalom!: A Critical Casebook.* New York: Garland, 1984.

Musil, Robert. *Tagebücher, Aphorismen, Essays und Reden.* Hamburg: Rowohlt, 1955.

Nandy, Ashis. *The Intimate Enemy: Loss and Recovery of Self Under Colonialism.* Delhi: Oxford University Press, 1983.

Ong, Walter J. *Orality and Literacy: The Technologizing of the Word.* London: Methuen, 1982, 31–57.

Outlaw, Lucius. "Toward a Critical Theory of Race." In *Anatomy of Racism,* edited by David Goldberg. Minneapolis: University of Minnesota Press, 1990.

Paredes, Américo. *George Washington Gómez: A Mexicotexan Novel.* Houston: Arte Pùblico Press, 1990.

"With His Pistol in His Hand": A Border Ballad and Its Hero. Austin: University of Texas Press, 1958.

Pateman, Carole. *The Sexual Contract.* Stanford, Calif.: Stanford University Press, 1988.

Pfister, Joel. *The Production of Personal Life: Class, Gender, and the Psychological in Hawthorne's Fiction.* Stanford, Calif.: Stanford University Press, 1991.

Porter, Carolyn. *Seeing and Being: The Plight of the Participant Observer in Emerson, James, Adams, and Faulkner.* Middletown, Conn.: Wesleyan University Press, 1981.

"Symbolic Fathers and Dead Mothers: A Feminist Approach to Faulkner." In *Faulkner and Psychology,* edited by Donald Kartiganer. Oxford: University Press of Mississippi, 1993.

Proust, Marcel. *A la recherche du temps perdu.* 3 vols. Paris: Gallimard, Bibliothèque de la Pléiade, 1954.

Ragan, David Paul. *William Faulkner's Absalom, Absalom!: A Critical Study.* Ann Arbor: UMI Research Press, 1987.

Railey, Kevin. "Cavalier Ideology and History: The Significance of Quentin's Section in *The Sound and the Fury.*" *Arizona Quarterly,* 48.3 (1992): 77–94.

Ross, Stephen M. *Fiction's Inexhaustible Voice: Speech and Writing in Faulkner.* Athens: University of Georgia Press, 1989.

Rubin, Gayle. "The Traffic in Women." In *Toward an Anthropology of Women,* edited by Rayna Reiter. New York: Monthly Review Press, 1975.

Schneidau, Herbert N. *Waking Giants: The Presence of the Past in Modernism.* New York: Oxford University Press, 1991.

Schochet, G. J. *Patriarchalism in Political Thought: The Authoritarian Family and Political Speculation and Attitudes, Especially in Seventeenth-Century England.* Oxford: Basil Blackwell, 1975.

Schwartz, Lawrence H. *Creating Faulkner's Reputation: The Politics of Modern Literary Criticism.* Knoxville: University of Tennessee Press, 1989.

Scott, Emmett J. *Negro Migration During the War.* New York: Oxford University Press, 1920.

Sedgwick, Eve Kosofsky. *Between Men: English Literature and Male Homosocial Desire.* New York: Columbia University Press, 1985.

Showalter, Elaine. "Feminist Criticism in the Wilderness." *Critical Inquiry,* 8.2 (1981): 179–205.

Smith, Henry Nash. *Democracy and the Novel: Popular Resistance to Classic American Writers.* New York: Oxford University Press, 1978.

Smith, Lillian. *Killers of the Dream.* Rev. ed. New York: Norton, 1961.

Smith, Paul. *Discerning the Subject.* Minneapolis: University of Minnesota Press, 1988.

Snead, James. *Figures of Division: William Faulkner's Major Novels.* New York: Methuen, 1986.

Spear, Allan H. *Black Chicago: The Making of a Negro Ghetto: 1890–1920.* Chicago: University of Chicago Press, 1967.

Spivak, Gayatri Chakravorty. "Subaltern Studies: Deconstructing Historiography." *Selected Subaltern Studies,* edited by Ranajit Guha and Gayatri Chakravorty Spivak, 3–32. New York: Oxford University Press, 1988.

Sundquist, Eric J. *Faulkner: The House Divided.* Baltimore: Johns Hopkins University Press, 1983.

"Faulkner, Race, and the Forms of American Fiction." In *Faulkner and Race,* edited by Doreen Fowler and Ann J. Abadie. Jackson: University Press of Mississippi, 1987.

Tindall, George Brown. *The Emergence of the New South, 1913–1945.* Baton Rouge: Louisiana State University Press, 1967.

Tompkins, Jane. *Sensational Designs: The Cultural Work of American Fiction, 1790–1860.* New York: Oxford University Press, 1985.

Trotter, Joe William, Jr., ed. *The Great Migration in Historical Perspective: New Dimensions of Race, Class and Gender.* Bloomington: Indiana University Press, 1991.

Tucker, Susan. *Telling Memories Among Southern Women: Domestic Workers and Their Employers in the Segregated South.* Baton Rouge: Louisiana State University Press, 1988.

Urgo, Joseph P. "*Absalom, Absalom!:* The Movie." *American Literature,* 62 (1990): 56–73.

Wadlington, Warwick. *Reading Faulknerian Tragedy.* Ithaca, N.Y.: Cornell University Press, 1987.

Weinstein, Philip. *Faulkner's Subject: A Cosmos No One Owns.* Cambridge: Cambridge University Press, 1992.

West, Cornel. "Learning to Talk of Race." *New York Times Magazine,* August 2, 1992, 24, 26.

Wilde, Meta Carpenter. *A Loving Gentleman: The Love Story of William Faulkner and Meta Carpenter.* New York: Simon & Schuster, 1976.

Williams, Raymond. *Marxism and Literature.* Oxford: Oxford University Press, 1977.

Williamson, Joel. *The Crucible of Race: Black–White Relations in the South After Reconstruction.* New York: Oxford University Press, 1984.

New People: Miscegenation and Mulattoes in the United States. New York: Free Press, 1980.

Woodward, C. Vann. *Origins of the New South, 1877–1913.* Baton Rouge: Louisiana State University Press, 1951.

Woolf, Virginia. "Mr. Bennett and Mrs. Brown." In *The Captain's Death Bed and Other Essays.* New York: Harcourt Brace, 1950.

Wright, Richard. *American Hunger.* New York: Harper & Row, 1977.

INDEX

231